The Science and Method of Politics

The
Science and Method
of Politics

By

G. E. G. CATLIN

1964

ARCHON BOOKS

Hamden, Connecticut

First Published 1927
Reprinted 1964 with permission in an
unaltered and unabridged edition

Library of Congress Catalog Card Number: 64-25412
Printed in the United States of America

TO THE SCHOOL FOUNDED BY
JOHN COLET AND DESIDERIUS ERASMUS
IN THE
LIBERAL HOPES OF THE ENGLISH RENAISSANCE,
TO ITS MASTERS AND SCHOLARS,
AND ESPECIALLY TO
LEONARD DART WAINWRIGHT AND L. CECIL SMITH,
THIS BOOK IS DEDICATED

CONTENTS

PART I

POLITICS, HISTORY, AND THE DATA OF POLITICS

PART II

THE METHOD OF POLITICS

PART III

POLITICS AND ETHICS

PREFACE

IT is three years since I started upon these studies on *The Science and Method of Politics ;* it is yet another six years since such thoughts as they may contain began to take shape in my mind. The thought that further delay is not likely to improve their value, whereas it may easily cause the book to assume some more pretentious form than that loose one of a pioneer attempt which alone is appropriate, has overcome my reluctance to publish what I could well wish to consider still further. I put this forward as an unsystematic contribution to what I am conscious is a very great subject and, I should add, since Aristotle, an almost untouched subject.

The events of the War and of after the War gave a greatly increased impetus to that revulsion against the doctrine of the omnicompetent national State which had already been assailed in England by the ancient Whig doctrine of Natural Rights, by the intellectual *élan* of the Tractarian religious revival, and by the rising forces of Trade Unionism. Prior to the Fascist reaction, the claims of the god-state throughout Europe were challenged by a reinvigorated ecclesiastical internationalism and by political pluralism in all its forms. The voice of Natural Rights was heard again in the land—and not only, from the mouth of Dr. Krabbe, in the Netherlands.

Pluralism confronted the theory of absolute State power with a realistic presentation of the facts of the governmental process ; while the ideal of national moral self-sufficiency, disclaimed with some hesitation ten years earlier by Dr. Bosanquet, was

in temporary disrepute. But, although the test
adopted by Pluralism of the value of State machinery
was pragmatical, Pluralism continued to concentrate attention on forms of social organization as
the instruments for the realization of a certain
ethical philosophy. It criticized political institutions, and treated the study of Politics from the
angle of this liberal philosophy. Just as the world
of the pragmatist tends to be an indeterminate
world of free will and of individual purpose, so the
pluralist treatment of Politics, with its pragmatic
tendencies, has been teleological and a reply to the
moral affront of the denial by the Prussianizing
State of individual values. It has not provided a
dispassionate study of actual human behaviour which
declined to entertain, save as a hypothesis, any
ethical dogma about human conduct, present or
future, but only concerned itself with observing or
discovering rules of political conduct.

In brief, the Pluralist, as the Catholic, philosophies of the State attack the dogma peculiarly
connected with Tudor England and with Nineteenth-
Century Germany with a dogmatism of their own.
These doctrines may well be ethically superior to
the dominant political philosophy of post-Reforma-
tion Europe, but they have no better guarantee of
issuing in practical political action more feasible and
efficient under the conditions laid down by the
habits of human conduct. They have been concerned with principles, the principles of a philosophy
in the party tradition, and not with any scientific
study of political behaviour.

Before, however, we discuss the ideal, it is incumbent on us, by virtue of the very importance
which we attach to that ideal, and to the achieve-
ment by man of control over his own destinies, to
study impartially and scrupulously what history
shows to be feasible in political undertakings, and
to make clear to ourselves the basal principles of

political method. The great conquests of man over nature have been due to the use of a few such well-founded principles of method, and to apparently minute improvements of technique in conformity with these principles : they have not been made by the re-discussion of the principles of the schools. In the words of William Harvey, " The method of investigating truth commonly pursued at this time, therefore, is to be held erroneous and almost foolish, in which so many inquire what others have said and omit to ask whether the things themselves be actually so or not."

History, however, as usually treated, whatever its literary, educational and antiquarian value, will not contribute to elucidate this political method, because the information which it supplies is not methodically arranged. At the best, the short-cut of a philosophy of history is attempted, which may be inspiring and even profound, but which lacks those exact qualities from which alone technical discoveries in the field of human behaviour may be expected. A behaviorist treatment of Politics, proposing to discover what, if any, are the rules of human social method, will be compelled, while thanking the accurate training of the modern historical scholar, to choose its own crucial researches and to compile its own relevant data. Until an intelligent diagnosis is possible of social ailments, based on a knowledge of the physiology of Politics, legislation which shall treat the body politic with the scientific confidence and with the prescience with which the physician treats the body natural will be impossible.

My profound thanks are due to Professor J. B. Black, of the University of Sheffield, author of *The Art of History*, and to Professor Wallace Notestein, of Cornell University, who encouraged me, when I first became interested in the relations of History and Science as the crux of the problem of the scientific treatment of Politics, to adventure to America in order to have free time for study. I am also indebted to Professor E. B. Titchener for valuable suggestions, and to Professor F. C. Prescott for his kind readiness to help me in the tedious work of revision. And especially the writer wishes to record the debt which he owes to Dr. Ernest Barker, Principal of King's College, London, who, first by his writings and then as tutor, inspired a belief that political thought is a mistress worthy of devotion, and to Mr. H. W. B. Joseph, Fellow of New College, Oxford, who inculcated the lesson that the most acceptable service of devotion is that which is precise in detail. To Professor H. J. Laski, who induced him to write by giving him the confidence that new contributions to thought, however imperfect, might yet be worth making, and to Professor H. E. Barnes, an indefatigable protagonist in the task of synthesizing History and the Social Sciences, who led him to the resolution to publish, it would be difficult for the writer to express sufficient thanks.

G. E. G. C.

New York.

PART I

POLITICS, HISTORY, AND
THE DATA OF POLITICS

INTRODUCTORY

What is to be expected of History. To know History is to control power. The twentieth century is marked by an interest in History, novel not so much by the closeness of its attention to the subject, as by the nature of its expectations from it. It is an age not so much of historical scholasticism, as of the renaissance of History as the record of human behaviour, in the hope that by the study of this record increased control will be gained by men over men's destinies.

For those who are willing to observe the signs of the times, the reasons are not, perhaps, too obscure for explanation. Men who have turned, with the passing of the theological ages,[1] from supramundane things to the affairs of this life, men who have sought in turn for an explanation of experience in the Classics, in Mathematics, and in Physics, are now turning back again to Humanism, to the new

[1] O. Gierke : *Althusius*, 1880, p. 66, " der göttliche Wille wird zwar als wirkende Ursache fest gehalten, allein er tritt in die Rolle der ' causa remota ' zurück." Not, however, until the last century (save perhaps before the Peripatetic School gave way before the puritan Stoics) has it been recognized how far morality and the refinements of life are contingent on the control over means, the choice of appropriate social organization and the mastery of environment, as well as on what Döllinger called ' the inner civilization.' The new truth has, of course, been exaggerated.

3

Humanism of History, for an answer to their riddle.[2] Concerned for a future which interests them more by reason of the hopes that they entertain for the temporal happiness of their children here than for the eternal happiness of their own souls hereafter, it is but natural that they should look for revelation in History, for the revelation of the future of the human race in the record of its past. A classical education was imparted by the Renaissance teachers, because they believed, unlike the mere grammarians, that in the study of the Classics was contained a gospel, the gospel of the way of life of the Ancient World. It has remained for our own generation to suspect in History a gospel of a new world other than this world to which we are accustomed, to suspect that it may faithfully reveal the real world of social cause and effect as contrasted with the world of comfortable private opinions and of ' the pictures in our heads.'[3]

This new movement of inquiry, as distinct from the old curiosity, does not look to History so much in order to become acquainted with events and conditions which will not recur and for the sake of a cumber of unprofitable detail, as in order to gather an omen of future progress from the previous continuity of advance, and encouragement from

---

[2] Significant in this connection is the amount of attention given by the general public to books on the idea of progress, or on national and racial retrogression or degeneration, which endeavour to argue from the tendencies of past history to the development of future events.

[3] W. Lippmann : *Public Opinion* (1922) Introd.

consideration of the improbability that a current of such great momentum will abruptly change direction. There are, again, those less sanguine, who are averse to all kinds of prophecy and generalization and to any implication of automatic progress. These dislike the historian undertaking the office of the haruspex, and prognosticating from the entrails of the past the specific victories of the future. But even these to-day persuade themselves that they will find in the problems and answers of dead men not a mere intellectual exercise, but a wisdom more profound than current opinion, and more humane than are the voices heard in the solitary meditations of the mystic and of the philosopher.

A vast accident, unallowed for in a civilization which seemed not only stable but placidly progressive, has caused yet others to lay their ears against the mouths of the silent ones, and to become consulters of the mummy-head of History. The war was a period in which men forsook ordinary ways, and, going beyond rule, became either more or less than themselves. It was a period of mud and doubt, of resolution and of conflicting maxims, of idealism and of passion ; a period when virtue seemed to compromise with virtue. The period has passed ; the thunder of the greater storm is, for the time being, distant. But, under the sullen skies of distress and discontent, it has left not a few who ask what are the causes of these social catastrophes ; whether it pass the wit of man to avert them ; whether they are indeed accidents or an ineluctable human fate ; what are the principles on which a society is founded wherein these disasters seem inevitable, even although the next one prove fatal.

Those who have so urgent a reason for seeking to understand the causes of the great movements in politics must look into the past of politics. They seek a wisdom which will enable them better to understand what is permanent and to control what is changeable in the complex civilization which men have, in part, created, and in which, until they attain full consciousness and mastery, men find themselves, in part, enmeshed. The study of past politics is that of History, although History is the tale of more things than of politics. But those who go to History because they seek not merely to survey present political detail but to understand the greater framework in which that detail is accidentally set, who seek to understand from the concrete facts of History the abstract scheme of Politics, to grasp, through a study of material, what is meant by such political formulæ as the ' Sovereignty of the State ' or the ' Rights of Nations,' must have a care lest, asking ' Why ? ' they come to be satisfied by being told ' What.' The reason why a nation creates or retains its institutions is not to be explained by a narration of events, themselves motiveless, but by a consideration of the play of human nature, compact of wants, fears and desires, upon the momentary situation, with its limited and determining possibilities. Inquiry must not be brained with the primitive stone-axe of a fact. But if these students of History are themselves content to be more patient in industry than intelligent in method, and omit to ask themselves what is the nature of their material and how it may most properly and most profitably be treated, they risk the reproach of the miser who amasses gold for the love of the hard-won particles in themselves, and without regard for their utility. The first consideration in constructing a scientific study of politics is, therefore, one of method.

CHAPTER I

WHAT HISTORY IS

History does not Comprise all Facts. What is History? Every fact is not of itself an historical fact. A mountain is a *fact* but not an *act*, and it is not historical. A thought is both fact and act, but it is not historical so long as it remains merely ' my thought,' untranslated into the world of things we see and hear, into the visible and sonorous world. A ' history of the world ' is truly so called only when it tells of the great process of mundane events, a process of change which, even when non-human, is of profound interest to man and of essential significance in the understanding of his history. If they were unchanging, not even the happy genius of Mr. Wells could hope to treat the ' eternal hills ' as having a story or a history. But fortunately hills themselves need not be regarded as ' dead things.' The record of the activities of Etna or of the creeping desiccation of Rajputana is of more interest to the historian than the biographies of all the individual shepherds of Sicily, or of all the coolies of India, would probably prove to be.[4] History

---

[4] The attempt to limit History to man, and to treat human affairs as qualitatively different from non-human, arises from a failure to recognize this external side to these affairs. It is a superstitious

should be no respecter of persons, and no adulator of man. Owing, however, to the anthropocentric prepossessions of orthodox History-writing, it has been customary to treat volcanoes and god-haunted rivers as inactive matter of no consequence, and disconnected from the affairs of History. The result has been to confirm the baseless belief that the study of the affairs of man is qualitatively distinct from the study of natural events. On the contrary, what is required is a study of happenings which control man, if man does not control them.

History is not Limited to Human Acts. Nevertheless, in order to be included in History, mountains, on the one hand, must find place in men's knowledge of terrestrial *change*, just as thought, on the other hand, must find objective expression in speech or autobiography. Despite Professor James Harvey Robinson, History is neither limited to man nor inclusive of thought which remains only thought.[5] History is not concerned with the eternal or with the subjective. When we pass on to judgments on character we drift away from History to psycho-

---

relic of anthropocentricism and, however convenient on occasion, is detrimental to clarity of thought and to a proper view of the relation of things human and non-human. Cf. Bernheim : *Lehrbuch der historischen Methode*, p. 5 (. . . " Nur der Mensch ist Objekt der Geschichtswissenschaft "), and G. Simmel : *Die Probleme der Geschichtsphilosophie*, p. 1, *contra*. The extremer form of this theory (that History is concerned with the individual) would lead to the conclusion, on the one hand, that the origin of the human species is no part of History (as it is not of the conventional text-books) and, on the other, that the biography of every trooper in Wellington's armies or of every warrior of Tchalka is of interest.

  [5] J. H. Robinson : *The New History* (Macmillan, 1912). *init.*

logical conjectures. History comes with *the know-ledge of the act*. It is irrelevant whether this act be the aimless one of a despot or part of the purpose of Providence in Nature, in the conformation of hills and the shaping of seas. To draw a distinction would be needlessly to bind our theory of History to the complacent conclusion that men have purposes, and that only men can have them. History is merely the movement of all moving things and the knowledge of the movement ; it is cognised change. There is no intellectually honest reason for permitting the title of History to be usurped by one privileged section of creation, namely, mankind, for the behoof of its own record.

Recorded History is a Fragment : much has been Forgotten. If anyone suppose that the historian is somehow concerned with *all* facts, and has no obligation to select, let him but remember that most of the data of history are lost, and that selection is not a matter left to our choice. It is very desirable that they should be lost, since these forgotten facts were doubtless chiefly the small dust driven before the wind. But our uncertainty as to the early civilization of China and India, our surmises regarding the Hittite Empire, our ignorance until recently about the Minoan civilization, show that, when so much has been but barely saved, the means of reconstructing what is of the highest significance may have perished beyond hope of recovery.

The statement that the data are lost is entirely true for pre-history, save for inference (often but too uncertain) about what has taken place, derived from the residual facts of stone and bone, of funeral pomps and of midden-heaps. The zoologist can know the animal from the inspection of its bone-structure, but the reconstruction of the historic acts, of that which changes, is dependent upon a more detailed and ephemeral record. And, in speaking about these primitive times, the veracity of genuine History fails us. The act is known to have been effected, but its time and place are uncertain and unverifiable. The historical fact is not like a rock, present to have chips chopped out of it for inspection at any time. The narration in cases of this kind is not the work of scholarship, grounded in such a way that it will never need to be substantially altered when re-told. We have here largely opinion and not knowledge.

Much is Uncertain. The statement that the data are lost is also true in grave measure of classical History. It is true, moreover, of modern History. Here the accumulation of our gains but serves to show us how vast are our losses. For when the record of a century or of a decade is known from the testimony of one author, such as a Gregory of Tours, the historian is tempted to regard this testimony as true. But it is not mere paradox to assert that the multiplication of evidence, by giving the possibility of criticism, involves the multiplica-tion of doubt.[6] In one sense, the more modern the

---

[6] The arguments for historical scepticism were elaborated as early as 1530 by C. Agrippa of Nettesheim : *De Incertitudine et Vanitate Scientiarum.* Cf. also Melchiorre Delfico : *Pensieri intorno all' incertezza e inutilitá della Storia* (1808).

history, the more uncertain ; so that the prudent
historian declines to write the history of his own
times. He waits for some of the sediment to settle,
and optimistically hopes that, when the waters have
cleared, only what was of no significance will have
disappeared from view. Few periods are more
heavily documented for the student than that of the
French Revolution, yet few contain greater obscur-
ities. Writings believed to be genuine, such as the
letters of Marie Antoinette, are discovered to be
forgeries ; authentic documents by interested men,
such as the Abbé Barruel, are perceived to falsify
the facts ; honest witness is defective from lacunæ
or lapses in the writer's memory.

Circumstantial testimony may indeed correct
bona fide direct testimony ; and to the credit of
human beings be it said that they are not usually
witting liars. But yet little attains to what would
be demanded by the rigorous standards of legal
evidence : the litigants being dead and unrepre-
sented (or representation being denied), the case
for the defence must often lapse. It is to the honour
of certain writers that, having turned History into
one protracted Last Judgment on the acts of statesmen, they are as untiring as barristers in marshalling
the evidence.[7] It is, however, Chance which, like

[7] The speed with which a beginning has been made in clearing
the ground as touching the incidents of the late war by eminent
historians working on rich and trustworthy material is encouraging.
When, however, the inquisitive historian has ventured to push too
intimately his inquiry, he is still met by over-ready patriots in the
lately belligerent countries, who loudly declare that for them these

some lean and beggarly attorney, selects for them at once the data and the verifying checks. Facts are not exhumable 'things,' but aggregates of acts bound together by hypotheses. To expect, then, to patch together a complete photostatic record of even the more important doings of man is to encourage a chimerical hope. History must be, not indeed 'Philosophy teaching by examples,' but a field, a part of Nature, from which must be selected evidence to build up or to corroborate the contentions of those who are seeking for an explanation of conduct, and thus to simplify and illuminate our understanding of our own human world of action. Each inquirer will inevitably have to select for himself what he considers important, and what he considers important will be decided by his own interests, prepossessions, and standards of value.

Much is Unknown to Record. Yet the historian's prepossessions are not, because he is an historian, therefore much sounder about grave problems than those of naïve laymen. It is vain to demand from him, in the moment of crisis, information even so important as the causes of the sinking of the *Maine* or of the *Lusitania.* The most learned and judicious historian, when he is suddenly consulted in some serious crisis, may well be at a loss, a 'plain man' among 'plain men,' and, after the event, have bitterly to confess himself to have been fooled by the

matters are a *cause jugée*. This is, doubtless, true. 'For them,' truth is relative. But the honour of countries is not vindicated but aspersed by the protests of such. This is not to deny that people with propaganda minds have propaganda value.

clever propaganda of politicians. How much the historian, and especially the academic historian, does not know, becomes more apparent the more modern the times. Not for his use are the recordless meetings of contemporary statesmen, but only the memoirs of their declining years. The prospects of precision and publicity of record may increase, in all cases not connected with war and secrets of state, when politicians come to regard their task as comparable to the passionless one of the physician, requiring accurate diagnosis, extensive information and comparative research, as well as personal skill, instead of resembling alternatively that of a leader of condottieri and that of a revivalist preacher. But it is, at present, precisely the important facts, relevant to the sultry or thunderous questions of the hour, which men are interested in concealing or distorting.

The Sensational is Stressed. Some facts, nevertheless, are unforgotten, unforgettable, and notorious. These are the foundation-stones of the historian. They may also prove to be his stumbling-blocks. Notoriety is the first principle of practical selection. It might even seem that, in this respect, modern history, with its complexity of petty detail, has small advantage over more remote history, where the more significant facts stand out like peaks silhouetted against the dawn. Here the task of emphasizing the important and significant (relative terms, these) seems less left to individual caprice and subjective likes. It is, however, the abnormal not the normal, which thus juts up and strikes our attention.

The abnormal may, indeed, be significant, but significance and notoriety are not synonymous. The significant is to be determined by the results, not by whim ; but the character of notorious facts would seem to differ as the notions of diverse ages vary about what is to be accounted noteworthy. The long obituary notices, which the modern historian might be tempted to dismiss as bare chronicle, were replete with historical interest to the man who wrote them for the interest of his world, not ours. An eclipse to the Babylonians, the name of an Olympian victor to the Greeks and Romans, the sanctity of a hermit or the suppression of a heretic to the Middle Ages, in more modern times an international exhibition to encourage peace and trade, or an opium war, an invention to increase the speed of production or the completeness of destruction, these things aroused popular zeal, were notorious, and seemed noteworthy. The only history sure of being regarded as of absorbing interest by all ages is the history of that which is by definition abnormal ; to wit, the history of crime.

The Significant Tends to be Passed Over. The notorious and the significant can more appropriately be thrown into sharp antithesis. The significant is that which is most influential in deciding the present and future fortunes of men. The normal situation of the past is the matrix of the body of the situation at the present, and the great inconspicuous normal forces of the past silently beget that which is determinant of the spirit of our lives at the present. Perhaps chiefly by reason of the superior imaginative value of the exceptional, attention has been devoted to the history of courts, of curious villainies, and of abortive conspiracies, of remote territorial exchanges and of recondite points of long-repealed law.[8] This seizing of salient and limited happenings, instead of illustrating vague ' social background,' has been justifiable for those who strove to write the history of a connected change and slow explication of causes ; it has been an error on the part of those who thought that History was a series of disjointed ' events,' brought together to exemplify the thesis that fact is more startling than fiction. The writing of History is the exposition, not of brilliant phenomena, but of substantial causes.

It may, however, be argued that the former process is unavoidable. The details which the crowd picks out for attention we may choose to term the ' sensational,' but the historian is no more detached. He will choose as important and valuable what seems to him personally, as the child of his age, interesting and significant in relation to the theories he entertains.[9] Each inquirer will select for himself what

---

[8] Doubtless the perennial notoriety of the Milos and Roscii is not that of the Ciceros and Cæsars. That the populace consider the latter to be more noteworthy, judging from the comparative prices paid for the autographs of their modern counterparts, it would be rash to conclude.

[9] C. Becker : ' Detachment and the Writing of History,' *Atlantic Monthly*, x. 1910.

he considers important, and what he considers important, within the field of his knowledge, will be decided by his *own* interests, prepossessions, and standards of value. History tends to become ' a pack of tricks we play on the dead,' or, according to Napoleon's plagiarism, ' a fable agreed upon.' But this argument may be carried too far in the direction of scepticism and subjectivism. The study of human History precisely resembles the study of natural History in that, to bear fruit, it must, indeed, be undertaken with a hypothesis, or valuation of what is probable, in the mind of the researcher.[10] And amid the immense field of facts available, he must certainly select by this test of his own estimate of what contributes to an understanding of a period or movement. But the actual field of knowledge is not indifferent, nor are the limits of it subjectively determined. Some of the facts which he himself would esteem most important to a true understanding are those which may be concealed.

He has, then, the obligation, not to publish all facts, but to demand that any fact be made public, and to make facts public on demand. And if, for the social sciences, information about certain facts is demanded as likely to have pragmatic value, it is his duty to satisfy this demand. An historian is not merely an obliging man with a kaleidoscope who will shuffle the fragments to suit his age's taste or his own whim.[11] Some assemblages of fact are not

[10] H. Poincaré : *La Science et l'Hypothèse, passim.*
[11] Cf. Sir Paul Vinogradoff : *Villainage in England* (1892), pp. 3 ff., for remarks on Sir Francis Palgrave's treatment of history.

c

merely pretty pictures, but determine to action and have pragmatic utility. Whether these facts are sound and representative History or biassed propaganda, depends on the calibre of the historian. And upon whether our facts are balanced History or the fruit of the will-to-believe, depends their use in diagnosing and curing the ills of society.

True History must Display the Real World : not that in which we Will to Believe. Each man lives in a world of his own construction. It is the obligation of the historian to refuse to come to terms with the beloved fictions of these myriads of private worlds, and to remain unflinchingly the hierophant of the real connected world of cause and consequence. The man of ' plain common sense ' is a convinced idealogue, confident that he is competent to form an opinion *a priori* on the way in which the sun goes round the earth, on the nature of the Absolute and the theology of the Trinity, on the existence or non-existence of Warm Mousterian man, and upon how the world may be made safe for Democracy. Germany was to be forced to pay to the last farthing, and the economic consequences were to be favourable to the victors. In contrast with this dreamworld, in which the consequence is own child of the wish, is the historical world in which he who wills the end must will the unpleasant but inevitable means, and in which the act is not dissociable from the consequences of the act. We may fashion for our own ease a toy world and play with it for a while, but the facts and their nemesis remain. ' Not

even the gods themselves can cause that which has
been not to be.'

The better the historian, the better he is able, by
comparisons, to estimate the degree of significance
in the relation of facts, to get the perspective of
reality. But to admit, in the abstract, that historical
facts have a certain objective (even if relational)
scheme of importance, is to aid us but little in finding
out what kind of things in particular are important,
of which we as inquirers may look for a knowledge
peculiarly through History. We do not look to
History for the way in which to cook our dinners ;
we do not look to History in order to learn how to
appreciate Beethoven's Sonatas. Is it for a new
theory of Medicine, or of Religion, or of Industrial
Relations, that we should look to it ? For what
kind of knowledge, then, is this material, which we
have delimited, peculiarly apt ?

The question is no light one. Learned men spend
a lifetime upon research into History ; time which,
with the same application of intelligence and display
of scrupulous care, might have produced in the field
of biology results of conspicuous advantage to
humanity. School children have their attention
turned to History in the confident expectation that
an acquaintance with the misdeeds of William the
Red will have a beneficial effect in encouraging them
to be good citizens ; but the endeavour seems slightly
misdirected. And if wise men prefer not to concentrate attention upon a merely utilitarian benefit to
humanity, but to preserve their precious ointment

for a better and more splendid use, they might be
expected to turn to the contemplation of eternal
things and to the service of the sciences of pure
speculation, to mathematics and to metaphysics.
Many, nevertheless, are to be found who turn to
History, expecting they know not quite what, and
after some years go unsatisfied away, and, not
unnaturally, sorrowing. Is History a treasure-house
as yet but partly rifled, the keys of most of the
treasure-chambers half-turned in the locks ? Or is
History a mausoleum, spacious, splendid, its walls
vivid with painted figures and its halls empty of all
life ? Is it that these men of old are vital enough
to do anything save beget a future generation, and
that we perchance pervert our natures by necro-
philia ?[12] As students of History, do we, Sordello-
wise, merely dream great dreams ? Is no more to
be expected of History than an old tale newly told,
some scholar's endless narrative devoid of mundane
utility ?

When a self-made millionaire, interested deeply, if
not wisely, in the cause of peace, declares that he is
not concerned with History, which has to do with
the past, whereas his business is with the future, the
laughter of the learned is like the crackling of thorns

[12] The fallacious implications of the dictum of the Abbé Mably,
' You will find everything in ancient history,' it is not difficult to
detect. But in comparing so-called ' modern ' with contemporary
history, we ourselves too easily forget the warning of Hegel : " Eine
fahle Erinnerung hat keine Gewalt im Sturme der Gegenwart, keine
Kraft gegen die Lebendigkeit und Freiheit der Gegenwart." (*Phil.
d. Weltgesch.*, Ed. Lasson, p. 174). Cf. also Emerson's essay on
" History," on the relative importance of past and present.

under pots. But it would be interesting to reflect whether statesmen reared in the conduct of affairs would laugh with them, or whether they would reflect that too tenacious a memory of the past has been a greater curse to peoples, and impediment to political vision, than ever an historic sense has been a useful guide in affairs to prudent action. The historical argument has often indeed been introduced, but it has been brought in more often to defend conduct otherwise desirable than from any genuine sense of the control exercised by the past over the present. And, if peoples have fought wars for their historical liberties, these liberties have owed more to man's myth-making powers than to his flair for historical accuracy. It was bad History and a great faith in the Magna Carta which nerved both Parliamentarian and Whig. It does not, however, follow that History is without use because it has been subjected to abuse. If too unforgiving a memory and too tenacious a knowledge of history has often hindered political experiments, historical ignorance, with its delusive world of passionate make-belief, has as often been the cause of political catastrophe.

How, then, shall History be so treated that it will prove of assistance in the solving of problems which are for our age intolerably urgent ? Or do we wrench it from its function in endeavouring to make it subservient to such ends ? If so, it is best to recognize the fact, and to admit that the historian seeks the ' truth for its own sake,' out of all relation

to any human need—a quest in which he will find,
it is to be hoped, few to impede or to follow—or,
it may be, only seeks ' to instruct and please.'   In
order to answer this question we must first ask how
historians have in fact understood their office.
Assuming that the task of the historian is to reveal
systematically and connectedly that real world,
without a knowledge of which it is impossible wisely
to conduct public affairs, to what method of treatment have historians subjected their data, and to
what treatment should they subject it ?

CHAPTER II

THE METHODS OF THE HISTORIANS

In order that the historian may write, some principle of selection is obviously necessary. The nervous system itself seeks to discover what facts it may safely leave to subconscious registration and discard from consciousness. The attempt to note every fact would be a monstrous nightmare were it not a ludicrous impossibility. As country after country contributes its record (and perhaps an Oriental Renaissance equal in significance to the Classical one of the Fifteenth Century, for which China will be the new Byzantium, is yet to come), it may indeed be hoped that the ' mind of the group ' is edified by the result, but the mind of the individual is certainly incompetent to comprehend it. The co-ordination and social organization of science, the linking up of the ganglia of learning, is a most pressing need ; and it would seem as if, in some very real way, individual knowledge must give place to a systematized and group knowledge with some central sensorium. Only thus can the unity and efficient employment of knowledge be reconciled with human finitude. The days of the polymath have gone. The days of the encyclopædia, of international institutes of intellectual co-operation, of international statistics, of international translation bureaux, of thinking recognized as a ' social act,' are coming. But, whereas in the physical sciences the data have long been arranged with a view to the yielding of practical and theoretical results, into the chaos of political history no such cosmic spirit has as yet been breathed.

I. *Why History is Written : the Writers of History as Massed Facts.* History has in large part been taught and written in a manner natural to the inertia which, finding in hand a large store of facts and anecdotes, naïvely assumed that, as ' knowledge,' this must be as valuable as it was vast. The temptation is almost irresistible to conduct the young through fields so easy of access, so spacious, so spectacular, and, like a wild-beast garden, so superficially interesting, even though the journey prove itself in no very specific way profitable, and the guides themselves have only sought an enjoyable if laborious afternoon. The radical assumption is made that all acquaintance is knowledge, and that all knowledge is valuable. The value of ' background ' is undoubted ; but that the background is valuable owing to its relation with the foreground does not appear to be a proposition which should require defence.

Most acts are trivial. Fortunately they require neither to be observed nor to be retailed ; not all things are worthy of inquiry and narration (ἱστορία). This reflection, if trite, is not trifling. The complaint of Lucian of the plague of history-writing which had befallen his land and time is not meaningless to-day. The historians have taken to writing—and a well-schooled age to reading—history as an amusement, as a trade, as a means of grace and even as a new religion.[13] But although most itch, not all have sought to learn the causes of this craving for historical knowledge, its proper limitations, or what precise satisfaction is to be expected from it. It is hoped, however, that by much writing benefit will somehow or other accrue. This faith in the mere cognisance of all mundane things, massed and motley, a faith in mere acquaintance with a loaded past, as distinct from a scholarly desire to found firmly our knowledge of ' things which lead to other things,' must not be permitted to pass without challenge. If History is, in Windelband's words, ' the memory of the human race,' it must not be a senile memory for anecdote and incident.

The error to which the scholars have tended has not been quite that of the pedagogues, or writers of historical jottings. To many it seems that minute medieval records have some value intrinsic in themselves, or at least bequeathed to them by antiquity—even though surely by no bequest can it be easier to come. Even when admitting that these researches might contribute to the general understanding of inherited ideas and habits of thought, or might form an historical prologue to some trenchant critique of an institution, they have yet

---

[13] E. Troeltsch : *Der Historismus u. seine Probleme*, p. 110. *Vide* also pp. 6 and 26.

been proud to feel that such studies had value apart
from utility. The highest ranges of science, they
have reflected, have been traversed only by those
inspired by a pure desire to know ; yet without
these speculative scientists many of the greatest
inventions of our age would remain undiscovered.
They ignore the fact that the speculative scientist
is sustained by a confidence in the ultimate fruitful-
ness of his knowledge, and burke the problem of the
precise utility of historical knowledge.

The historians, we are told, cultivate a pure and
not an applied science ; but to the question : ' Why
write History, if it is a science, and not, as a poetical
art, justified just in the writing ? ' they do not seem
to have found an adequate reply. Too often they
have merely stilled all doubts by the reflection that
at least they write it more conscientiously than
others. Their very enthusiasm for the means leads
to a frivolous scepticism about the end.[14] History,
at last, has to be excused as supplying, for the
serious student of Dante, pleasing addenda to his
knowledge, or as indispensable for the needs of the

[14] Nietzsche : *Thoughts out of Season*, Eng. ed. 1909, p. 30, " The
knowledge of the past is only desired for the service of the future
and the present, not to weaken the present or to undermine a living
future." Cf. Lord Macaulay : *Miscellaneous Writings*, ed. Routledge, p. 138, " No past event has any intrinsic importance. The
knowledge of it is only valuable as it leads us to form just calculations with respect to the future." Also Lord Morley's remark will
be recalled : " I do not in the least want to know what happened
in the past except as·it enables me to see my way more clearly
through what is happening to-day." And, again : " It may perhaps
be successfully contended that the true conception of History has,
on the whole, gone back rather than advanced during the last

intelligent traveller in his walks round Paris. That History should be eyed with a view to the bearing which this or that problem will have upon the problems of Economics, Politics, Psychology, Æsthetics, or on the art of life, is ignored or forgotten.[15]

II. *History and the Humanists : Moralists and Artists.* The most obvious and usual method of escape from treating History as an amassment of detail, as a confused heap of facts, and from treating ' historiography ' as a record of all historical events or as disjointed memorabilia, annals, notes of strange happenings, is to treat History as a subject for epic prose. Clio, along with her sister scientist, Urania, finds herself placed among the Muses.[16] The criterion, thus, whereby certain facts are related, certain omitted, certain deeply chiselled into high relief, certain indicated by a careless stroke, becomes that of a literary fittingness responding to a desire for æsthetic pleasure. One admires each historian according to his different genre, the *lactea ubertas*, the Claude-like facility of a Livy, the cold clarity of a Cæsar, the Rembrandtesque shades of the well-

hundred years . . . vast and countless accumulations of insignificant facts, sterile knowledge and frivolous antiquarianism " (*Diderot*, II, p. 212 ; and cf. also *Voltaire*, p. 310).

[15] *Vide* H. E. Barnes : *New History and the Social Sciences*, and review by the present writer in the *New Republic*, 18. xi. 25.

[16] A. Birrell : *Collected Essays*, I, pp. 274–5, " To keep the past alive for us is the pious function of the historian. Our curiosity is endless, his the task of gratifying it. . . . History is a pageant and not a philosophy." The historian, that is, is a tabarded herald, not some mere pretentious Puritan fellow, buzzing about truth. Cf. also G. M. Trevelyan : *The Muse of History*.

named Tacitus. This school of the literary conception of History, which desires the choice of some
subject ' comely and pleasing to the reader,' the
school of Dionysius of Halicarnassus, is with us yet.
So long as the interest be stimulated, the philosophy
be exemplified, and the pageants of these new poets
of Parnassus do not cease to please, who cares for
more ? But there is a difference. Among those who
would array History in a gorgeous robe, some care
much for the philosophy and little for the facts,
others much for the detail and little for the philosophy. Neither, it may be suggested, is the most
helpful attitude for the historian, but both attitudes
are conceptions of History so common as to be worth
examining.

(*a*) *The Moralists : the Distinction between
Homily and History.* The educational importance of
the moralising school, which seeks by History to teach
the people to be ' better men and better citizens,'
is not to be denied. The reason why Livy was so
worthy an instructor of Roman youth was because
he made all history into one long gallery of memorial
busts, into one long oration of the ancestors to stir
their descendants to mighty deeds. And yet his
treatment is not above the suspicion that it did but
decorate with mirrors, and did not pierce with
windows, the ' private worlds,' the national prejudices of his hearers.

The modern historian, who depreciates the part
played by the English at Agincourt or who discusses
the diplomatic incidents preceding the battle of

Copenhagen, cannot hope to have a like hortative and patriotic effect. Unfortunately Livy was an effective historian precisely because he was a bad historian, who caused the good, because it was good, to triumph, and the evil to fail.[17] Those who aspire to write true history may well find that they remain ineffective as popular moralists. The honest study of History, in its crude and unselected condition, can no more be considered a moral training for the young than can the partaking, in all its variety, of crude experience be commended for juvenile education. The indecent verity can by no means always be adapted to the terms of polite melodrama ; the ' evangel of History ' is not to be taken so cheaply.

History represents ethical operations, if at all, on a scale too superhuman in universality and complexity for its examples to do other than confuse the faith of a novice. History has the ethic of the Creation, not of the conventicle, and although its actors are rightly judged by the morality of their time, the moralities of epochs are judged by it. This is not to say that they are condemned, or that in a strict historical judgment there is room for condemnation. That ' what is, is what ' (there and then, not here and now) ' ought to be,' is perhaps one of the profoundest, although certainly one of the most controverted, dicta in philosophy, and it may

[17] Of the historians of the Middle Ages, Professor Gooch writes (*History and Historians of the Nineteenth Century*, Introd.) : " History was a sermon, not a science, an exercise in Christian evidence, not a disinterested attempt to understand and explain the course of civilisation."

well be, that it is the function of the historian to
justify each age and every country as indispensable
to one process. History has no irrelevances.

Nevertheless, the apparent failure of a Marcus
Aurelius and the apparent success of Louis XI, the
conquests of Mongol and Turk and the wastes where
stood Ephesus and Carthage, the famine which
scourges the undue fertility of the East, and the
sterility which dogs the aristocratic cultures of the
West, the probably superior ability of extinct
paleolithic man, are not consoling, if they be virile,
subjects for study.

History as Liberator from Conventions. It is more
obvious to find a moral value in History in that it
confronts those conventions which our age regards
as ' of course,' with times and places when such
seemingly fundamental proprieties were regarded as
' of course not,' as indifferent or as immoral. The
idols of no age are too sacrosanct for comparison
with the old worm-eaten idols—not even the idols
of the present decade. History, like Geography,
introduces us to other climes ; it is the temporal
Geography of the human race. It gives, with the
one hand, freedom from the stereotyped reasonings
and inappropriate loyalties which we have inherited
from ancestors for whom these were meaningful.
It gives, with the other hand, a cure for the blindness which imagines that all might be well with the
world by to-morrow's sun, could men but be
persuaded to make a new resolution. History, by
its method, is able to provide a moral discipline ;

in its content, presuming that we do not regard it
as but the record of an unordered struggle and an
uncertain conquest effected over circumstances by
man, it has a certain wry morality, a superhuman
ethic. ' Because,' it may be said, ' virtue cannot
be dissociated from what by the nature of things
must predominate, permanent victory in History
must be the epiphany of the good.' But this ethic
the moralistic school has taken much too cheaply.
It has presented something which, at the best, is
naïve, and, at the worst, dishonest. Yet in its
treatment of History, at least, it is not guilty of
frivolity.

(b) *The Artists : the Distinction between Story and
History.* Among the advocates of a semi-rhetorical
presentation of History are also to be counted those
who would reject with contumely this notion that,
like some moralizing playwright, it is the duty of
the historian so to present the past that it plays
pedagogue to the future. History is story, not
homily. To these the many-coloured facts in all
their variety are sacred just because they are bubbles
and drops—caught as they stream past—in the
tumbling current of life itself. Usually, although
rather inconsistently, lovers of this full motley hue
have been adherents of the ' literary tradition ' in
history. Haters of a heavy-seated seriousness, they
are confessed amateurs of a good tale, in which the
light and shade are not lost. The literary presentation of History may, in such hands, without doubt
be quite free from any desire to point a moral, it may

be blameless of all *Tendenz*. Or, rather, the tendency may lie precisely in the intrinsic necessities of artistic presentation. A Tacitus, even when he forgets his castigation of empurpled vice, may still love to preserve a sombre mien ; a Gibbon, even when not impelled to display his enlightenment, may still seek to preserve his piquant antithesis and pompous serenity.

The manner of art and of history are not the same, for no good artist is ever content to be merely a mirror. This distinction is too often obscured by adherents of the literary and epic tradition of history-writing. The mannerism of the historian may be a glory to his art, but they are a danger to his History, to the bald, balanced, interminable narrative. In a certain essential sense *historia* must always remain a tale untellable, even if it command the finest rhetoric. Every presentation, however skilful, must have its perspective and its side unpresented. It may yet well be that the spirit of life is better caught, if this is what we seek, in the leaping period and in the graphic page than in slow-footed documented compilations. Historical narration, it may be felt, should be a resurrection, a blush of life in dead limbs. But this is surely no more than to admit the right to select the more significant things, for the writer to emphasize their significance in an artistic, a dramatic form—the right, in brief, to typify. It is to adjudge Aristotle justified when he declared Poetry, the presentation of the concrete type, to be ' more philosophic than History ' (which we must hold to as being the presentation of the particular), as the interpreter of human experience.[18] Intending to write History, we end by writing Poetry.

History has not so profoundly to do with ' Personality ' as it pleases the Epic school to suppose. The analysis of character being hypothetical, and its matter psychological, it falls (as distinct from the facts of external behaviour) even less than the inference of incidents within the strict field of History. Rather it falls within that of dramatic art, which is entitled to make assumptions more or less hypothetical about the individual, and so to construct a scheme of motives. The biography of a Cromwell or of a Lincoln admits legitimately of either treatment, but, to the degree that life enters in, the presentation will swing towards tragedy. Thus indeed the drama and other fiction may convey more typical truth than the cumbrous detail of facts. Shakespeare's ' King John,' it may well be, is more humanly valuable than any documented survey of that monarch's reign. But it is not therefore history.[19]

The Distinction between Typification and History :

---

[18] *De Arte Poetica*, colon 1451 b, ed. Teubner, 1878. The opinion is echoed by Goethe. The idea of resurrection occurs in Michelet.

[19] Cf. Macaulay : *Miscellaneous Writings* (ed. Routledge, 1893), p. 140, " Sir Walter Scott . . . has used those fragments of truth which historians have scornfully thrown behind them in a manner which may well excite their envy. . . . But a truly great historian would reclaim those materials which the novelist has appropriated. . . . The perfect historian is he in whom the character and spirit of an age is exhibited in miniature." We have here a prophecy of the coming of Mr. Lytton Strachey and of the substitution for

Truths Poetical and Historical. We learn, indeed,
more of Agamemnon, king of men, or of Haroun,
Commander of the Faithful, perhaps more of eternal
human nature, from the Homeric poems or from the
Arabian Nights' Entertainment than from any
collection of Mycenæan or Saracenic antiquities.
But it is the meaning of these persons, not their
corporeal performance, which is important. That
existence can be predicated of these men contributes little, it may be argued, to the richness of
what is presented. Although Trojan Hector and
German Siegfried were, we suppose, men who
walked a world such as ours, it remains more or less
irrelevant whether either of them was this or that
man here or there ; enough that they were men of
like passions to ourselves. The historian, however,
must not permit himself to substitute the truths,
profound though they be, of mythos for historical
truth. History, as Niebuhr says, requires the
positive. Its servant must sacrifice, if need be,
inspiration for veracity, fullness to the admission of
ignorance. He builds not a dream world, but one
where fire burns wood, a world of determinate cause
and effect, the actual public world of which we
ourselves are the specific effects and caused products.

To this conclusion it is no answer to object that
the *Iliad* itself would lose half its value did Hector
of the glancing helm, ' splendid Hector,' not corre-

the historical novelist of the novelist-historian. But a biography
of an individual cannot be the history of a society or period, even
in miniature, in any sense in which an illuminating work of fiction
might not be.

spond to facts more dear to us, as facts, than all the
tale of Orthagoras of Sikyon or of Cypselus of
Corinth or of many strange dead worthies ; did not
Hector correspond typically and in the poet's wise
to actual facts, which experience remembers as
characteristic of men whom we ourselves have loved.
Homer, on his poetic plane, is true, and even true to
facts. But the poetic and dramatic plane is not the
historical plane, and any compromise between the
two involves a confusion of function, and, usually,
an underestimate of the seriousness and scope of the
dramatic method. There may be a strong argument
for nurturing the people, as Plato proposed, on a
splendid myth, but let us not pass this myth off as
based on ' cold facts.' And by these are to be
understood experiences not inherently improbable,
and established as having objectively occurred by
a consensus of testimony among the best witnesses
available.

Carlyle is too ambitious and too unreliable to be a
great historian, but he is a master of great fiction
and should be honoured as such. Gissing, Hardy,
Galsworthy may be invaluable interpreters of their
generation. In writing the biographies of the great,
it may be possible for anyone so skilful as Mr. Lytton
Strachey to combine the office of novelist and
historian. Biography may yield, to a psychologist,
insight into the influences at work in human
character and in the building of human institutions,
such as will seldom be provided by conventional
history. But the biographies of little folk are

uncollected and uncollectable ; the very names of
these people are forgotten, and their bones have gone
to add to some new limestone formation. Clio is a
convinced lover of the great, whose biographies, if
important, are few. But the many who have no
biography have made history ; the great ' persons '
in large measure did but ' mask ' this anonymous
action. There is grave risk, if history-writing is
assimilated to biography, that the proportions of
the real world of History will be distorted, and the
weightiness of causes misestimated.

The adherent of the Romantic school is not guilty
of falsification, any more than is the artist when he
offers us a picture in lieu of a photograph. Some
delicate miniature of a biography may be of profoundest interest to the student of psychology. And
on a broader canvas the poetic method has its own
justification. But it is not to this school that we
shall look if we desire to study the ' effectual truth
of things ' apart from its æsthetic value, and apart
from all suspicion of an anthropocentric presentation.
The impressionism of Art is different from the
flickering lights on the mirror of History. To
apprehend the character of the latter, confused and
trying to weak eyes, is our present problem.

III. *History and the Philosophers.* (a) *The New
School of Croce : Immersion, not Dissertation.* Historical studies must be ' soaked in the concrete.'
A new school of History, guided by Benedetto Croce,
would so far admit this as to find the æsthetic

appreciation of the past, not in artistic selection and in the use of the historian's pen as though it were the painter's brush, but in a ' living into ' that past in all its detail both great and petty. This method, the inquirer is told, is the way to find out what is important in History and to discover its meaning. The desire to be gratified is not artistic or moralistic, but philosophic, and what plain men (although never Signor Croce) used to call religious ; and it is gratified by care for the body of detail within which slumbers a revivable soul.

The Neapolitan School has not a contempt for facts as ' mere dross ' ; it is only if the dry bones be complete and form a skeleton exhumed intact, that the spirit which breathes in the valley can re-cover them with the integuments of flesh. But this school has principles of valuation which show that, if too subtle for the literary, it yet belongs to the congregation of humanist historians.

The Crocean School deserves thanks for insisting upon the possibility of *penetrating* History with Poetry, as distinct from confounding their substance —upon an intellectual making alive ; and for its protest against the frivolity of those who, speaking of ' experience in History,' after deliberation refer us to the Anglo-Saxon compurgatorial system. (Not that this may not contain a human problem, but that in fact for unguided students it does not.) Ruthlessly Signor Croce condemns the drag-net scholars of detail who, after their deep-sea dredgings, imagine that, like the fisherman of the *Arabian*

Nights, they have got the genius of History corked up in their antique bottles.[20]   Vigorously, again, he attacks what he calls the ' Naturalistic school,' which seeks to import into History the methods of the physical sciences, and which he accuses of that error which is the opposite of meticulousness, that of undue generalization and systematization after the fashion of the traditional sociologists.

Such a criterion as : Does this serve causally to explain what follows ? he rejects.   Rather he would ask : Why are we interested in an explanation at all ?   To which he replies : Because all life that was may have value for the understanding of the life that is, when thought re-lives that past and makes it present ;   because different men are faced with different problems, and different features of the past, enlivened by this interest in a solution thrust on men by the present, are, for inquirers, living and contemporary.   The answer to the question : ' What facts are of historical significance and what are trivial ? ' is that in every case the problem, which gives meaning to the facts, is prepared by the actual

[20] The statement of M. Lot (*Les Derniers Carolingiens*, 1891, p. xiv), be it here said to avoid misunderstanding, that " Au fond le détail c'est toute l'histoire," is typical of an attitude which deserves the deepest respect.   The wilful intrusion of hypothetical specula-tion—Carlyle's ' peripatetic philosophers on the bank ' throwing their speculations into ' the stream of narrative '—is a perversion of the function of history-writing.   But selection no less than collection is essential to the process.   And to assert that a piece of history-writing is no more than detail, ' collection des faits,' in Taine's phrase, is to be like the man who would define a picture as an aggregation of granules of pigment.   Cf. Croce : *Theoria e Storia della Storiografia*, ed. 1920, p. 64.

circumstances of life and solved by each thinker's own thought.[21]   There can be no answer *a priori ;* different men, different ages, different countries will appreciate the past, each after its own fashion.

What are the problems prepared by life ?   Surely, although some may have a craving to understand the secrets of Greek painting or of Byzantine art, to probe into the authorship of ' Homer ' or of ' Shakespeare,' or to spy out the ways of fourteenth-century Treasury clerks with an interest seldom felt for those of the twentieth, there are problems more vulgar, more universal, more profound.   The diversity in value of the many interests of life, history, and thought, Signor Croce probably would admit.   The historical facts are noteworthy because not only my interest, but also (or why an histori-ography ?) that of many thinking men, is con-centrated upon them.   The task of the historian is not soliloquy.   History may be written, as by the Father of History, that the glory of great deeds may not pass away, or to vindicate justice against triumphant oppressors, *ne virtutes sileantur.*   But it is also written because heroic situations or avoid-able tyrannies may recur ;   because History, if it is the record of progress, is also the record of degeneration and of ancient wars to be fought anew.   History supplies food for thought—an undecaying food for ever-recurrent thought.

For Croce, the endless and objectless world-process, as known, is History, and, being known by

[21] Cf. Croce : *Theoria e Storia della Storiografia,* pp. 144 ff.

thought, its knowledge in all its tissue of variety is also philosophy. History is the very intellectual vision of the

> Murmur of living,
> Stir of existence,
> Soul of the World.[22]

This process, every moment of which issues from all previous moments and is related in its entire contemporary extent, is something at every point unique, and is incapable of repetition without difference. Hence a conclusion of the first importance : *There can be, from the nature of the case, no science of History*. For science is concerned not with the ' content ' but with the ' form,' the ' form '

---

[22] It does not appear that Goethe considered that it was owing to the mediation of History, but thanks to the inspiration of far more musical things, that the seer was able to exclaim :

> Das Unzulängliche
> Hier wird's Ereigniss :
> Das Unbeschreibliche
> Hier wird's gethan.

But for Croce, History, as distinct from historiography, is not mediated ; or, rather, the medium of historiography has been made, by intensive thought, a perfect one, and the words no more interfere with the spirit than does the music with the meaning of Magnificat or solemn Te Deum. The theory is well enough. The question is of the possibility. Perhaps occasionally we can not only think with a statesman through the more intellectual of his problems (for although we have many things similar to the past, true ideas alone we have in common with it), but may also catch the authentic sound of the tread and the march and the hurrying thud of the millions who have gone to make the History of man. A great literary historian may have power to enable us to stand beside Pericles as he delivers his Funeral Oration, or hear the hush after Lincoln's speech at Gettysburg. But surely the experience is rare. And yet the ' situation ' is intrinsic to the solution of the ' problem.'

which can ultimately be reduced to a formula. And History, like Nature for the Nature-lover, like the rainbow for Keats, is essentially ' content,' full of the unique joy of things not recurrent.

That the waters of events know no return is seen to be true when we consider thoughtfully even inorganic ' natural ' things and the passage of the seasons. The same sea which went out with the ebb does not come in with the flow, neither is it the same shore which it washes, nor does the same sun shine upon it. In the same way, but more patently, Jamshyd has gone and Cæsar has gone. The existence and maturity of the physical sciences must not, however, lead us to a false distinction between ' Nature ' and ' Man,' but rather to the true distinction between the method which considers ' content,' the unique and changing object of experience, and that which considers ' form,' the abiding ' universals ' under whose ' idea ' thought detects similarity, cosmos, recurrence, methodological principle, amid dissimilarity and chaotic variety. And, so long as we regard History as the whole riot of human experience, it is essentially regarded under the species of ' content,' and must be treated by an appropriate method.

It is impossible to establish a ' law ' of the unique, or to construct a schematic science of the unrepeatable. Until life is reduced to the terms of anatomy, History cannot be reduced to a science, for it is *savoir vivre*. It is the self-consciousness of man, because it is his consciousness of the world as not alien, but as at one with himself, intelligible and rational.[23] What is unrepeatable in fact and unseizable by the abstractions of science, is repeatable, Croce holds, for thought and by an ' empathic ' experience.

Although the Neapolitan school may be non-theistic, non-teleological, denying that the task of philosophy is to concentrate on certain ' fundamental problems ' and condemning mysticism as an enemy of the rational spirit,[24] the attitude of this school to History may not inappropriately be called religious. It offers to man through History a method of reconciliation with his world ; it is a doctrine of Salvation by Historical Atonement. The individual loses, and finds, himself in an experience not individual. This humanistic philosophy of the Absolute declaring itself in Time is, as philosophy, most valuable. Once again men turn from the transcendental to the incarnate. But it does itself injustice by calling itself a theory of History.

Freely, however, Croce admits the validity, within its limits, of a more pragmatic treatment of History.

[23] Croce : *op. cit.*, p. 286. Croce seems to waver between a conception of philosophy as reflection on the historical process of the spirit (a question of History), and of it as a knowledge of the categories of the process in the apprehension of historiographers (' methodological moment of historiography ') (a question of the History of history-writing). *Vide* Collingwood : *Hibbert Journ.* XIX, 2 Jan., 1921, pp. 276–7 ; also, on the modifications which the Crocean doctrine has undergone, *vide* C. Barbagallo and O. Masnovo : *Storia e Storiografia nel Pensiera di B. Croce* (Nuova Rivista Storica, iv, 1920, pp. 54 ff.). Cf. also Droysen : *Grundriss der Historik* (Leipzic, 1882), p. 33, " Die Geschichte ist das γνῶθε σαυτόν der Menschheit im Gewissen." Also, on the difficulties involved in the notion of a ' Science of History,' *vide* Dilthey : *Einleitung in die Geisteswissenschaften*, 1922, I, pp. 86–112.

[24] B. Croce : *Logica*, 1917, p. 307.

" Indeed we should be exercising our right and bowing to a rational necessity, which is that of naturalizing, when naturalism is of use, but not beyond those limits. Thus the naturalising of the facts and the external or casual binding of them together are altogether justified as *puro naturalismo*." The process is, of course, ' economic,' utilitarian ; it is the convenient abstraction, as a ' law,' of certain of the determinate workings of History. If we are discussing Reality, the search for causes is futile, a fool's chase starting from an arbitrary selection of ' major causes,' which obscures recognition of the fact that the number of causes is infinite,[25] since the whole is cause of the whole. So be it. But when we are concerned merely with the means to an end, we are entitled—Signor Croce himself permits us—to ignore the real verity, to ask only ' What works ? ' ; to be satisfied with the ' abstract ' or ' general truth,' and to utilise the ' working hypothesis.'

The Crocean school seeks to teach us a new attitude towards experience. But its ' empathic ' method is that of Poetry and Religion, appropriate to the reconciliation of the spirit. But we, while admitting the inadequate nature of formal ideas, the externality of the practical reason, shall proceed to

[25] But, as Professor S. Alexander in his admirable remarks on causation well points out, it is not true that a search for causes cannot stop short of taking in the whole universe. This ' assumes that the operation of the stars is a motion which interferes with the causal act by which a man knocks another down ' (*Space, Time, and Deity*, I, p. 289).

cut up the living body for the furtherance of our researches into the anatomy of society. There may be no ' fundamental problems,'[26] but not all problems are equal. There are problems of the age, which render certain facts more significant than others. And there are helpful and purposive, as well as aimless and narrative, methods of treating the facts. There is, alas ! much history-writing which is neither exact and useful nor poetic and illuminating.

(b) *The Hegelian School : History as the March of Reason.* ' Sciences of History,' like sciences of the Universe or of God *an sich*, are sciences falsely so called. The establishment of this contention we owe, in no small measure, to Croce. The flood of events is too full to be pent in the mill-race of a system. Yet no review, however brief, of the attitude adopted by historians towards History can ignore the treatment of History, as reduced to a rational and expoundable plan, of Croce's great master, Hegel.

The Hegelians have seen in the flood a current, in the current a drive, in the drive a logic. *This* social situation, thanks to the continuity of History, was, they held, indisseverable from, and followed from, *that*. Further, granted *this* situation, then *that* followed. So far as the idea is actualized of the State as *summum bonum*, so far, by the logic of the premise, men will regard the interests of lesser and other groups than that of their State as subordinate.

[26] B. Croce : *Theory and History of Historiography*, trans. D. Ainslie, p. 154.

Moreover, some ideas take a grip on so vast a part of the field of History, so take body as facts and establish themselves as in the nature of things, move by their logic so many men in the same way, that, without denying that the *whole* present situation proceeds from the *whole* past, it is possible and appropriate to speak of major and more universal causes. The ' idea ' is constant in the method of its unfolding and operation, whosoever or whatsoever may be the subjects affected. Patriotism, enemies, wars, form a sequence which holds, whatever the country. Subjectivity, objectivity, synthesis, holds not only of oriental, Greek and modern civilizations. Human life is not logic, but the logic of the external situation (which is yet itself but consequence of an idea working itself out in negation of ours)—the enemy,—or of the idea within—patriotism,—controls human life.

To affirm, with Hegel, that ideas have such an inextinguishable cunning in germinating in the minds of men that their truths, once sown, can never be permanently suppressed, is not indeed to assert that human history is overruled by some external and knowable Fate, or even by an Idea which, although immanent, may yet have its sure operations foretold by men. To deny, however, the possibility of a system, such as the Hegelian, tending to the simplicity of a geometric diagram, or of unconditional dogmatism about the course of future evolution, such as is implicit in Hegel's philosophy of History as ' the development of the idea of

freedom,' is not to deny the great Hegelian contention of the rationality of the historical process, or to
make of actuality a monstrous and whirling Charybdis.

But the Hegelian philosophers of History have
been less fruitful in illuminating the problems of
human experience than they might otherwise have
been, for two reasons : their tendency to take first
the idea and descend thence to the facts, and their
belief that History is a process to an end.

The sanctity of the actual merely because it is the
actual, and thus something more divine than any
subjective whim or convenience or system, has been
a favourite theme with those who have seen in the
chain of events the coming to pass of the Divine
Purpose and in the writing of History its declaration—the revelation of the march of God in the
world.[27]   Nevertheless, despite their great respect
for the actual as a category, despite their belief that
events have displayed the slow ' process of God
against the Gentiles ' or the sure dialectic of Reason,
few have been more culpable of a masterly dragoon-
ing of the facts than have these very thinkers
(daring pioneers, be it nevertheless remembered)
from Augustine to Hegel.   The actual course of
events was for them holy, because History declared
the purpose of Reason or God.   There should have
resulted a school of historians exact, dispassionate,
scrupulous, reverent ; introducing, unlike the trivial
Protagoreans, measurement of which the measure

[27] Hegel : *Grundlinien der Phil. des Rechts*, ed. 1840, p. 313. Cf.
ibidi : *Vorlesungen über die Phil. der Weltgeschichte*, ed. 1840, p. 12.

should not be man, even preferring perhaps the objectivity of a statistical method. . . .

Nothing could be further from the facts of the case. By a natural human failing, they speeded across obstacles to a conclusion. To them, it sometimes seemed, it was given, as to seers, to anticipate the world process, and to perceive, as a welcome support to their own theories or to the cause of which they were partisans, what the latter end would be. In the light of that end it was possible to interpret facts or to neglect them. Such a procedure seemed to be but a justifiable corollary of the rule of Reason over Matter, Spirit over Nature.

It must be forthwith pointed out that the great master with whose name this method of interpreting History is especially associated was the readiest to exclaim that knowledge had reached but one further stage, that the Spirit was not yet spent, that all highhandedness in arranging the facts was but a confession of immaturity in the system. The Hegelian system, it must yet be admitted, most easily tends, in inferior hands, to fall into the error of wrenching facts, because it inclines rather to a teleology which indicates a goal, even if an indefinitely distant goal, in true liberty, than to a methodology which more modestly contemplates the persistent forms of the ceaseless phases of the spirit, moving from problem to problem.

Hegel was an Icarus whose exploit was so grandly conceived that it serves rather for an incitement than for a warning. The great merit of this treatment of History is that it insists that there is a logic in the historical process which is too profound to be turned aside at the pleasure of the individual will, and that whoever would understand this process must study this logic in things, supra-individual and displayed in events, and (as they have been called by Durkheim) these more abiding 'social facts.' But it is the shortcoming of the Hegelian philosophy of History, if shortcoming it be, that it gives to men a faith to live by and an ideal towards which to strive, rather than increases insight into the precise manner of the working of things. It is in accord with its intention to enable man to gain greater control by knowledge over his destiny and the spirit of man over the matter of nature, including his own, but this aim is not fully effected by its method. To the philosophies of History after the style of Bossuet and Herder, in which a bold dogmatism of theory was encouraged by an inadequate acquaintance with facts, return, in these days since Niebuhr, is improbable, despite the works of Oswald Spengler. But the Philosophy of History of Hegel deserves, not imitation, but more consideration than it receives.

IV. *The Writers of History for History's Sake.* The custom of adducing facts which he knew to be wrong to support theories which he suspected to be so, aroused at the end of the last century the wrath of the greatest of English historians since Hallam, an unashamed lover of pedestrian veracity.[28] The

[28] W. Stubbs : *Lectures on English History*, ed. 1906, pp. 194-5, " Philosophy in its modern use is generally an attempt to find the

exact spirit of Stubbs was revolted by so cavalier a manner of reaching conclusions. The scientific school of historians cultivated a humble industriousness which declined to believe any fact too minute for their notice, any subject too trifling for an excursus. . . . The mark of the Merovingian Kings or the itinerary of a twelfth-century baron were alike not amiss as subjects for investigation. The labour not only of scholarly Germans but of such British men of learning as Madox, who regarded the writing of History as ' almost a religious act,' prepared the way for this firm basing of History, so that the historian seemed to rival the chemist and the biologist in the claim to be ' scientific.' The claim was of deep significance, even though, for many, ' science ' was but an innocuous synonym for accuracy,[29] and to a few, such as Professor Freeman, only a terminological weapon whereby

wrong reason for events or phenomena . . . perfect knowledge is independent of and perhaps inconsistent with, any generalization at all." The creed of the late Bishop of Oxford and of his school will be found in the words of Dom Mabillon : *Acta O.S.B.*, I, i, " Maxime interest sincera secernere ab spuriis, certa ab incertis, ut rebus pie ac sancte gestis sua constat auctoritas." It is, however, perhaps well for many Englishmen to remember Fueter's comment on Stubbs (*Gesch. der Neueren Historiographie*, p. 488) : " Like Waitz, Stubbs was more a learned research scholar than an historian." But it would be absurd to dismiss such men as Dr. Stubbs or the Maurist Fathers as mere ' carters of bricks.' It is gravely to be regretted that the present Benedictines cannot afford to follow the brilliant example of St. Maur on the old scale

[29] Complementary to the desire to be accurate (to avoid errors of commission) is the desire to be impartial (to avoid errors of omission), to attain to what has been called ' mental objectivity.' Cf. A. Rhomberg : *Die Erhebung der Geschichte zum Range einer Wissenschaft*, p. 86.

E

to abase the pride of the physicists. *A priori*
dogmatism about the conduct of men and affairs
was put at a discount. Ideas, which had masquer-
aded as certainties, were placed against their social
background and themselves made matter for scientific investigation. *The whole field of human affairs
was reduced to the first stage of scientific treatment—
accurate observation.*

The Pious Antiquarians. For some the value of
every record as a human document, the stirring
of dead leaves, still vermilion and gold, which tell
of past autumn glories, makes a strong appeal. It
is surely a depressing thought that a chilly day has
ere now made bonfires of Bible codices, or that some
careless clerk may, by the ignorant burning of a list,
blot out the last remembrance of a thousand once
living persons. The astonishing toil of scholars
in deciphering palimpsest seem a light labour of
love if thereby but a fragment of the treasures of the
past are brought to knowledge again. The bundles
in every solicitor's office may well appear, not ' the
white sepulchres of the dead,' but the last tenements
of hundreds of human souls still replete with wills
and aspirations. Although a life spent in the
meticulous examination of this human débris en-
veloped in parchment would seem to be the result,
not so much of a sublimation, as of a perversion
of the social instinct, even the most prosaic must
find it comprehensible that some such mausoleum
as the London Guild Hall or the Vatican Library
should possess all the pathos of the deserted streets

of Herculaneum or of the wind-swept halls of Karnak.

These writers often endeavour to stem the tendency of History to concern itself with 'public affairs' and to forget the little human things; they try to correct the 'snobbery' of History.[30] The romance of past deeds, great or small, is indeed very real, and only becomes injurious when it enervates or dissipates the zest for the romance of present activity, or when interest in it becomes an excuse to defend our failure in facing this life. But the romantic antiquarians, as a school, have been regarded by most research-workers as weaker brethren, although their dominance is less harmful to History than the régime of the commentators who guard the coffins of the great and ignore their thrones.

The Scientific Historians. Others, who have little feeling for these pathetic relics of humanity, for this jejune and dusty immortality, who have little sympathy with the man who would twist a rose-

[30] The significance of this attempt to rescue from the all-smoothing hands of Time some few distinctive traces of what once meant so much to the hopes or pride of this or that one of the children of men, the conviction that History is, in a sense, not so much a going along with the Hours as a strife against them, Professor R. Eucken (*Phil. d. Gesch.* in *Die Kultur der Gegenwart*, I, vi, pp. 269–71) well brings out. But the attempt is hopeless save in the case of those who have entered into greatness. History must usually content itself with treating of the anonymous as a mass, or of the few known individuals. Most, however, of these more important things, which the superciliousness of 'public history' ignores, are infinite repetitions with a difference of a few great themes, love and strife, birth and death. This is why Poetry is a better interpreter of what is humanly important than is 'political history.'

garland from the deserted garden to place on the owner's tomb, who dismiss the whole conception of History as 'pedestrian Poetry,' πεζή τις ποιητική, with a shrug, are yet moved by the hope that every document which they deem important may be collected, docketed, stored. At last, all present fields of research having been allotted or exhausted, they expect to see historical studies dig downward into archæology. Patient burrowers, they hope to unearth the bone-strewn graveyards of the remotest history of the race (for a bone is a document to him who can read it).[31] Church Fathers and Positivist philosophers, who declared that astronomy as a human study was a vain thing, have been put to ridicule, and a like fate is perchance in store for those who contemn archæology. It would be dangerous to declare that the most trivial fact is of no human interest or social importance, since we do not know the links which the future may require in order to connect its theories. The capture of facts may not have any more significance than the

[31] J. H. Round : *Feudal England*, ed. 1895, p. 539, ' Historical research is about to pass, if indeed it is not already passing, into a new sphere—the sphere of Archæology.' It is scarcely possible to exaggerate the importance of the preparatory work which might be done by local clergy and by solicitors in gathering together the genealogical, social, and archæological details of parishes.   As Bishop Creighton remarked : " The history of England is at bottom local history."   Such work may be the ' hack work ' of History, which prepares the way for more ambitious schemes, but it is also the ' collar-work.' Histories of the world will doubtless be written and superseded as long as the world lasts, but histories of the village may rescue much which is passing into oblivion while we wait.   But the local historian needs to be guided by some central research body.

capture of beetles by a man who keeps toads,—it is one kind of pursuit among many. Or it may have great significance.[32]

That man would be rash who would venture to condemn, whether in history or in chemistry, disinterested research. But it seems not to be too

---

[32] It must never be forgotten that without a Blondus and his like there would have been no Machiavelli. But it must also be remembered that a Blondus is justified in his works because a Machiavelli came into being, and that a Machiavelli is not merely epiphenomenal to the studies of a Blondus. It would indeed be an excellent thing if someone would do for Gibbon's *Decline and Fall* what Machiavelli did in his reflective survey of the *Decades* of Livy.

That history should be written by statesmen such as de Comines, Machiavelli, Guicciardini, Bacon, Clarendon, Morley and Rosebery, or at least by men of broad experience such as Voltaire, Gibbon, Macaulay, Bryce, that it should be true as Bolingbroke, himself a statesman, wrote (*Letters on the Use and Study of History*, p. 10) : ' In fine to converse with historians is to keep good company,' is most desirable ; that it is not now entirely true is a deplorable symptom. For Bolingbroke's opinion of the mere antiquarians, ' who deserve encouragement whilst they continue to compile and neither affect wit nor presume to reason,' *vide* the ' *First Letter* ' (and also Laski : *Political Thought from Locke to Bentham*, p. 106). Cf. also Nietzsche, *op. cit.*, p. 24. Both condemnations are sweeping and grandiose but not quite unmerited. It is impossible, however, to refuse a certain sympathy for the erudite Wagners, each one of whom digs for treasure ' und froh ist wenn er Regenwürmer findet '— so few are prepared to dig.

How important information may be lost through culpable indifference was shown by the way in which documents important for local history were sent to be boiled down into pulp during the late war, and is further illustrated by an incident related by Dr. Hubert Hall : " A well-known Colonial antiquary, suspecting that Washington's first American forefather went to Virginia from Barbadoes, made some attempt to trace the matter. To his disgust, he learned that the papers in question were believed to be among some bags of old records that, a few years ago, were cast into the sea. The Colonial Secretary of Barbadoes of that day had himself photographed as he sat on one of the bags with a pipe in his mouth."

utilitarian to demand intelligent investigation ; that is, purposeful investigation.   But what purpose is there, or can there be, in historical research ?   The answer is surely clear.

The most recondite studies have not been in vain if they have corroborated, or thrown doubt upon, opinions formed in those more fertile fields by the study of which chiefly we are able to understand an age, and thus to appraise our own inheritance from it.   A history of Gallo-Roman agriculture may throw more light upon the customs of the English peasantry than some more direct method of attack, may tell us more about the phases of the evolution of the human spirit than a brilliant description of the courts of the Cæsars ; the curiosities of Montesquieu or strange golden boughs plucked from the tree of Anthropology may be more fruitful for thought than the platitudes of Livy or the scandals of Suetonius.   The mistake has been, not in asserting the value of these researches, but in denying their utility, and in declining to examine their comparative utility.   In a petrified past the humanist can find no pageant ; History must be made contemporary.   The scientist, seeking a present truth, a ' word of power,' can discover no profit in a useless irrelevance.

Unimaginative irrelevance, however, neither exact, nor stimulating, nor useful, but merely garrulous, has been encouraged by the pernicious doctrine that ' the only lesson of History is that it has no lesson,' taken not, in the sense of its author, as a condemnation of satisfaction with *narrative* History, but, in a sense the contrary of Hegel, as teaching that History provides much enjoyment but no arguments. Far from History providing no arguments, History, in the broad sense of our original definition, provides every argument that has ever been adduced, for all argument is from our knowledge of the changing yet recurring world of experience. And that human History is singular in not providing, when properly selected or 'reflective,' matter for deductions, is, as has been said, an unfounded hypothesis based on the ancient saw that 'History does not repeat itself'; a saying which, taken precisely, stultifies all learning by experience and negates the value of memory. The true cause of trouble is that we have as yet devised no adequate method for learning some of those lessons of History which are of especial importance to us as human beings. For this we have to thank the absence of scientifically gathered data in which our casually-minded ancestors saw neither use nor emolument, and their flattering belief in the unaccountably free qualities of the human will, which it was impious to suppose did not defy prognostication.

The Difference between Exact Science and Scientific Exactitude. The 'scientific school' of historians has laid stress upon its accuracy. Accuracy is not science. But accuracy, the exact learning which can cite for its statement the recorded fact, which understands the meaning of measurement, which can support a judgment not by rhetoric but by the precision of figures, which knows its statistics, this may not present an attractive form of History, but, for our purpose, it presents the history which matters. The 'blue-book,' and the critical guide to the 'blue-book,' are, relative to this purpose, the most important forms of History, just as they are, relative to their importance, perhaps the most neglected. Here we escape from the whim-world made by passions and alluring opinions to the world of what 'actually does happen.'

The school of documentation, precisely because it has been engaged in the re-writing of History and in the writing it more accurately, has lent colour to the popular fallacy that History is especially concerned with the past. On the contrary, it may be suggested that, to the precise degree to which History becomes out of touch with the practical problems of our own age, it approximates, if it is to remain valuable, to Poetry. This is not, of course, to put forward the absurd thesis that historians should concern themselves only with the occurrences of the last two or three decades. Biology bids us research deep into the remotest antiquity of the race, and yet the problems of biology are not lacking in instant importance. But it is to suggest that the History which is not Poetry shall be taken seriously, with a sense of proportion and with a confidence in its practical value.

On the whole, men have decided that History, the study of change and, above all, of human change and behaviour, is not a 'useful' subject, or one to be taken quite so seriously as Mineralogy or Botany. The motive, perhaps, which most men have had for undertaking the study of History is that stated by Polybius : It is to be studied as a method of vicarious experience of the fortunes and misfortunes of others, and as a training without tears preparatory to one's own experience. But it is well recognized that this utilitarian hope has not been adequately fulfilled ; the voice, though grandiloquent, has been too incoherent, the risk of mistaken inference too great, to justify popular confidence. Something less than Polybius's expectations, are those generally entertained ; a few hints, some heroes, a vague ' cultural background.'[33] The disappointment has been, in no small measure, due to an inadequate appreciation of what was impossible, and to an inadequate attention to the most fruitful method of compassing what was possible. Men of old were accustomed to endeavour to bind the moon by spells, and to sprinkle their fields with blood in order to increase the size of the harvest. The same narrow and unintelligent

[33] Polybius : *Hist.*, ed. Teubner, 1882, I, 33. That Polybius states rightly what are the fruits which it is desirable that History *should* yield—τὰς τῆς τύχης μεταβολὰς γενναίως ὑποφέρειν—even the least pragmatic ' scientific historian ' would probably admit. But in practice to guide oneself, as do spasmodically Members at St. Stephens, by analogies from general history is, as Guicciardini says, ' *molto pericoloso.*' History, Thiers declares, is like a father instructing his children (*Hist. du Consulat et de l'Empire*, Paris, 1885, XII, xviii). This sentimental simile is misleading. Faust's warning to Wagner, that history is merely the limited opinion of one elderly gentleman deceased about other gentlemen also deceased, is saner and safer.

conservatism lasts on in the habits of human thought to-day. The historians who have for long turned and re-turned the mould of the ancient fields, view with suspicion as an adventurer or charlatan anyone who would suggest sinking a shaft to tap the mineral wealth beneath. With the French superintendent of taxes they are tempted to ask : ' When everything goes so happily, why trouble to change it ? ' If History is to yield any answer to the question as to how man shall so control his circumstances as to avoid the evils which History shows him to be repeatedly inflicting upon himself, there must be not only an accurate *record* to provide subject matter, but, as organon, a well-thought-out *method*.

CHAPTER III

THE USES OF HISTORY

The Poetical and Utilitarian Treatments of History.
It is to History that men, seeking a cure for those
social diseases which History itself reveals to them,
naturally turn for a light to show them the way out
of their difficulties. They desire to know ' how it
happened before.' They have in History interests
undoubtedly more dilettante and less crude ; but
they have this abiding interest.

This interest may receive satisfaction in two
fashions, the utilitarian and the religious. From
an increased knowledge of his environment, natural
and social, material and mental, man may hope
more and more to control that environment rather
than to be controlled by it ; to be his own master
instead of being the servant of inanimate nature,
of the nature of the society in which he lives, and
of the nature which, imposed upon him by his
ancestors, he bears about with him. He cannot
escape this heredity and environment, but by
consciousness of its structure and processes he may
become free in it, and not ignorantly bond. So
long, however, as he obstinately prefers his pleasant
wish-world to the real world of actual effects, he
remains a dreaming slave, and his merely arbitrary

legislation remains futile when it runs contrary to the more permanent things. The objective world decides. History, as the knowledge of the natural laws of that world, is the only final legislator. We cannot understand the structure of that which is changing without understanding the manner of its growth. History has the record of this growth, and to History men must therefore turn in search of the old, long-sought things : in search of power and the control which comes with power used with wisdom, in search of the means to carry the warfare for control over the physical world into the kindred field of control over human nature and over the social environment.

Or this interest may receive a religious satisfaction, the satisfaction of the poetic mind in the object of its inspiration, and the sense of union with that which one has freely chosen as an object of devotion. The religious and the poetic outlooks are frequently distinguished. There is no space here to do more than assert that the religious and poetic outlooks are not different in essence but only in emphasis ; that the religious attitude is not only passive but also active, and that the poetic and philosophic are not alone creative ; that the non-utilitarian attitude towards History, wherever it is of any profundity, may no less appropriately be described as religious than it may be called 'poetical.' Reconciliation and release for the human spirit are here directly provided ; there is that sense of something greater than ourselves with which we may identify ourselves, which is the essence of religion. History, which is the mighty purview of an unlimited experience, may give to us satisfaction by inspiring us by noble examples to action, by providing us with demi-gods. Or, more profoundly and more conservatively, its study may fill men with a recognition of their own puniness in the age-long process, and with a consciousness that ultimately satisfaction is to be found, not in reforms and strivings, but in the peace, austerity and resolution of soul which come with the faith that History is the process of the divine, self-justifying Idea, and that those who are on the side of the reasonable have in that their sufficient vindication and reward.[34] " Truth abideth and is strong for ever ; she liveth and conquereth for evermore."

History, it may then be objected, is not mere data for the sciences peculiarly the social sciences. It is,

---

[34] This is not to be read as condoning the error of *basing* Religion upon History, instead of valuing the particular historical phenomenon by the tests of psychological value and metaphysical verity. Recently there has been a tendency for theology to degenerate into a combination of ecclesiastical history and literary criticism, and religious thought into a moist humanism. Religion is enriched by knowing itself, not by historical details, save as these serve to base a general affirmation of the actuality of the religious drama. The deepest things in life have their fount in thought, not their chief foundation in fact. Religion is founded upon piety towards what *is* (which has its epiphany in History), not upon any documents. Still less, as Hume long since showed, can historical evidence be adduced to prove that which does not conform to History's canon of probability. History, it is sometimes said, is concerned with the unique. On the contrary, what is entirely unique, as a miracle, no History research can disprove—or prove. We here leap off the earth of probability and the whole territory of historical canons.

by philological derivation, the knowing (ἴστω) of
life ; historiography is the record of that knowledge.
To substitute laws for this universal experience, or
to maintain that History is merely some primal
stuff which should yield itself to be cut up by the
sciences,[35] is to substitute knowledge of the abstract
for knowledge of the concrete, the indirect for the
immediate ; it is the curse of Shalott, thanks to
which we see not life but merely a reflection. It is
irrelevant here to inquire whether this be not the
defect, if defect it be, of all knowledge by ratio-
cination. It is no true reverence, but rather a
prejudiced indolence and a timid scepticism, which
impels us to cling to the conception of History as
' methodless stuff,' a teeming chaos and a riot formless and inane.[36]

[35] Few would desire, in the words of Professor Troeltsch (*op. cit.*,
p. 102) : ". . . die lebendige Gottheit an menschlichen Messen zu
messen." But the endeavour to raise the methods of the Natural
Sciences and of History into world-outlooks and, then, to put them
into opposition, is mistaken. Naturalism and Historism are both
premature and one-sided views of life. Nor is it clear that an ideal-
istic Historism will necessarily save the value of individuality, in
any simple sense, any more than Naturalism. Certain indications
rather point to its presenting experience as a standardless and futile
flux. Values are too little intellectual to be destroyed so easily by
a naturalistic hypothesis, while Historism, with its love of the
changing and of the moment, is probably a graver obstruction to
the finding of values in the Absolute than some Spinozistic treatment
of Naturalism. It is a capital error to consider the onlooking
scientific view and the inlooking, empathic or poetic view of History
as mutually exclusive.

[36] F. J. Teggart : *Theory of History* (1925), pp. xiii–xiv : " It is
remarkable, indeed, that the fact should not have impressed itself
more generally in the minds of contemporary scholars that when
established modes of procedure have brought to the surface irre-
concilable views as to method and aim of inquiry in any field, the

Some will always find in History a simple æsthetic enjoyment, a quite human sympathy. They will suspect that anyone who proclaims a complete theory of life does but announce his own incompetence in living. Some will find in History the breadth of spiritual experience, demanding the height of intellectual energy, and, sailing with the swift mind over a sea of problems, may choose to call the very reflection on History itself by the name of Philosophy. To assert, however, that History is indispensable as a step to something beyond itself and has a utility, is not at all to deny that it is valuable, treated from another standpoint, in and for itself as a species of Poetry or of Philosophy.

It is with the less intuitive, with the less direct, with the utilitarian satisfaction and with the means to its attainment, that we are here concerned. We look to History for enlightenment as to the nature of the society in which we live, as to what is

time has come for a far-reaching inquiry into the theoretical foundations of the subject in question." With Professor Teggart's conclusion that " the type of inquiry initiated by Hume and Turgot will, therefore, call for the assemblage of historical data upon an unprecedented scale," in order to make possible a scientific study of " how things work," I heartily agree. With his belief that, e.g. Chemistry " inquires into the nature of things," whereas the social sciences inquire " how things have come to be as they are," I am unable to agree. Chemistry is not metaphysics, and cannot ignore the temporal order in which the atoms come together to constitute the molecule ; and the study of a social culture is not only concerned with the time factor but, *qua* social science, with the possibility of repetition, the constituent needs and circumstances being the same. The inquiry into the actual details of growth is historical and not scientific, save in a Linnean sense. I regret that I did not see Professor Teggart's book until after these pages were written.

permanent and what alterable. We desire to understand the structure of the social environment, and
we shall only understand it by knowing its past
and its growth.[37] The essence of the study, however,
is not the growth, but the structure itself in its more
permanent parts and the consequences flowing
persistently from this fact of permanence. This
environment, be it noted, includes the mental
environment. Not the least important part of
History is the History of ideas, of the development of
the directing ideas of great minds, but also of those
conventional ideas to which men are giving daily
expression in action, ideas which are lasting social
facts.

These ideas are not uncertain, ephemeral thoughts,
a tenuous sort of stuff. " By words we govern men."
Conventions are not changeable at will; they
are more abiding than men, more abiding than
boundaries and states. Only those who understand
how a convention has been built up, and against
what background it has taken shape, can by their
criticism dissolve it. To explain is not to explain
away, but to understand is to know how to attack—
and how to defend. Voltaire so nearly succeeded

---

[37] J. H. Robinson : *op. cit.*, p. 21 : " Could we be suddenly en-
dowed with a godlike and exhaustive knowledge of the whole history
of mankind . . . we should gain forthwith a godlike appreciation
of the world in which we live, and a godlike insight into the evils
which mankind now suffers, as well as into the most promising
methods of alleviating them, not because the past would furnish
precedents of conduct, but because our conduct would be based
upon a perfect comprehension of existing conditions founded upon
a perfect knowledge of the past."

in his onslaughts upon Christianity, because he seemed to explain the very course of development back to its source. Voltaire failed because he was wilful, and not patient enough to study History respectfully and to see the needs of human nature, lovely and unlovely, declared there. The conventions of great religions do not arise from the void, nor can they be imposed by calculating craft upon a hostile or unreceptive human mass. Voltaire and Gibbon, Sir James Frazer and Mr. H. G. Wells, dissimilar though they be, all alike become dangerous when they offer to explain to us the origins of the structure of things.

History includes the history of ideas. It also includes the record of the changes which take place in things. Is the burying of Pompeii under the ashes cast out by Vesuvius to be excluded from History because this burial was not due to human agency? The division between Natural and Human History is an intolerable consequence of human conceit. The religious value of the History of Nature may conceivably be inferior for those who do not believe that ' the gods are in all things,' but as touching the pragmatic value no difference can be established between the two, except in relation to the particular end in view. And the division is mischievous as encouraging the view that man lives in a moral world of his own, which only occasionally and accidentally is impinged upon by the inferior world known to Biology and Physics. What we are we owe in large measure to our society, and

F

what our society is we owe to the reactions of a nature, once not human, upon an environment unconcerned with the troubles of man, and as yet unmodified by his handiwork. In the utilitarian treatment of History we shall, then, be concerned both with the growth of ideas and with the relevant changes of the physical environment.

But History as the known series of things is phenomenal, not substantial ; we can trace back to its course the series, but we do not, by unintelligently following along, explore down to the founts of action. No number of ' World Histories ' of themselves enable us to understand why things grew to be thus or thus, and hence, the cause being removed, how they can become otherwise. The facts being at length declared or more strikingly presented, men's ' common sense ' enables them to leap to a judgment as to the cause, their everyday knowledge of human motive enlightens them.[38] But this popular psychology is not due to knowledge of the tale of History. No amount of running, in narrative histories, over events which lead up to a great war will of itself explain the origin of great wars. We do but skim the surface ; we are told how, but not why. As to why, we are left, at present, to make the untrained conjectures, based on private experience, of the ' plain man.' The work of Rousseau did to France no small harm

[38] This is doubtless the ground for Mr. Shaw's remark that ' the man who writes about himself and his own time is the only man who writes about all people and all time.'

because it lacked the stable learning and dis-
passionateness of a Montesquieu. Its theories often
did violence to experience. But the *Contrat Social*
of Rousseau stirred more than one generation and
more than one continent because it sought a cause
where Montesquieu had presented a fact.

Yet to Montesquieu we owe the beginning of the
greatest discovery in the history of history. What
no account of an isolated event will tell us, we may
learn from a comparative study. Popular psychology
in explaining causes leans for support on generalization from a multitude of experiences. If History,
then, is to be useful, we must generalize. But we
must generalize, unlike the ' Scientists of History,'
in the limited matters capable of generalization.

Men, as they grow more enlightened, discover
themselves to be involved in a social system of
which they are, if co-operating, yet involuntary
members, and in which they act, even if in good
faith, yet blindly, and suffer in consequence hope-
lessly. The rise of the demand to understand this
course of events, this underlying system, is the
complement of the attempt to build up an educated
citizen body, and is a demand which cannot be
treated with contempt. Slowly the Platonic argument that politics requires wisdom, not enthusiasm,
is beginning by its cogency to find its way home.
Whether this demand is to be met in the schools,
where the possibilities of education are indicated, or
in the universities, in which education should have
its rebirth, or in adult schools and in the education

of public life, it is no part of our business here to discuss. The point to be made is that the demand has not been met by the historians, upon whom schools, universities, and other educational agencies must rely, in a fashion by any means satisfying.

The moralistic school, while keeping alive the sentiment of the glory of an ancient tradition and of the heights of human accomplishment, tends to degenerate into apology or polemic and to become dishonest. The romantic school has presented us with a poetry of personality, full of subjective valuations. The philosophic school has produced poetry after a more metaphysical style. It has not indeed charted the ocean of History, but it has proclaimed the depths of it. The scientific historians (if it is permissible thus sharply to differentiate schools divided only by period or emphasis) have had the merit of providing a positive treatment, but there has been too little attempt to reduce the chaos of the facts to a cosmos, to penetrate below the surface narrative of how things happened, or to connect events by anything other than the chronological sequence, which may obscure instead of elucidating causes.

It is rash to speak of a ' New History ' in contrast with the old. The attempt methodically to write impartial History is as old at least as Niebuhr, if not as old as Thucydides. The purposive and selective writing of history, although for partizan purposes, is only too old ; Hotman's *Franco-Gallia*, if not Livy's *Decades*, is written emphatically enough in relation to contemporary needs. The ' synthetic ' writing of history, borrowing contributions from the conclusions of all relevant sciences, and picking up promiscuously unconsidered trifles of stray knowledge, is as old as Voltaire and Condorcet, as old as Bodin and Montesquieu, as old as Herodotus himself. The endeavour to detect principles of social method will be found in Taine. If anything is ' new,' it is the combination of these methods, and the production of a history accurate, impartial, serviceable, ecumenical.[39] The difficulty, of course, is not here touched upon of how the individual historian, who is no superman, can avoid being departmental, any more than the specialist in chemistry or physics. But the ideal, because not immediately practicable for individuals, is not valueless as a guide showing the lines along which a utilitarian history-writing may be expected to develop.

Institutional v. Chronological History. Slowly the attempt to write, at once or in part, histories of civilisation in general, which itself succeeded the uncouth annals and showy philosophies of history of an earlier age, is giving way to the writing of histories of conventions, and of the institutions in which these ideas embody themselves so far as geographic, economic, and other determinant conditions permit. Already we have histories of the Idea of Progress, of Toleration, of Nationalism, histories of Representative Government, of the

---

[39] For a full discussion of this question, and bibliography, *vide* H. E. Barnes' *The New History and the Social Sciences* (1925).

Party System, of the Art of War. It must be recognised that this task of indexing history cannot be carried forward until the chronological histories of countries are in a satisfactory condition. But it is suggested that institutional History is the next step, a grade upward in the rationalising and systematising of History for utilitarian ends. That, for these purposes, the history of our own time is chiefly, though by no means solely, important is patent, even admitting that the liberating effect of History, considered as an educative discipline, is greater, the further removed are the times described from those dominated by our own Time-spirit. This reason is not an adequate one for neglecting contemporary history; although education is important, the value of history is far greater than its mere value for pedagogy.

Contemporary History. For the purposes of the social sciences, it is the study of contemporary history which matters first, then that of recent history, then that of the earlier history to which academic historians have traditionally devoted their time. This is not to be guilty of the puerile doctrine that exact ancient history ' does not matter.' It is merely to say that, for certain practical purposes, it is less important, while vast untilled fields of contemporary social reports await the attention of the trained student. ' And the labourers are few.' The value, considered æsthetically and in its ultimate bearing on the conduct of human life, of Greek or Renaissance history may well be far greater. Its superior attractions for the student, with a well-defined field, a more perfected technique and established method, neat problems of recognised value and a better opportunity for displaying sound scholarship in a 'workman-like job,' are obvious. Even here, however, we must insist that, for the man of energy, no age or tendency of thought can be more interesting and adventurous than he may find his own age and contemporary tendencies to be.

The Prospects and Performance of Psychological History. Moralistic history and heroic biography may be educationally suitable for children at their most impressionable age ; romantic history will arouse the serious interest of schoolboys and is good reading of a winter's night or before setting out on the 'grand tour'; scientific history, chronological, and documented, is indispensable to supply framework to the student and edited data to the expert.[40] The immediate future of history-writing may well lie with institutional histories. Nevertheless the institutional history will be no more adequate than its predecessors if it present, not a record of intelligible growth, but a wooden structure of accomplished facts piled together. To make this growth intelligible, it is necessary to assume a certain consistency in human methods and a certain uniformity in human motives. These suppositions will obviously be not only of such a character as

[40] With the temporal framework supplied by chronological history should be coupled the spatial framework supplied by Geography. The importance for the study of History of the latter subject is too often forgotten.

will provide the simplest explanation of the facts before us in the particular case, but will also be based upon general psychological convictions about human behaviour. The fount of historical interpretation must be found in our understanding, scientific as well as amateur, of human nature. Hereby we are able to bind together otherwise disconnected detail, and to show events as incidents of one rational process.

Psychological hypotheses are, however, as yet uncertain and unsatisfactory expedients for improving historical presentation. If, at the present stage of our knowledge, too many hypotheses are intruded, scholarship, lifted high into the air of conjecture above the ground (alone genuinely historical) of known fact, is likely to suffer the fate of Antæus. It will be well to be satisfied for the present with the minimum number, the simplest and the least controversial of such hypotheses, of a kind that the plain man has long since conceded and has ceased to regard as more than ' common sense.'[41]

Granted that there is a certain consistency in human behaviour, a method even in madness, it may well be supposed that there will be a recurrence to old methods when men are faced with situations sufficiently similar to be susceptible of like pragmatic treatment. Situations *en bloc* do not repeat

[41] Psychology is here considered as making a contribution to the understanding of human motives, in those cruder and more fundamental forms which hold good for large groups. The contributions which Psychology and Medicine may make to the understanding of the conduct of individual historical personages it would be rash at present to estimate

themselves, and there can be no science of history
or of experience as such. But there may well be a
study of these recurrent methods or expedients, of
these abiding social forms (particular content apart)
which owe their permanence to the partial constancy
of the needs and impulses of human nature. Here
is an appropriate field for generalizations which are
not mere averages.

From a study of any two of the three terms, human
nature, environmental difficulty, and social expedient,
a deeper understanding of the third is acquired. The
first business of the politician and of the student of
Politics may be to know, not libraries, but men. But
the great problems of politics cannot be decided by an
amicable dinner-party. Not only men have to be
consulted but also facts, the facts of the permanent
social structure which we may study in relevantly
written history. Because part of the social situation
changes more slowly than the rest, old methods are
in part appropriate and new ones can be discovered
and applied for the future. The expedient which
proved most rational in coping with a past difficulty
will again be utilised in dealing with a situation
approximately similar, and these recurring expedients
may fittingly be described as social ' forms ' (εἴδη).
Such a form is monarchy, recurring under whatever
name when there is pressing need for unity of
command. Such a form is the electioneering
system, if not in its historical incidentals, at least
as embodying the representative principle. Such a
form is war, to which there is always a tendency to

have recourse so long as the approximately same situation is permitted to recur.   If it is to be averted, a new expedient must be found for avoiding and anticipating this situation.   It is profitless to weep, once one is in the toils of the logic of a ' political situation.'

Comparative History. Institutional history is a step forward, but it is not enough.   The distinction between the principle lying at the foundations of an institution or of the method which is common to its operation, wherever it be in any proper sense found, and the mere accidentals which surround it in this or that place, must be made by the use of a further expedient in historical treatment.   History, written institutionally, ' indexed,' may show us the stages of growth of the institution, but it requires a comparative history to distinguish the principle of the institution from what is incidental to a particular place or age in which it may be found.   A comparative history, which is more than a narrative compiled of chapters treating, in an abbreviated and inadequate fashion, of the history of many countries, should, as Bryce asserted, be able to assist us here. For a political science is concerned with human social experiences, not as they have been used, but as their past indicates that they are likely to be used again.

History is merely Data. History is our storehouse, not only for the study of old social expedients, such as the jury or Parliamentary systems, but also for those hints, guided by which and by our analysis of

the particular situation, we may plan new expedients
whereby to meet most efficiently situations without a
precedent in our own local experience, which a
changing civilization throws up. Thus, in dealing
with the unrest of the poor in our new industrial and
urban civilization, England has borrowed ideas of
methods of alleviation, e.g by giving a large measure
of economic security in ill-health and old age, from
the earlier experiments of Germany, a country of
the same general type of civilisation. Japan is an
obvious instance of a country which has used the
recent and contemporary history of other countries
for its own advantage. More and more, comparative social study comes to be of recognized
importance.

But the contemporary history of home affairs—
to be found in ' blue books,' and technical reports
of health, employment, crime, and the like, and
such remoter history as is strictly relevant—alone
can give us a real and technically exact presentation
of the actual situation which is the field of our social
engineering, or (to use the more Platonic metaphor)
which is the patient of our social therapeutics.
Unless we desire always ' to bolt the door after the
horse has gone,' or to leave these matters entirely to
politicians happy in their ignorance of history, no
substitute can be found for this study of contemporary history. History is not and never can
be a science; but it provides the data for the social
sciences, whether considered as theoretic studies of
method and form, the counterparts of mechanics

and chemistry, or from a more specific and utilitarian standpoint, as the counterparts of engineering and pharmacy.

Symbolic History. These data must be as scientifically prepared as must the data of the observer for the consideration of the physical scientist. They must be prepared in the most convenient fashion. We must not be surprised if we are asked to see in quantitative statements, in statistics, the most suitable fashion, for many purposes, of communicating our information about social facts. We must settle our minds to talk of a ' symbolic ' history, that is, a historiography expressed in numbers. As Professor James Harvey Robinson admirably says, we must not lecture on bubonic plague instead of typhoid ' because it is more interesting,' and we must so study and lecture on typhoid as to enable practitioners to get results.[42]

Human interests are manifold. Thus Astronomy relies on its recorded observations for its mathematical predictions, Biology educes out of historical data the doctrine of evolution, Economics out of its historical data the ' law ' of supply and demand, Psychology from biographical data a corroboration of its theories, and Medicine derives guidance from statistics in formulating generalisations about hygiene and genetics. Every *a posteriori* science, not merely indirectly through its records, but in its essence as concerned with what is liable to genesis and change, with ' act,' rests on historical

[42] J. H. Robinson : *op. cit.*, p. 11.

data. The sciences are children of History and of Logic. Each of these sciences requires its own departmental historian. Many already have them.

Political Science and Political Data. Historiography, however, still records a vast field of data hitherto employed by no science, even in these days when the general annalist disburthens himself of the responsibility of recording all those portents, curiosities and genealogies, the noting of which the astronomer, anthropologist and sociologist find valuable in ancient histories. The question naturally arises whether all the data concerning human interrelations yield no generalizations, and their study, called ' political,' merely answers to that mental activity which searches for " a spectacle magnificent, various, interesting,"[43] or to that creative phantasy which, more subtly, seeks either to project the features of life on an heroic scale against the screen of historic names,[44] or, again, to inject into bygone ages a virility and simplicity corrective of the vices which certain minds ever mark in their own. Thus we get the myth of the ' gifted Greeks ' or of ' the simple Teutons,' of

[43] Hume : *Essays*, ed. 1875, II, p. 389. This instructive occupation is, therefore, to be commended to " those who are debarred the severer studies by their tenderness of complexion and the weakness of their education." Cf. *contra* Lord Acton : *Lectures on Modern History*, ed. 1906, p. 2 : " For the science of Politics is the one " (?) " science that is deposited by the stream of History, like grains of gold in a river of sand."

[44] The myth which gathers around Charlemagne *à la barbe fleurie* or the disproportionate exaltation of the first five (or three) centuries of Christianity, compared with modern religious practice, may be cited among instances.

Augustus and of Charlemagne, of the ' Golden Age ' and of ' Merrie England.' It is probable that it is of this science of Politics that we must inquire for an answer to those problems which we propounded when we first turned with our questionings to History.

The Methodology of Politics. The social student, although he may admit that, philosophically considered, ' all things flow and nothing abideth,'[45] and that History is of events unique which will never recur, will yet detect, so far as this political material is concerned, similarities in individual and collective conduct, sometimes transient, sometimes recurrent, and will select the more persistent from the more passing forms.[46] This meeting of certain

---

[45] Professor Xénopol (*Les Principes fundamentaux de l'Histoire*) makes an interesting distinction between ' faits successifs ' and ' faits co-existants.' The distinction in the text is between the more abiding form (the precondition of Science) and the flux of content (known in History). It seems to be dubious whether M. Xénopol could sustain his statement (p. 4) that there are in Nature repetitions of which it can be said that " le temps ne modifie aucun de ces phénomènes."

[46] Cf. Spengler : *Untergang des Abendlandes*, I, p. 7 : " Ich trenne der Form, nicht der Substanz nach mit vollster Schärfe den organischen von mechanischen Welteindruck, den Inbegriff der Gestalten von dem der Gesetze, das Bild und Symbol von der Formel und dem System, das Einmalig-Werkliche vom Beständig-Möglichen," etc. Also H. von Treitschke : *Deutsche Geschichte im XIX Jahrhundert*, IV, ed. 1889, p. 469 : " Die Staatslehre muss Gattungsbegriffe und Imperative zu finden suchen, während in der Geschichte doch überall die unrechenbare Freiheit der Machtkämpfe und des persönlichen Willens wirkt." Also Menger : *Methode der Sozialwissenschaften*, 1883, pp. 12 ff. ; and Rickert : *Die Geschichtsphilosophie (Die Philosophie im Beginn des Zwanzigsten Jahrhunderts*, II, pp. 59 ff.) for the opposition of the scientising tendency to pure Historism.

social situations, approximately the same, by the
same general method, is a matter of the first importance for the student. He may not understand, and
he need not concern himself, with the ultimate
purpose. His task is to note this rational ' form '
or *schema*, this manner-of-working, as it recurs in
human history. Within the terms of this form he
will find human life repeating itself, since, having
the same desire, so far as they may, men use the same
means. No chess-players ever yet repeated the
identical game of chess, but no successful chess-
player asks better than that he may perfect and
repeat his appropriate method, and, having started
with Queen's Gambit, he will not play as for Fool's
Mate. So too in life.

For the social scientist the study of History is the
study of human method. He requires " political
understanding and interpretative power."[47] But
he must forget the great romance of History, he must
turn his back on that vague mystery called the
' Philosophy of History,' he must renounce hope of
one science of History, and he must concentrate his
attention, like some chemist or botanist, upon
studying whether his materials do not supply him
ready to hand, if they are subjected to suitable
treatment, with more than he can require for the
construction of social sciences which will yield
results. Part of this material has already been
wrought into shape by the economists and other
scientists for the benefit of their particular disci-

[47] Lucian : *Opera*, ed. Teubner, III, p. 20.

plines. But that part which is peculiarly relevant to political problems (using the word 'political' in the broad, Aristotelian sense) still awaits an ordering hand.

A. *The Quantitative Method.* We have in abundance, if in chaotic confusion, the clinical data of the body politic, the events of past and current history, of how individuals behave in society under various conditions. Scientific tabulation seems to depend upon a far greater use of the quantitative method, corrected by intensive local studies. Statistics will show when events of a certain kind, if measurable, as are crimes, follow or appear in conjunction with events of another kind, such as good or bad rates of wages. It thus becomes possible to sort out that important type of behaviour called crime into kinds which, saving reasons to the contrary, we may ascribe to misery, and those which we may ascribe to the passions or ambitions of men enjoying a certain measure of well-being. If we studied comparatively the 'symbolic history'—the statistics—of the birth-rate, immigration, health and mortality, of the trade-returns, wages and employment, of savings, insurance and expenditure on certain commodities and luxuries, of crime and lunacy, of education, of the national budget, we should be able to reach much better conclusions about the fundamental traits in the life of a people than we can do at present in these days of ill-co-ordinated, incomplete and recently compiled tatistics.

B. *Local Studies.* How far political phenomena
are profitably reducible to measurement, there has
been no serious endeavour to discover. And if such
generalised observations, as these are often mere misleading averages, were corrected by past and present
descriptive history, with its ' atmosphere ' and opportunities for psychological insight, and especially
by detailed studies of the conditions of selected
localities, we should be far advanced not only
to an understanding of the forms assumed by our
legal and political systems, but also to a diagnosis
of our social diseases so impartial and accurate, that
we should be able to administer appropriate and
scientific legislative or administrative remedies.[48]

[48] Instances of the detailed studies here mentioned can be found
in the Pittsburg and Springfield surveys of the Russell Sage Foundation of New York (Cf. Harrison : *Social Conditions in an American
City*, 1920). In England similar surveys of the lives of towns, in
their health, education, etc., have been undertaken, e.g. in the cases
of West Ham (*West Ham, a Study in Social and Economic Problems*,
compiled by E. G. Howarth and M. Wilson, 1907) and of Reading,
Northampton, etc., in 1915 and 1925 by Professor A. L. Bowley and
a colleague, while more limited surveys have been undertaken, e.g.
at Sheffield, from the point of view of industrial conditions (*The
Equipment of the Worker*, ed. H. Freeman, 1919) and of town-
planning (*Sheffield Civic Survey and Development*, P. Abercrombie,
1923).
    There appears to be no adequate study in existence as to where
the quantitative method can be applied with prospects of sound
results in the field of Politics. The need for the extension of this
method is urgent (C. E. Merriam : *New Aspects of Politics*, 1925,
pp. 106, 131 ; discussions in the Annual National Conferences on the
Science of Politics, printed in the *Amer. Pol. Sci. Review, passim*).
An admirable study of the quantitative method is provided by A. L.
Bowley's *The Nature and Purpose of the Measurement of Social
Phenomena*, 1915. Most of the valuable work which has at present
been done trenching on the political field, has been from the economic
or fiscal side, e.g. the work of the National Bureau of Economic

G

C. *Theory of Social Structure.* Symbolic and descriptive history alone, however, the statistics and narrative account of political phenomena, are not sufficient. The reaction against the statistical school of the followers of Quetelet, led by Lilienfeld with his theory of society as an organism, may well appear not to have been a change for the better. The inadequacies of the one were probably less misleading than the metaphor taken for scientific verity of the other.[49] Nevertheless, statistics are unintelligible unless we approach their interpretation in part by the deductive method with an hypothesis.

Such hypotheses need, in order to be more than disconnected guesses, to be based on a grasp of the fact that social phenomena are interconnected in a social system, and that this system is not merely

Research, of New York, and the Bureau of Municipal Research, New York.

The study of non-voting in Chicago is open to the objection, admitted by the organisers (C. E. Merriam and H. F. Gosnell : *Non-Voting*, 1924, pp. 18–19), that voting, like most acts regulated by *governmental* action, is affected by arbitrary and artificial conditions which impede conclusions of broad applicability. This objection, however, may prove far from decisive (*vide infra*, p. 261). On the other hand, research into more fundamental *social* phenomena, such as that of Durkheim upon the statistics of suicide, and of Benini on the ' sense of kind,' may be suspected of being too ambitiously planned.

There is, however, a crying need for quantitative surveys of specific problems upon a compassable scale. The work of the Galton Institute, e.g. upon alcoholism, and upon the relations of wage and size of family, although largely biological, is of the greatest political significance.

[49] P. von Lilienfeld : *La Pathologie Sociale*, 1896, Introd., pp. xviii–xix.

amorphous or a sand-heap of events, but a structure bearing marked characteristics which change more slowly than the stream of current events. The industrial structure or the moral conventions of a country outlast the lives of particular business undertakings or of individual reformers or conservatives. But our knowledge of the physiology and morphology of societies is still in a rudimentary condition, confused by much bad biology, worse philosophy, and not a little political partisan propaganda. Until precise and systematic knowledge has been carried further by the fundamental study of political structure and institutions, as built up in the endeavour of human beings rubbing against each other to find a *modus vivendi*, and by the detailed survey of compassable areas of human life by the quantitative and descriptive methods, we cannot hope to answer the simplest questions about social disorders, or to cure them except by the rough empirical methods of barber-surgeons.

The Limitations of History. The problems both of how to understand social movements and of how to forestall or meet disastrous consequences which may flow from them, we propounded for solution to the historians. It is now clear that for an answer, if there be any, we must turn to Political Science. The historian's business is but to ascertain and present the complete truth about what we may happen to be interested in, not (save as a layman with singular advantages) to expound, reflect upon or draw deductions from it. His work may have

explosive and devastating results where the truth
has hitherto been intentionally concealed, or where
the traditional opinions entertained by the mass of
men can be shown to be wide of the real world of
attested fact and consequence, where denial involves
rejecting all reasonable probability, and introducing
miracle or a personal revelation that one's belief or
party is right. But social therapy is not his affair.
Nor is there any short cut to knowledge by means of
a science of History ; the historian scarcely climbs
to the peak of Pisgah, and certainly is not, as Enoch
and John, translated up out of space and time, to see
a revelation.

The Poverty of Political Science. The misfortune,
however, is that there is as yet no such thing as a
political science in more than a barren name. The
very field of what is to be understood by Politics
has not yet been satisfactorily defined and has
received little close attention. A perfunctory para-
graph, based on the assumption that the community
is a sociological synonym for the State, and that
Politics has to do with the study of government,
especially as exemplified by Athens, Rome, four Western European states in their post-Napoleonic period,
and the United States of America, is usually considered
sufficient. Certainly no recent definition of Politics by
a principle, such as is a commonplace in Biology and
as has been considered worthy of heated discussion
in Economics,[50] has attained acceptance, while the

[50] The definition of Biology as ' the study of the general vital
phenomena common to plants and animals ' (J. A. Thomson:

Aristotelian definition has been generally departed from. The hope of a political science must be in getting away from essay writing and *a priori* theory, and in re-basing itself on observations of social behaviour; that is, on History. As in our definition of Politics, so in our method, we could do worse than cry ' Back to Aristotle.'
The Prospects of the Advancement of Political Learning. Better, however, than to return to Aristotle is to imitate him, in his attitude of the natural scientist towards social phenomena. The quantitative as well as the descriptive method must be used, and it must be recognized that the generalizations of historians of the past and of the present can be expressed in symbols as well as in words. But generalizations are not proved conclusions, with which to remain content, but tentative hypotheses to be tested by well-planned observations. It is necessary to proceed from superficial and isolated generalizations to closer investigation and a better understanding of the structure and growth of social organization. With this understanding it should be possible again to approach

Science of Life, 1899, p. 1) does not appear to have been seriously challenged. The economists have made a serious attempt to define their field by what is common to the subject matter or is brought together as a consequence of the angle of approach, and have not been content with mere exemplification of the objects studied, e.g. ' states ' or ' civilised governments.' Hence they have not felt their time to be wasted by a protracted discussion, among other things, of whether the Wealth, of which some would consider Economics to be the study, is all fungible wealth or only tangible wealth. The theory of Politics has scarcely attained the maturity of discussing these preliminary questions (*vide infra*, p. 210).

more intelligently particular problems and render fruitful detailed research upon them. Intensive local studies, the statistical and descriptive information in special subjects for larger areas, and investigations into the characteristics of the more permanent framework of society relying upon anthropological, economic and social history, serve, if properly conducted, to fertilise each other. From this combination of methods a political science, rightly so called, may conceivably be constructed.

Already by economic history we mean the history of the economic structure of communities, of its changes and altering technique, and of the commercial and industrial relations of men. The economist has been permitted a free hand in arranging, for his convenience of information and illustration, the data of economic life. But by political history we often mean nothing so constructively selected, but rather a narrative of wars and peaces, laws and parties, without more serious attempt at connection of incident and incident than recognition of the brute fact that they happened in successive spans of time. In this more ancient and orthodox field, the conservative tradition of the annalist has been stronger. There is no 'new science' of History, such as Vico dreamt of. And whoever would construct out of History (and it is from observation that it must be constructed) a science of Politics, must abandon the notion of History as a plain tale of the recorded human past, and, in this ' great instauration,' must be bold enough to adopt a new method, a new way

of going about things, concerned as much with
contemporary reports as with ancient records, as
much with a numerical as with a verbal description
of social situations and movements, as much with
local studies as with world histories, and more with
the relatively permanent structure of social organisation for itself, than with the relatively ephemeral
events for themselves.

Systematic observation shows us in social life
' forms,' recurrent methods, such as war, of dealing
with approximately recurrent situations—historical
clichés, as it were. Human beings in the mass do in
fact seem to react to approximately repeated situations in pragmatically the same fashion. The
student must detect and use these ' forms ' as his
novum organon in the elucidation of political history.
It may be that he will be able thereby to build from
the wilderness of scattered stones (composite, at
that), called facts, a new city among the cities of
knowledge. At least he may be confident that it
awaits the builder, and that the greatest practical
need of our day is that it shall be built and built
speedily.

PART II
THE METHOD OF POLITICS

CHAPTER I

THE POSSIBILITY OF A POLITICAL SCIENCE

Concerning the Disrepute of Political Science. " The Sciences," says Schopenhauer, " in that they are systems of concepts, speak entirely of universals, History speaks of particulars, which betokens a contradiction."[1]

Schopenhauer's criticism is appropriate. History is not and cannot be a science. To speak of it as such involves a complete misconception. Its function is to reveal to us the real world undistorted by subjectivism, to provide us with the facts irrespective of our tastes or dislikes. The task of the historian is not moral exhortation or vaticination, but, among other things, the preparation of trustworthy data for those sciences which undertake to study the structure of society. Historical treatment may, indeed, be ' scientific,' that is, accurate and systematic ; but accuracy is not science.

It is, however, owing to dicta such as this of Schopenhauer that Political Science, something very different from History but, like all the observational sciences, founded on record and history, has

---

[1] A. Schopenhauer : *Werke*, ed. 1888, III, pp. 502 ff.

come to be eyed as an illegitimate science, 'a bastard child of Philosophy.' An indolent unwillingness to make distinctions, which are easier to dismiss as ' artificial ' than to examine, has led men to assume that, since most of the history which they read is entitled ' political history,' therefore the studies of history and of politics are much the same thing. And the argument which showed History to be no science has been used with apparent cogency to prove that Politics is not one. It has been the purpose of the preceding chapter to clear up this fundamental question of the relation between History and Politics, and to indicate that, whatever we may discover Politics to be, History is something wider than it, different from it and, in one sense, subsidiary to it. Arguments as to the nature of science applicable to the one discipline may be inapplicable to the other.

This point requires stressing the more because there is a strong tendency at the present to decry ' abstraction,' and to reduce back again to history even those social studies which have attained some measure of scientific standing.[2] The critique of the

[2] A science, here and throughout, is treated as a *corpus* of certain knowledge, and (as certain knowledge) valid prior to particular experiences and despite appearance to the contrary. It can thus predict, and in its statements stands in no need of reiterated verification. It is, however, infallible just so far as it is abstract, logical and *a priori*. Cf. Professor Karl Pearson : *Grammar of Science*, ed. 1911, I, p. 87 : " Law in the scientific sense is thus essentially a product of the human mind and has no meaning apart from man. It owes its existence to the creative power of his intellect. There is more meaning in the phase that Man gives laws to Nature than in its converse that Nature gives laws to Man." But although scientific law is

abstract method, often founded upon a misconception of what is meant by ' natural laws ' (which are quite falsely supposed to have as much objectivity as the Twelve Tables or the *Code Civile*), itself stands in need of criticism. To this matter it will be necessary to return. It is sufficient here to say that, if by abstraction (as in the case of Pure Mechanics) we risk losing touch with reality, by reducing the social sciences to collections of social studies we risk permitting them to descend to anecdotal incoherence. Unending description has small pragmatic value. Because the historians have hitherto been too little generous, too strait-laced and ' snobbish ' in their supply of data valuable for the understanding of human nature, because every man must be, therefore, in part his own ' dry-as-dust ' in *ad hoc* researches into recent blue-books and into the contemporary history of the slum and the suburb, the workshop and the church, there is no ground for confusing our minds by identifying the social sciences with contemporary social history. This history will supply us with the facts, dispassionately

a priori to any particular experience and is thus in a sense independent of facts, it is in its genesis *a posteriori* to the body of observation and deductive from facts. A scientific law is valuable because it indicates that a certain sequence of events or regular relation must follow in theory and will highly probably follow in practice, since the hypothetical clauses of the law are founded upon some well-observed ' manner of the working of things.' In looking thus for a ' law ' in Science, we look for a logical structure superimposed upon the observation of a highly frequent occurrence. So soon as this abstract logic is lost, whatever name we may continue to use, we have passed from the realm of Science into that of History, even if of History treated schematically.

tested, of the social structure. But such empiricism is not enough.

The Unpopularity of Scientific Methods. The ' *politike episteme*,' the political science, which Plato so properly regarded as 'wisdom,' as a science of method to be utilized by the expert, has been confounded with 'political' or 'constitutional' history or the 'history of government,' whenever it has escaped from its customary fate of being treated as a collection of essays and *belles lettres* on political themes, such as 'Liberty.' But this study, of which the founders of Philosophy were the nursing fathers, has fallen into contempt for yet other reasons than that it possesses no graver weight than is due to the unaided genius of individual thinkers and essayists.

Any attempt to make Politics more worthy of the name of a science has met with little academic collaboration. The metaphysician dislikes its empiricism, the natural scientist suspects its human uncertainty, the historian abhors its attempt to theorise ; each makes a peace offering of it to the others. It has been left to the unsympathetic guardianship of the moral philosopher, to the unappetizing nourishment of local and arbitrary fact served up by the lawyer, to the occasional help of the suspect follower after psychological opinions, and to the unscrupulous attentions of men of affairs.

Moreover, when political science has become logical, it has been its misfortune to become objectionable to the tastes of the mass of men. When the early economists seemed to justify, by an 'eternal law,' the more shame-faced operations of business enterprise, their explanations were well-received, as meeting a popular need and as satisfying the public conscience. Quite other was the fate of the premature use of the abstract method by Hobbes to develop a doctrine of sovereignty which, if entirely acceptable when later applied by the prosaic Austin to the British Parliament, was detestable when applied by its originator to the Stuart kings. And the dispassionate scientific honesty of Machiavelli, before Hobbes, had scarcely contributed to render a frank treatment of the subject acceptable to ages more squeamish than that of the Renaissance. It was safer to practise, along with the great Frederick, Machiavelli's doctrines, and to write a book against his name. Political science in the modern period has had a bad start. Economic Science by its early utterances pleased the dominant class ; Political Science in its early utterances displeased the insurgent and victorious classes. And yet, unless Politics ventures, as Economics ventured, to clear for itself the forest of detail by the use of abstract hypotheses and of a scientific method, it can no more hope to advance to the status of a science than Chemistry could advance without the atomic theory.

The Unpopularity of Determinism, and the Barbaric Pleasure of Free-willing. Recent years have, indeed, seen a violent reaction against economic determinism.

And, although men will glibly enough admit that such or such a war was 'under the circumstances, inevitable,' a deterministic treatment of Politics has little enough to expect in the matter of popularity. Politics, in common with Theology and Economics, has suffered from the obstinate insistance of the man in the street that 'he would have his own opinions about these matters' (although, as Herbert Spencer wistfully remarked, no layman would venture to express an opinion on quaternions or on the physiological theories of Helmholtz), and from his conviction, either that all conventional opinions are beyond challenge, or, at the opposite extreme, that 'it is all a matter of opinion.' That there can be 'no liberty of conscience' in matters of science is unpalatable,[3] and this distaste, combined with an anthropocentricism, to which the belief is natural that not the facts but man's wishes and aspirations and his convenience are the measure of all things, leads to the ready denial that there is or can be any science of Politics. It is yet the argument of this present study that a scientific method is necessary in the treatment of Politics. Although it may sometimes go sore against the grain of the 'plain man' to permit his theoretical prejudices and personal interests to be overridden by the conclusions which may be derived from available knowledge, to resist such conclusions is to court disaster,

[3] A. Comte : *Early Essays* (edit. Routledge), p. 97 : " In Astronomy, Physics, Chemistry and Physiology there is no such thing as liberty of conscience."

even when one dignifies one's obscurantism by the name of democratic sentiment.

The danger to science, due to this anthropocentric bias of human thought, is an ever-recurring one. To be deposed from being sultans of creation offends too bitterly the vanity of men. When the ordering in their courses of stars is under debate, the passions of most men, who are neither mathematicians nor theologians, remain unaroused. But against the discovery of unaltering rules in political life, the protest of unsystematic common sense is even more vigorous than cogent. The fear of men is very deep-seated, as they see domain after domain of Freedom and Chaos being reduced to scheme and order, lest they themselves should in due time be placed in the humiliating position of automata. The objection to determinism is emotional. This fear, which prefers to law even a barbarous whimsicality of action such as primitive men attributed to the forces of nature, is yet grounded on a delusion and evoked by a bogey. No science can remove the values discoverable in experience by Poetry and Religion. They think too highly of science who are so much alarmed by it. Schematism, which is external and pragmatic, cannot cut down into the life of personal freedom.[4] But the menace from

----

[4] It is significant that the demand for freedom of will and action, although often made in the name of the higher human values, is by no means distinctive of the deeply religious consciousness. Rather it reminds one of the dismay of the savage when he is robbed by his enlightened white instructor of the freedom of action of his suns and moons, or of the Hellenes denouncing Anaxagoras for impiety

science is often felt, not so much because it dissolves the highest values, as because it touches a private, ego-centric and quite ungodly pride in, and a barbaric vanity about, our liberty as lords of the world. The time has come to fling this child's tinsel crown aside, take stock of our position without prejudice, and find our place, wherein we can best do what we may do.

The Method of Approach : I. Human Nature in Politics v. Scientific Politics. It is frequently and rightly insisted that Politics must not, through undue absorption in system and machinery, lose touch with the individuals, each with his own idiosyncrasy, who make up society.[5] This protest, as was indicated in the preceding chapter, is entirely justified if it be directed against the tendency to be satisfied with a description of institutions and governmental machinery, which ignores the thrust and nature of the forces, thanks to which these institutions take shape or this machinery works.

in reducing Helios to the rank of a celestial body. Doubtless, in a certain sense, they were right—Helios was much more than a minor star—but not in the scientific sense. The weakening contradiction, however, between the affirmation of arbitrarianism, popular in an age inspired by faith in the power of every individual to progress to a happy future, and the assumption of determinism, which lies at the root of most of our scientific methods and inventions, is common to twentieth-century thought (Cf. A. N. Whitehead : *Science and the Modern World*, 1925, p. 112).

[5] W. Lippmann : *Preface to Politics*, ed. 1914, p. 32 : " That is just the deepest error of our political thinking—to talk of Politics without reference to *human beings*." But cf. p. 300 : " Real statesmanship begins by accepting *human nature*." There may be a difference (italics mine). For the protest, referred to in the text, *vide* especially the distinguished work of Professor Graham Wallas.

It is especially the danger of lawyers to rest satisfied when they have presented the reader with a documented statement of the character of the social order which in fact obtains and which the courts are prepared to maintain, even though these facts, left by themselves, furnish no more enlightenment concerning the cause why they have come there, or should be there, than do the devices of heraldry. The subject termed 'Government' is a relatively unimportant part of Politics, but even Government is much more than the description of the governmental machinery of kings, parliaments, presidents and ballot-boxes, however sacred some may deem these stage-properties of the science.

But this protest would be beside the mark if it meant, not that we should study psychology and the more abiding and reliable characteristics of human nature, or the influence upon human conduct of the partially determinant factors of geographic and economic conditions, but that Politics should never ascend above retailing what old women may happen to have said to canvassers at election time. These comments are doubtless full of racy wisdom ; but Politics is something more than this. If the study of Politics is to be profitable, the statements of this science, although lacking in that metaphysical and absolute certainty which Kant endeavoured to give to Ethics, must possess as permanent and general an application as is practicable. The clever remark of de Maistre, that he had never met 'man,' was scarcely helpful, since by parity of reasoning it could have been shown that he had never met the French or the Germans, with whom he claimed to be acquainted. So far as is useful we are concerned with the political conduct of any man ' of like passions with ourselves ' ; to a less degree with the political method of a certain age or even of a certain people ; and not very much with the conduct of my eccentric neighbour next door, save in so far as his failings are ' very human,' i.e. he confesses unabashed to motives which most men experience, but few admit. The effect of the activity of ' human nature ' in politics must be considered a pledge of uniformity and order, not a plea for inconsequent chaos.

II. *The Free-will Objection v. Hypothetical Determinism as the Basis of all Natural Sciences.* The objection to the scientific treatment of Politics on the score of the freedom of the will is of all objections the most obstinate and fundamental, even if of less practical importance than the preceding. It demands such brief notice as is here possible. This objection does not take the form of the assertion that human beings never repeat their actions or that there is no such thing as habit. But, while reluctantly admitting force of habit and the tyranny of custom and of rules of conduct, it is commonly asserted, in effect, that it is the moral privilege of human beings at any time to break out into inexplicable and, thus far, into irrational action. This is stated, by those who have a simple faith in human freedom of will, to be a fact of experience.[6] Any statistical attempts to neutralise by averages the significance and the essential individuality of actions are rejected —and indeed rightly rejected.[7]

[6] Professor Bergson, in the course of a defensive argument which makes large play with the fact of our ignorance of our own motives, admits : " In this instance I am a conscious automaton, and I am so because I have everything to gain by being so. It will be found that the multitude of our daily actions are performed in the same way. . . . Moreover, we will grant to determinism that we often resign our freedom in more serious circumstances " (*Time and Free Will*, Eng. ed., pp. 168–9). This admission is quite enough for the present purposes of Politics, which can afford to neglect ' great and solemn crises.' The politicist is concerned with action and not with ' the inner world of conscious states,' where determinism, we are told, ' loses every shred of meaning.' The social sciences, as a matter of method and not of philosophical dogma, must be frankly behavioristic. They are not concerned with intention or appreciation, save so far as these show themselves in historical action (*vide supra,* p. 9). As M. Bergson admits : " When we turn " (in science) " to our conscious states we have everything to gain by keeping up the illusion through which we make them share in the reciprocal externality of outer things. . . . The greater part of the time we live outside of ourselves. . . . We live for the external world rather than for ourselves " (*ibid.*, p. 231). Cf. Graham Wallas : *The Great Society* (1910), pp. 24–5.

[7] Sigwart : *Logic*, Part III, § 101 (1895, trans. H. Dendy), pp. 502–4 : " All that statistics corroborate in such cases is that causes which we have known in some other way have taken effect, and have not been checked by others, and they afford a measure for the relation between their efficiency and that of all the others. There has seldom been a more senseless statement propounded than that it has been proved by statistics that marriages are not based, according to the ordinary belief, upon individual inclination, etc., but are regulated by a law which, regardless of the heads and hearts of individuals, makes marriages depend upon the price of corn. . . . Any formulation of real laws can refer only to the activity of the efficient units, of individuals, and must be based upon psychology." " An average . . . by itself does not even justify us in expecting that the majority of the particular instances in a region will approximate to it " (*ibid.*, p. 487). The average may, however, indicate to us that the rule of the ' head ' may dictate a relationship between the

A norm itself, however, is not denied by voluntarians. It is not asserted that the abnormal is normal to men, that the idiosyncratic and unexpected is more common than the general and anticipated. But they do assert that the more important and decisive events are just those which seem to indicate a voluntary breaking through all laws and breaking away from all rules. Thus norms of action are merely superficial, based on aggregations of similar (and these the less significant) actions, not on examples of underlying and over-ruling forces or principles. History, it would seem, is a sand-heap which becomes no transparent vitric mass, but separates out into individual and dissimilar granules, under the heat of analytic thought. Events are not links in any chain, predestined beforehand, even if humanly unpredictable ; still less are they ripples on the surface of one ' many-dimpled ocean.'

It is impossible to conclude on this subject here ; the argument, as John of Salisbury said long ago of that concerning universals, has taken longer in the discussion than the empire of the Cæsars in the building. A few remarks only are possible.

The tendency of modern thought may not unfairly be asserted to be opposed to both determinism *ab extra*, i.e. by physical forces exclusively, and to the arbitrary voluntarism of which the logic must end by defending an irresponsible and irrational will, *causa non causata*. On the contrary, it favours

price of food and the willingness to marry which may come as a surprise to the preconceived opinions of many.

a doctrine of determination from *both* within *and* without—self-determination in the light of total (super-individual) experience. It is favourable to determination of the entire present by the entire past. And, while denying that mechanical causation is an adequate explanation in the realm of matter, it is inclined to assert the possibility of an ætiology of the very extravagances of the mind.

Modern thought may equally fairly be asserted to tend towards the obliteration of the sharp division between the freakish whimsicality of man and the servile monotony of the natural world and of the animals,—the ' spirited things ' (anima-lia).[8] Human actions are individual ; human beings are individual. And this individuality is important for many purposes. So also chemical reactions and the behaviour of stars are individual, and this kind of individuality is important for some purposes. But for the purpose of the physical and the social sciences it is the common characteristics which have pragmatic value.

The physical sciences have built up all their achievements by emphasizing the orderable and determined side of nature and overlooking its many-

---

[8] Bernard Bosanquet : *Three Chapters on the Nature of Mind*, 1923, p. 75 : " I think so or act so because what I am shapes itself so." On p. 40 Dr. Bosanquet speaks of " the seamless continuity by which the individual passes into the universe," and hereby corrects a one-sided doctrine of ' inner ' determination. More explicitly on p. 58, he writes : " Surely the typical and fundamental act of mind is that self-assertion of the objective by which, through the mind and by means of its psychical matter, it asserts and constructs itself, and controls the mental behaviour, both theoretical and practical."

coloured variety ; they have ignored the content
for the sake of the method or form. For Astronomy
a star is not a world of unexplored things, but a
fiery mass, of determinable conduct. Similarly,
without committing ourselves to any crudely
materialistic psychology or ' doctrine of reflexes,'
it is at least possible to treat the subject matter of
the social sciences in a deterministic fashion. Moreover, any such treatment is as admissible in
philosophy as it is hopeful by scientific analogy.
Modern philosophic voluntarism rather assumes
the attitude of scepticism towards a too mechanical
doctrine of causation, with its Cartesian imagery
of the impact of solids (as billiard-ball causes
billiard-ball to move), than endeavours a defence
of the naïve and positive dogmatism of the plain
man. But to doubt, wisely enough, the adequacy
of our present notions of cause is not freely to accept
the introjection of arbitrary events into the world
of our experience. So far as man is rational he is
under the logical law of reason ; he is incarnate law
as well as law-giver. It may also be that his sensa-
tions, motions, even aberrations, are no less certainly
under law, though it be the law of his body and of
the organ which reason uses.

The plain man, however, still tends to be dis-
satisfied. Free-willing is a fact of experience and—
which is more to the point—a fact very dear to him.
But, it may be said, it is also a fact of human
ignorance, of our finite limitations. The human
memory is like a lamp struggling to illumine a vast

room ; what comes from out of the dark into the light seems to come spontaneously from nowhere. This seeming freedom and spontaneity is a necessary and healthy illusion of those who cannot bring all that determines them to action into consciousness, no more to be deplored than the limitation which prevents us from seeing with our eye the structure of the atom. We are not concerned to deny consciousness of purpose. But the purpose may not be of ' our ' making in any precise sense ; this immediate experience of freedom may be no more to be trusted, as a scientific truth, than that which shows us the sun going down in the west, though, like this experience, it is to be enjoyed. That men are reluctant to abandon the free-will doctrine surely renders suspect the very doctrine which they seek to defend ; they adhere to the more naïve theory, not because it is true, but because they will it to be true—in brief, because they have an interested motive in adhering to it.[9] It is hard to

---

[9] The popular aversion to the talk of ' laws ' in human affairs is, partly, a healthy scepticism about the omniscience of *savants*, partly because these ' laws ' are visualised as external and tyrannical, and the plain man is provoked into a determination to ' do as he pleases,' as, in the light of his past experience, he is fully entitled to do. Certainly no self-determinist would deny him his right, but would, on the contrary, point out that it is the most natural, rational and explicable affair in the world, this mulishness. Many men imagine that the determinist position involves that those who have hitherto let down pint-buckets into a well must ever after continue to do so, and cry ' kismet ' when the drought comes, instead of letting down gallon-buckets in faith, in order to test the capacity of the well. This is an error. The plain man needs rather to be reassured that in the discovery, as far as is possible, of the laws of human conduct, lies the hope of maintaining a stable, although not a static, society,

abandon the ' wild lawless freedom.' But it is only
for those who do not clearly distinguish the realm
of science, which is a realm of means, from the realm
of values or ends,[10] that so many experiences of
worth in life seem to be degraded by a determinist
philosophy.

Politics must view social phenomena externally,
considering without moral *parti pris* the appraisals
of value and conventional estimates which it
observes that men, in given places or times, in fact
entertain. It must merely regard them as but
added factors in the total situation, to be dispassionately weighed when they are shown by
results to incline the balance towards this or that
action. The appreciation of the meaning of the
phenomena it must leave to art and religion, which
alone are competent to give us ' empathically ' a sympathetic understanding of the personal experience.

since thereby irrational and revolutionary experiments may be
avoided, or at least their ultimate failure predicted as *contra naturam*.
The day will doubtless come when the plain man will appeal as
unhesitatingly and, it is to be feared, as uncritically, to ' political
laws,' as he did, in the days of Archbishop Whateley, to ' economic
laws ' as to a new Pentateuch.

[10] It is not the opinion of the present writer that any *ultimate*
division between the realms of science and of values is tenable.
This would be the old fallacy of the ' two truths.' The estimate of
values must be influenced by our *whole* experience and by our entire
knowledge of truth. Similarly there can be no ultimate division
between self-determination and hetero-determination. The ' internal ' and ' external ' parts are, as factors, mutually reactive. The
physical world may be external to us, but the world of mind is not
our private and sealed-up possession, but something greater than
ourselves. Thinking, it has been happily said, is a social act. And
it depends, for its content, upon external civilisation and material
technique and conditions.

Pure politics is limited to ' naturalism.' That is the price paid for its method. But its method may attain results, and this resulting knowledge of social workings may give us, as every practical science should, increased control, the control of men over the hitherto alarmingly uncontrollable behaviour of man.

So far as the above argument be true, so far the contention holds that human conduct is not a mere pattering of the leaves of isolated phenomena, brushed up afterwards into heaps called ' generalizations,' but is something which proceeds thus or thus because, granted the circumstances, it must so proceed. It has a law. But, it must be emphasized, we are not here, in Politics, concerned dogmatically to assert a determinist theory, or to lay down a philosophical position. Leaving the drawn battle of the philosophers, it is sufficient if we assert that the voluntarian is at least as suspect as the determinist ; that he is not entitled to thrust the burden of proof always on his opponent's shoulders ; that for us the *onus probandi* will rest with him ; and that for our purposes we shall adopt the hypothesis that human conduct (as distinct from human value) is as completely determined by the antecedent situation as physical action, although human conduct is not solely determined by ' external causes '—any more than is, it may be, physical action.[11] We adopt as an hypothesis that which,

[11] Cf. the pampsychist philosophy of Professor J. Ward (*The Realm of Ends*, 1911, *passim*) which, whatever its intrinsic value, should serve to give pause to dogmatic dualists. Μέγας ἐν τούτοις Θεός, οὐδὲ γηράσκει.

as a thesis, is maintained by the great authority of Immanuel Kant.[12]

It is, at least, possible to affirm that, whatever may be valuable or good or desirable, certain things are theoretically impracticable. Here we are not concerned with whether it is good to build any bridge or this bridge, but with the conditions under which bridges can, or cannot, be built. In pure theory we must first study strictly as historians, without pride or prejudice, what mankind does, and hence state tentatively (the scientist's hypothesis) what men, on certain presuppositions, will do.

As a result of this study it should be possible to construct a plan of action which will not indeed correspond to the precise conduct of any man, but which will yet be useful as indicating the probable conduct, granted such or such a social situation, of every man. Machiavelli, without explicitly enunciating any doctrine of determinism, sketched out numerous such sequences or schemes of conduct, and his practical advice would have been futile if there were not a very considerable measure of consistency in human conduct, and of constancy in human method. " Men are born and live and die, always in accordance with the same rules ": a statement which, if open to challenge, yet indicates

---

[12] Kant: *Idea of a Universal History*, 1784 (trans. De Quincy, *London Magazine* x, 1824): " Whatsoever difference there may be in our notions of the freedom of the will metaphysically considered, it is evident that the manifestation of this will, viz. human actions, are as much under the control of universal law as any other physical phenomena."

the direction of Machiavelli's own thought. Hobbes' belief in determinism was expressed with his customary downrightness, and if the crudity of his belief damaged his philosophy, its vigour gave fearlessness and distinction to his interpretation of human nature. It is at least significant that the two most outstanding of political writers have adopted the deterministic hypothesis in their treatment of the subject.[13]

It would, however, be both mistaken and unnecessary to commit ourselves to any such position dogmatically, in the present state of our knowledge and of the philosophy which we are able to construct from reflection upon it and upon our natural prejudices. If the determinist theory is the more acceptable, there is no initial difficulty in the idea of a social science. But it must be insisted that if, on the contrary, some ' arbitrarian ' or ' voluntarian ' or other such ' free-will ' or ' free-willing ' theory be sounder, it is perfectly legitimate in science to treat social data *as if* determined (by its own whole past), provided that useful results are thereby attained. In mathematics, we may intercalate a number to solve an equation and eliminate it before we present the answer. So, in social science, we are entitled to the liberty of our hypothesis, if thereby we can in fact get results.[14]

[13] Machiavelli : *Discorsi*, I, xi, and Hobbes : *Eng. Works*, ed. Molesworth, II, p. xxii, and VII, p. 184. Cf. *infra*, p. 218.
[14] *Vide* H. Vaihinger : *Philosophie des Als Ob*, and H. Poincaré : *La Science et l'Hypothèse*.

III. *Social Conditions may be Determined, but are so Complex as to be Unpredictable.* Other thinkers do not deny the necessity which controls all events, but they do deny that it is possible to foretell what shape this necessity will take. The past waves which broke on the beach we can understand *must* have been, the future waves by the same token we are sure will be, but what form these many-shaped waves will take we cannot say. The past wave was of such a kind, definite ; the future wave will also be of a definite kind, but who can tell of what kind ? Each wave, even if the curve of its crest and the drops in its foam were necessarily of a certain kind or quantity—even if it was predestined, and, as the Scripture says, numbered,—was yet also unique. So each man is the product of the multiplying out in his person of a myriad factors, and nowhere else in experience are combined those precise factors, which in themselves are resultants changing moment by moment. History may be the record of the decreed, but it may well be objected that it is not a book of prophecy.

This objection, so far as it is directed against all prediction of *detail*, as distinct from hypothetical prediction of the general *form* of action consequent upon the fulfilment of any certain given conditions, cannot be too readily conceded.[15] But, when it is

---

[15] The distinction between the science which deals with the *form* of social relationships (of individuals *as* related, not merely of individuals who *happen to be* related) and the *content* of social life, is well drawn by Simmel (*Soziologie*, 1923, pp. 3-4 ; and N. J. Spykman : *Social Theory of Georg Simmel*, 1925, pp. 26–27,

directed against any attempt to make statements concerning conduct which will be true of the future as of the past, it must not be permitted to pass unchallenged. Human nature is not so irrational as is here pretended, or the emotions and passions of men so unlike.

In part the objection derives its force from the immense complexity of human phenomena, which seem to defy analysis or simplification. The search for ' causes ' usually, it must be confessed, merely results in the grotesque. The objection here urged is as natural to the ' concrete ' mind, which runs to the multitude of things, as it is unsatisfactory to the theoretical mind which, when it ' breaks up ' its experiences, only finds broader unities. Of the very waves one must remember that, although we cannot foretell their height, still we build towns on the shore ; men look forward to the day when seismography will predict the tidal wave.[16]   In

and 38). I am, however, unable to agree, as pointed out elsewhere (*infra*, p. 175) with Simmel in his differentiation of Sociology as the general science of the relationship of persons in civil, ecclesiastical and other societies, from the social science of Politics which presumably deals with some specific relationship, i.e. governmental, or perhaps, for Simmel, with mere ' content '—the subject of the social historian. To the mind of the present writer this deprives Politics of all *raison d'être ;* it becomes a mere historical study of (civil) governmental activities.

[16] J. S. Mill : *Logic,* 1879, Bk. VI, § i.   Mill, while (p. 486) condemning the pseudo-scientific language in which the Benthamite school wrapped up the polemic of the day against the self-interestedness of monarchies, is himself of the opinion that a social science of ' tendencies,' although not of ' prediction,' i.e. hypothetical and formal, not particular and contentual prediction, is possible, and must be abstract to the degree of only considering the influence of a

short, we may know all, or almost all, that is useful.

Now Politics confessedly desires to be a pragmatical science, not indeed in the sense of a craft or technology, but in that it abandons hope of mathematical accuracy. It only aspires to meet the two tests of prediction (if this is done, then that will, *ceteris paribus*, happen) and of positivity, i.e. that the *corpus* of its results is not a matter of shrewd opinion, liable to dialectical objection and perhaps sewn with logical fallacy, but is a matter of selected experiences or experiments which, on repetition, are found to yield to each observer the same conclusions. It would be a science precisely in the sense in which Economics is a science, no more and no less. Politics, in brief, should be a positive science, not a conglomerate of historical excursus, of *belles lettres* about ' liberty ' and the like, and of debating points prepared for a party platform.

Politics is a science of prediction. Daily and hourly we make predictions, sufficiently accurate for our practical purposes, about human actions, and, although some of these predictions may be mere predictions of content and detail, and, as such, be only superficial in their regularity, some may be predictions of method and form. That my morning train will leave at the same time to-day as it has

few predominant factors in the determination of social affairs. Among them, infelicitously, as most of us must think, he lists ' national character.'

left for the last year is a practical certainty, but nevertheless dependent upon the good pleasure of the railway company as set forth in their time-table ; but that the controllers of the railway company will run the service at a real and permanent loss, as they understand loss, or issue the time-table as a hoax on travellers, is contrary to all that we know about the workings of human conduct. Similarly, that every body of men in power will tend to acquire to themselves more power is not a statement which need fear serious challenge. And these consistencies of conduct are sufficiently formal, recurring age after age, although varying con-tentually with the particular conditions (for History never identically repeats itself ; the context taken as a whole is different), for it to be possible tenta-tively to put forward hypotheses as to concomitant or consequent lines of conduct, which hypotheses, upon constant re-verification, can be accounted laws.

Politics, moreover, is a science in that it consists of a body of verifiable and systematic knowledge, gathered by observation and experiment. That Politics can become an experimental science has been asserted by Bryce and others,[17] but is frequently denied. It is alleged that, although legislatures may ‘ experiment ’ and learn by experi-

[17] J. W. Garner : *Introduction to Political Science*, p. 23. Pro-fessor Garner is, however, here referring to legislation which can only be called experimental in the sense that it is empiric, not in the, alas ! rare sense of an experiment thought out, controlled, and scientifically observed.

I

ence, their experiments are not such in the precise sense of a series of exact observations of some process under prepared and controlled conditions, of a kind to exclude unintended interference. But, if I observe the amount of intoxication in ten overcrowded areas and in ten adequately housed areas of the same general type, observe the changes in the statistics of intoxication after clearing a congested area (perhaps cleared at my suggestion), and the change when an area, put under observation at my suggestion, becomes more crowded, I have conditions which are experimental in the same sense as a piece of chemical research may be called experimental. In both cases, in order to establish a conclusion (as to the chemical process, or the fact of partial dependence or complete independence of intoxication upon bad housing), it would, of course, be necessary to repeat the experiment many times. In states more expertly managed than at present, it may be thought economical in the long run to do this.

IV. *The Objection that no Social Science can Account for Great Men.* Politics has, however, to consider the case of the ' beasts and the gods,' the great men and the insane, who are (*contradictio in adjecto*, it may seem ; but the popular phrase is, as ever, significant) ' a law unto themselves.' As anatomists, not builders of constitutions, as political physiologists, not political artists, we cannot afford, with Aristotle, to pass these people by on the other side. If the course of political action be determined by the personalities and vagaries of great men, then the analogy of politics to everyday experience, with its monotonous repetitions, will not hold. But those who have fallen under the influence of such tragedians as Carlyle, and accept the 'great man' interpretation of History (in the more pompous sense of the term, which excludes everyday, menial experience), have to explain not merely why the great man comes to have such or such ideas, but also how he induces other men to act contrary to expectation and common fashion.

The lives of men of genius are either consummate expressions of the spirit of their age, or initiate new movements because these men have combined in some unusual fashion the old movements or old knowledge ; these are men who take the trouble to look at the old world in a new perspective—as it were from between their legs. But, whatever the nature of their contribution, it is still a contribution merely of content, affecting the detail of history, not an innovation breaking through all preceding method and upsetting our notions of human psychology. Politically, the highly successful man is a man of singular intelligence in using his knowledge of how men habitually act. Hence he gets the reputation for being, in the current phase, 'a man who knows the ropes,' i.e. understands opportunities in the 'system.' A Napoleon or a Mussolini is a man who understands human nature better than his neighbours, better than ' the children of light ' ; who knows precisely how far he may take liberties with circumstances ; who is extraordinary chiefly in the keenness of his sense for the possible.

Whatever, moreover, be the individual force of the great man in overthrowing institutions erected in response to past human needs, or in breaking up this or that shell of convention with which, in forms comparable but not identical, human desire perpetually encrusts itself, the results of his action will soon tend to conform to general type.   First the revolution, then the reaction, then normalisation ; new appearances, but still the old desires ; new devices and machinery, but still the old manner of working of human beings in society and much the same forms of conduct.   The New France of *liberté, égalité, fraternité* carries its frontiers to the Rhine ; Soviet Russia does not neglect to maintain prestige in the East.   Not that there is no progress, for perhaps there may be better machinery and less friction ; but this greater social harmony is secured not by hectoring, but by recognising the permanence of human desire.

The law of gravitation, or the form of the parabola described by a ball, are not put to fault because no one can predict the force or directive drive or individual character of the human hand which threw it.   Politics is not concerned with whether the ' great man,' a subtler and more complex and unaccountable man than his neighbours, cannot break through the ordinary rules of action and be an eccentric to its laws, the perpetual surd of genius.[18] For Politics does not pretend to be a science of all human action equally, any more than physicists hold it within their province to account for works of art or for the effect of human action upon matter. Politics is not a philosophy or even a complete psychology. It is concerned with the form of human action in a certain aspect of experience, and, primarily, with the more ordinary manifestations. It may admit that some day it will be called upon to explain, not only the more general form of human action (which is of especial practical importance) in the field of the interrelation of human wills, but more recondite cases. But it will no more attempt this task at present than will a chemist begin an analysis of highly complex substances in the field of organic chemistry, while his knowledge of inorganic chemistry is still inadequate. It is, however, as absurd to object that the social sciences cannot explain the career of a Mussolini or the effects of a protective tariff,[19] as to ridicule a Paracelsus because his chemistry could not explain ' something so simple ' as the organic matter of an oyster.

V. *The Objection that Life is not Departmental and*

[18] Most people in most of their actions, perhaps, resemble more closely the ball than the great man. But it must be agreed that " the causes of production of great men lie in a field wholly inaccessible to the social philosopher " (William James : *Will to Believe,* 1911, p. 225). He can point out the circumstances which will check their conception ; he has not the knowledge to state what the circumstances are under which they will be conceived.

[19] Alvord : ' *Musings,*' *American Mercury,* viii. 25, p. 436 ; J. S. Mill : *Logic,* Bk. VI, § i.

that Experience is an Indivisible Unity. But a graver difficulty than that of the eccentric actions of the exceptional man faces any theory of political method. Grant the determinate character of human action and the recurrence of similar action with similar situations ; grant formal predictability, and that even the exceptional man, who is to an unusual degree determined by himself—his own past—has yet to conform negatively to the limits set by the present social situation ; it yet does not follow that we can distinguish political action from action in general, or distinguish political motive from the complex mass of human motives, or predict anything about political conduct until we know a vast amount more about social conduct.

The great man who breaks through those external institutions and constitutions, which are built up by the mentality of the common man as the vital forces of the body build up skeleton from fluid and gristle, presents less difficulty from the point of view of method than the men who, a few for the whole of their lives and many for part of their lives, act on psychological principles other than those which we have thought fit to isolate for the better convenience of study. Such is, apparently, the philanthropist *sans arrière pensée*, in economic theory ; such is, apparently, the neurasthenic or 'weak-willed' man, or the unambitious man, or the monk or recluse, in political theory. This difficulty is not so much substantial as methodological. It raises the question of the practicability of discussing experience in a certain aspect and with emphasis on certain selected kinds of situation. To this subject it will be necessary to return when the nature of the political situation and the utility of the fiction of a political man are discussed. It is only important here to call attention to the general character of scientific method.

The method of science is, starting from the concrete, to abstract until a stage be reached when it is possible to state a formula which meets every instance *in that aspect* (*or those aspects*) of the phenomenon which is relevant to the inquiry being pursued, whether it be the weight of the object, its shape, its force, or some other characteristic, and whether all together or in isolation. The method of philosophy, on the other hand, is to synthesise these abstract conclusions with each other and with immediate experience, and to 'return to the concrete.' These formulæ of science, like the older magic, are ' controls ' by the aid of which we can do things, but what may be the effect upon our lives as a whole, if we choose to do them, it is no part of the scientist's business to decide. The physical scientist, for example, may abstract for his study the field of chemistry, and, although he may be interested in biochemistry, it is not his concern whether a certain process, chemically efficient if applied in industry, has evil psychological effects or is undesirable when taken in the entire context of experience and life. —*This Objection proves too much.* To this it may be replied that the chemical process is theoretically effective and could at any moment be put into operation by human agency, even if in practice unapplied, whereas political action, as distinct from action due to an incomprehensible mixture of human motives, is in fact never observed. Without elaborating the objection that the chemical process yet does have more than chemical effects, and can never be observed, even in a laboratory, just in a world of ' pure chemistry,' it will be enough to point out that, were there no ' purely political action,' there might yet be enough action of a dominatingly political nature for the political hypothesis to have practical utility. It is sufficient here if reasons be given for believing that to set out in pursuit of a political science is not an enterprise in its very nature futile. Whether it will succeed must be decided, not by subtle *a priori* argument, but by success. Arguments parallel to the objection raised here would undermine many other sciences besides Politics.

It is, then, asserted that Politics as a science has a right to be departmental and abstract, in its treatment of experience and of that section of experience covered by the term 'human society.' Physicists might claim, as certain of the more ardent do claim, to regard the province of psychology as part of their own sphere ; but it is found to be a more convenient method of treatment to separate the field of ' voluntary action ' and of psychical causation from the field of ' mechanical action ' and of physical causation,[20] although these fields are in experience

[20] B. Russell : *Analysis of Mind*, ed. 1921, p. 301.

inextricably joined. Similarly the fundamental differences of conduct, if any, of the sexes, differences of the conduct of men at different ages or of men of different races, are questions of the highest importance to the politicist, but it is not the function of Politics to enlighten us upon them, any more than upon the mind of Luther or upon the creed he believed. It is only entitled to consider these questions in so far as they affect the nature of the social structure, or challenge the suitability of a certain kind of social structure, whether ecclesiastical or civil. Again, the law of decreasing returns in agriculture is one of which the politicist must take incidental cognizance, but it is not one which he will regard as proper to his province, or in relation to which he will particularly concentrate his study of human conduct. It is a problem which would as much concern food-consuming automata living in isolation, as a society of wilful human beings. It is matter for the economic, not for the political specialist. It is only to be considered in so far as it affects (as the difference between extensive and migratory agriculture and intensive agriculture does affect) the form which human society takes.

We need not, therefore, be deterred from proceeding because of the reflection that the political situation is no more separable from the economic than the economic from the religious ; or that political action even in a political situation is not, always, guided by chiefly (or, often, by solely) political motives ; or that the texture of the political structure does not confront the attention of the casual observer. It is only here claimed that human action may for certain purposes be considered as determined by the action of past upon present experience, and by the interaction of man and his environment ; that this action is for many practical purposes and in the mass at least negatively predictable as to certain forms of action, though not as to detail—there are certain things that a statesman cannot afford to do ; that the existence of men of unusual power need not interfere with the utility of these predictions ; and that a method of treatment is not invalid because it is departmental. The question is whether it is fruitful.

Little, however, must be expected from all these negative statements of possibility, unless we posit a simplicity of human motive and, indeed, in the particular sphere of human activity with which we are immediately concerned, hypothetically a single consistent motive. The delimitation of this sphere as a department of observed human behaviour, and the choice of a suitable dominant motive as the principle in our hypothesis of the grounds of behaviour, must mutually influence each other. Hence, we could regard Politics, from the side of subject matter, as having for its field all behaviour resulting in the control or collaboration of one will over or with another. Or we could regard Politics from the side of the attitude of the participants, as the study of the activities of the will in satisfying the hypothetical desire for mastery over, or collaboration with, other wills. The value, however, of this hypothesis will be assessed by the light which it in fact throws upon the interpretation of history.

VI. *The Objection that Men do not Act according to Intelligent Self-Interest.* Regarded from the side of the psychological approach, the objection to hypothetical prediction is not entirely due to maximizing the complexity of social conditions, or to emphasizing the importance of the ' freedom of the will.' At least in part it is due to a fear of underrating the non-rational, ' unscientific ' elements in the nature of man. It would be easy to predict human conduct with some hope of success if men were entirely logical beings who, being faced with a situation, always responded to it in the wisest way, as the philosophers of the *Eclairecissement* and the Benthamites imagined, or in the way most conducive to their own interests. If so, instead of responding to apparently similar situations in widely divergent fashions, their action would be closely dictated by the situation, and could be anticipated to be similar when a similar situation arose. But in fact men are creatures of emotion and sentiment, erratic in their conduct. Not only is the whole situation complex and unrepeatable, but human nature is complex, and unlikely to react to these situations only in terms of their similarities.

Objectors have expatiated on the infinite variety of political phenomena, and upon its kaleidoscopic shiftings and absence of strict recurrence. The

obvious consideration that if no two human beings
are the same no more are any two leaves, that if
history never repeats its events neither does or can
the water ever return in the same stream, does not
seem to occur to these critics with sufficient force.
The objection which they presume insuperable is
indeed the elementary obstacle of difference in unity
which every natural science, by the establishment
of units of measurement and standards of reference,
has to overcome. The vagaries of human conduct
cannot exceed in multiformity the luxuriance of
natural variety. But science is concerned, not with
the essence of experience, but with the form, and
just as it is mistaken to divide between our æsthetic
appreciation of beauty in Nature and of beauty in
human things, so it is mistaken to make a division
between the scientific treatment of the inanimate
world and of human society. The division is
between the æsthetic and the scientific, the contentual and the formal ; not between the natural
and the human.

The Rational Element in Human Nature. Man is
not, it must be admitted, a pure intellect ' without
confusion of substance,' so that his conduct can be
plotted out, according to some simple rational
' form,' detected as underlying the riot of differences
in actual behaviour. His life is not guided by a fully
conscious pursuit of pleasure, or of self-interest, or
of self-fulfilment, and the intellectual hypothesis
about his actions (that he is guided by rational
self-interest—or rationally consistent altruism) is

thus never fulfilled by the facts. He is not a hedonist, although philosophers may think that he should be. What he would do, if he were what he is not, is not what he will do, and is of merely academic interest.

The Instinctive Element. Granted, however, that man does not act entirely from comprehensible rational motives or from predictable habitual ones, what are we to suppose that he does act from ? Here we are often referred back to the so-called ' instincts,' or even to the ' unconscious.' The unconscious, with its irrational instincts, its inexplicable presentiments, its unanalysable intuitions taking shape in consciousness, may, we are told by anti-intellectualists, have its own ' reasons ' which can neither be justified nor altered by the abstract understanding. It seems doubtful whether all this means very much more than that this Unconscious of von Hartmann, or Will of Schopenhauer, or Libido of Jung, although ' very cunning and intelligent,' does not subserve ends which can be related directly to the preservation or happiness (as he esteems it) of the individual, and is therefore irrational or ' not understandable,' judged by these all too human standards. But it does not follow that action dictated by this *libido* is by any means unpredictable, although it is, so far as we can see, purposeless ; rather there is likely to be in it a primitive simplicity. Nor, although resistant to frustration, need it be uncontrollable, any more than such a specific ' instinct ' as pugnacity is uncontrollable. All civilization is one vast dam thrown across the river flood of ' human nature ' ; it is only a bad dam when it holds the waters stagnant, without due outlet or use, until, mounting against the repressing walls, they burst forth. Instinctive action may be and often is both antici- pated, *ceteris paribus*, and advantageously counter- acted or controlled.

When we descend from the dangerous heights of the philosophy of the Unconscious to the working assumptions and experience of practical psycholo- gists, we discover that it is far easier to predict what their so-called instincts will lead an ' irrational ' crowd to do, then to what his intelligence will lead a man of high education. Although social action is seldom of so simple a nature as to involve only the lower nerve-centres and better understood reflexes, social action, from its collective nature, tends rather to inhibit or discount than to stimulate the subtler and more differentiated expressions of feeling. We are, moreover, in the first case concerned to analyse the general social structure, that which has been built up by the mass of men, as the shell is fitted to the back of the snail, to suit their own needs in getting through life. Here we have to deal with the simpler feelings such as move men in the mass. All profitable social work and intelligent legislation acts upon this assumption of the ' averageness ' of human nature. And we are entitled by experience to assume a certain ' method ' in the conduct of the average man.

It is probable that the present condition of our psychological knowledge will admit of no greater exactitude than the construction of a few hypotheses based on these major probabilities of human action. Indubitably so-called 'instinctive response' is uncertain; indubitably chance has its place in deciding the fashion of action. It would certainly be a delusion to entertain the hope that we are yet in a position to predict detailed action by noting 'influences,' after the fashion of the astrologers. Innumerable accidents may deflect the course of events when there is anything approaching an equilibrium between the directive forces. Even to speak of such forces as though they were distinct entities, between which the soul vacillated or was in suspense like Buridan's ass, is nothing but a clumsy metaphor. But be human nature as little guided by 'intelligent self-interest' as one may choose to maintain, there is no objection to assuming motive and method, and to positing hypothetically some one or few dominant motives, as the starting-point for experiment.

VII. *Factors Incalculable.* This assumption of method in human action and structure in human society does not, of course, at all involve the refusal to admit how important a part the incalculable plays in the determination of affairs,—not only events, but even the shape of institutions. For institutions cannot be entirely separated from events, or historical 'form' from historical 'content.' The tales of Achilles told to Alexander, the success of the Cæsarian operation with Julius, the shape of Cleopatra's nose,[21] the drunkenness of the men of Barfleur on a wild night in 1120, the internal cancer of Napoleon, may, each of them, well have changed the course of history. Great is the realm of what Frederick of Prussia called ' the Lord Chance.' There are certainly times when civilization is patient of one of several directive impulses, and when great destinies find as their executive instruments a few individuals.[22] No ' science of politics ' absolves us from individual moral obligation to serve the public weal ; it may merely indicate to us how we can avoid frittering away our energies in a steamy and futile enthusiasm, which runs counter to the channels dug deep by centuries of use through the obstacles of environment.

It would, however, easily be possible to exaggerate the importance for English history of the Norman arrow which slew Harold. It is not, indeed, because it is without consequence that Politics neglects the accidental—what may too lightly be termed ' les contingences négligeables '—but because it is too prolific in possibilities. And happily this neglect is permissible, because these possibilities are, broadly, possibilities of historical ' content,' and not of psychological ' method ' or of social ' form,' as

---

[21] Pascal : *Pensées*, I, ix, § 46. Cf. Burke's dictum : " The major makes a pompous figure in the battle, but the victory depends upon the little minor of circumstances."

[22] This would appear to be the meaning of Professor Troeltsch's remark (*op. cit.*, I, p. 107) : . . . " Die Weltgeschichte ist ungeheuer aristokratisch . . . Gnade und Erwählung sind das Geheimniss und Wesen der Geschichte."

manifested even, e.g. in so detailed a matter as
the governmental constitution of eleventh-century
England under the Normans after Harold was slain,
which, granted the facts and context, must have
taken some such shape. In Politics we are entitled to
simplify, by abstraction—by taking, as hypothetical,
frequently recurring historical situations; and by
' formalism,' in asking how a human nature assumed
constant will react to these situations, and what
method it will adopt. Thus, for two unknown
variables, are substituted a known variable and a
constant. Politics is not, then, an inherently impossible science. We turn to consider its method.

*The Assumption that Human Conduct is Similar in
Similar Situations.* This assumption, such as Bryce
made,[23] of actual constancy in human nature, is
probably cautious enough if we consider men in
certain abstracted fields of activity which are the
chosen subject-matter of our study, and on that
side of them which is brought out by the type of
situation selected. But it can be further safe-
guarded. Politics cannot stand still until Psychology has completed its investigations; rather it
should seek the advancement of knowledge by
boring through the mountain from the other side,
seeking to meet Psychology half-way. Politics may,
therefore, aptly safeguard itself from the dangers

---

[23] Lord Bryce : *Modern Democracies* (1921), I, p. 15. It should,
perhaps, be added that the assumption of constancy in human nature
is more cautious than the assumption that " there is in the phenomenon of human society one ' Constant '. . . . This is Human
Nature itself " (Bryce, *ibid.*), which is a highly ambiguous assertion.

K

besetting generalization from the average, by the construction, for purposes of argument, of an abstract ' political man.' It does not matter whether we may happen to believe that the man we meet in the street, in those situations and affairs with which we are alone concerned, acts very much as we postulate that the political man acts ; we merely ask that he should be accepted as a scientific hypothesis. It will then be our task as observers and historians to see how much of political fact and theory we can explain and cause to become intelligible by this hypothesis.

Some day we may be able to understand the laws which govern the meteoric careers of great individuals, human eccentrics, although we may suspect that these men are but superlative instances of the operations of the motives which dominate the many. For the present let us concentrate our attention on the regular movements of the ordinary planets and moons, on the movements of the common folk, both great and small, who go on their daily and monthly and yearly courses around their accustomed suns. History, which tells of all experience, can never be a science. No such objection can be urged against this social astronomy, Politics, so long as it admits that it utilizes a working fiction, the ' political man.' It is not fruitless to inquire how this laboratory creation will behave, and then to compare with this how men do in fact behave in political matters. The same expedient of an artificial single-motived man was utilized not unsuccessfully, *so long as its limitations were remembered*, by the economists in the pioneer days of Economics, when it was hard to see the wood for the trees of detail.

The Hypothesis of ' the Political Man.' Human action is neither arbitrary nor essentially unpredictable, but it is highly complex. As a matter of method in research it is, then, here proposed to overcome this difficulty of actual complexity by conscious ' formalism,' and then to test by History the value of the hypothesis. There are, however, difficultieś in the way of this particular method. The objection to the use of a concept comparable to that of the ' economic man ' is threefold. It may be held that the adoption of such concepts leads to a distortion, or at least to a biassed appraisal, of the importance of the social facts which History and observation show us. Or we may hold that this particular concept is no longer the most useful—is, in fact, obsolete. Or again, it may be held that it is not even a good working hypothesis, and never was. But none of these objections are fatal to the use of such a fiction as that of the ' political man.'

It may be suspected that those who approach a field of scientific research without some systematizing hypothesis, founded on the conclusions of ' the first view,' and who proclaim that they approach the subject without any ideas of their own or preconceived notions, do actually approach it, not without hypotheses, but merely unaware of their hypotheses, and full of the popular and uncritical prejudices of their time.

Whether the doctrine of the ' economic man ' is now the most useful hypothesis in the field of business experience, despite its difficulty in dealing with the facts of gregariousness and of indolence, of the ' publicly minded ' citizen, and of the negro on the Nyassan highlands who will not work for a wage ; whether our observations in this field are now sufficiently systematic and our psychology now sufficiently subtle for some other hypothesis to be made better fitting the facts, or for subordinate principles to be laid down, is a matter for the economists among themselves. There is not the least intention of arguing here that the rudimentary psychology and dogmatic individualistic philosophy of Adam Smith and Ricardo are satisfactory for the treatment of modern economic organization. We are not here concerned with the suitable technique or method for the adult discipline of Economics, but for delivering the infant science of Politics from the matrix of general political experience. No defence is intended here of classical economics. But that a crude psychological hypothesis, after a century of economic research, is proving inadequate and outworn, is neither surprising nor an argument against the employment of such a hypothesis by a science which is at present only where Economics was a century ago.

That the hypothesis is fundamentally false and contrary to all the observed facts, whether it be the classical hypothesis of the ' economic man,' or this, yet to be developed, of the ' political man,' is a thesis only tenable by those who decline to split up or abstract human operations. A parallel refusal to split up experience, a refusal at least as logically sound, would, as has been shown, stultify Physics as this refusal stultifies Politics. It is fundamentally due to the refusal to distinguish a pure from an applied science or a practical art. Just as, in particular crafts, a man develops a technique without, by becoming a technician, ceasing to be a man, so in certain definable situations it is certain sides of a man's self, certain only of his faculties and emotions, which are to a dominant degree called into play. And, being called into play by this situation, it becomes conventional that they *should* be so called, and the initial tendency evoked by the situation is confirmed and becomes habitual even apart from the precise demands of the situation. Thus it is appropriate enough to expect and assume a distinctive psychological attitude characteristic of the business situation (in part recognised in popular parlance as 'business morality'), and a distinctive psychology of the political situation. The experience, approach, and scale of relative values of the business man and of the statesman are not the same. This is not to say that the business man is not a human being, or the citizen not a good family man. But we can usefully divide the treatment of human behaviour according to the situation, and thus the question resolves itself into one of the appropriate distinction of social situations.

The fatal mistake of the classical economists was that, using a psychological hypothesis, they did not perceive the limitations of their own expedient, but foolishly treated their experimental fiction as an established fact, and their abstraction of human nature as the whole of it. The same disastrous error was made in Politics by Thomas Hobbes two centuries before, with that dogmatism which was customary to him and with a one-sidedness which was pointed out at the time.[24]   The efforts of Spinoza to ethicize that which was mistaken for a theory of human nature did little to quiet outraged convention, while they led yet further away from the recognition of the utility of the doctrine as based on a deliberate abstraction.   It is more important to have a hypothesis which, even though wrong, is recognized to be a hypothesis, than to have a sound hypothesis and fail to distinguish it from a complete and proven theory.

The important thing about the use of fictions, such as those of the economic or political man, is that they are an admission that the collection of facts in history, whether economic or political in their predominant bearing, must, if they are to be lent any internal unity or rational explanation in terms of motive, be approached psychologically, with some assumption of what it is that induces man to do this or organize that in a particular way.   And in the present state of our knowledge this must be done by the social scientist, as distinct from the

[24] *Vide* the present writer's *Thomas Hobbes*, 1922, p. 32.

professional psychologist, by bold, if well-selected, hypotheses. This does not mean that the social scientist should be ignorant of psychological advance, or a dilettante dabbling in speculations of his own.[25] It does not mean that the hierarchy of the sciences can be completely ignored. It does not mean that it is marvellous that, despite its early beginnings (along with Economics) in the Aristotelian school, no science of Politics has been achieved while there has been no developed Psychology, no extensive Anthropology and no scholarly History. But it does mean that, unless the social sciences are to mark time for a century, they must take those tentative conclusions of psychological research which seem most illuminating for the treatment of the various social fields and, treating them as assumptions for the explanation of social conduct, utilize them until the point is reached when they cease any longer to furnish a plausible explanation of the more recondite facts. And the fewer such hypotheses, on the principle of ' Occam's razor,' the better.

A Scientific Treatment of Politics will Expose much Uncritical Theory. Politics, so treated, can, then, afford for the moment to risk the accusation of being ' abstract.' It is abstract, not in the sense that it is theoretical, or out of touch with human behaviour. On the contrary, it is positive and *a*

---

[25] *Vide* the argument of *The History and Prospects of the Social Sciences*, by K. W. Bigelow, Roscoe Pound *et alii*, 1925, edited by H. E. Barnes.

posteriori in treatment. If the objections to a determinist treatment of social phenomena have, in the preceding pages, been successfully rebutted, a political science is, at least, not impossible. It is submitted that it should be the duty of Politics as a science to ground itself upon the humble facts supplied by Blue books and records,[26] and to break up the film of conventional interpretation by thrusting the probe of research into curious exceptions. It will be its task to study the side of human nature displaying itself in a type of situation marked and delimited by a certain kind of conduct recurrent in history, and falling within the general scope of the statesman's or the citizen's experience, such as the struggle for political control. And it will look to psychology for some tentative clue to the explanation of this behaviour. It will then lay down hypothetically a rule founded upon this marked, if one-sided, human tendency thus displayed, and by

[26] It seems regrettable that so many students who have been taught to regard the Public Records Office as a Mecca of all historians are ignorant of the very approaches to the Home Office Library. It is impossible to exaggerate the importance to be attached to reliable collections of detail, leading on to quantitative social surveys. But it is undesirable that these surveys, unsystematized by any political theory, should remain mere disconnected monographs. To apply to Politics a remark of Professor J. M. Clark's about Economics : " There is need, great need, for a common discipline which shall animate these special studies, co-ordinate them and interpret them to each other and to the intelligent reading public as well " (*The Trend of Economics*, 1924, p. 76). The four services which Professor Clark is of the opinion that such a discipline should render are the provisions of a scientific procedure, of suitable hypotheses, a summary and generalization of the results of inductive study, and ' an orienting of economic (or political) life.'

a logic confessedly as abstract as that of Hobbes, but justifiably, because consciously, abstract, pass from conclusion to conclusion, just so far as these conclusions throw light upon human conduct and suggest schemes for corroborative experiment, or starting-points for further research and helpful arrangement of material. This must by no means be understood as debarring some other hypothesis, perhaps equally fundamental. All that we ask is that the new hypothesis should with consistency explain as much of human conduct in the past and to-day as does the earlier hypothesis.

Human nature can only, as yet, be reduced to what is manageable by science by means of intentional abstraction ; we can no more compass all society within the scope of Politics or Economics— not to speak of one theory of Politics or Economics— than Psychology can compass, along with the mental form, the whole content of mental experience. By this means we may hope to attain an inadequate, but still serviceable, explanation of certain fields of social activity ; the hypothesis may be expected to explain something. And, just in so far as the hypothesis is followed out to its logical extreme, and it is shown where it becomes inconsistent with the facts of human experience, we may hope to attain an adequate critique of those fallacious human convictions, such as many of our beliefs about the State or Sovereignty, which are founded upon the belief in the entire adequacy and objective truth of what we know to be merely a convenient hypothesis, such as that of the unalterable self-assertiveness of human nature. If we were to assume that human beings in politics are moved by a lust for power, and were to discover that this hypothesis, raised to an absolute principle, leads to absurd conclusions, we should be able to criticize, with a force denied to the man who had never allowed this hypothesis, a doctrine of Sovereignty which, constructed in an age of which the violent experience might easily lead to a confusion of the hypothesis with the whole facts, happens to be based upon it. It is reasonable to suppose that in many cases relative truths have been raised by unscientific theories to the level of being absolute ones,[27] and upon a partial experience a dogmatic political creed has been built, just as the early physical philosophers asserted that Nature did, or did not, 'know a vacuum;' whereas modern science can allow the truth in different senses of both contentions. Such, then, is what may be expected from the treatment of Politics from the

[27] J. A. Fairlie: *Politics and Science, Scientific Monthly*, January, 1924, p. 27 : "Until after the middle of the nineteenth century most of the writers on Politics gave little attention to the detailed investigation of data, and their writings were largely legalistic deductions based on *a priori* generalizations. Then attention was given to historical records and the comparison of official documents and legal institutions. In the latter part of the century Mr. Bryce led the way to a much broader scope of personal observation, including the examination of legislative procedure, political parties, and other extra-legal practices and customs, in what President Lowell has called the Physiology of Politics." Professor Fairlie himself enters a strong plea for the increased use of statistical data (pp. 27–8) which is already available, or could be procured were there not the insistent belief that Politics, as an 'Arts subject,' can be studied 'on the cheap.'

side of Psychology and by the hypothetical assumption of a dominant motive in political activities.

The Subject-matter of Politics. Over against and supplementary to the study of Politics from the side of a psychological hypothesis, which may give order to the data, is the study of the actual political process, as detected from the intelligent observation of the field of political activities.

The adoption of hypotheses, for what they are worth, does not destroy the possibility of a strictly behavioristic treatment of political action, which declines to assume as axiomatic certain 'fundamental principles,' or to consider it to be its first task to examine these rationalizations of conduct, or to preface its studies by a declaration of ideals or of what, in the mind of the writer, should be the specific aims of political action or the utopias which ought to be built. All this is of the first importance in itself, but these matters are essentially problems of ethics, of what is desirable. And discussion of the desirable, to be convincing, presumes a preliminary discussion of what is possible ; the architect presupposes the engineer.

To the nature of the subject-matter of Politics far too little thought has been given. It has been assumed off-hand that the subject-matter of Politics is the State or states, regardless of the fact that the State, in the modern sense, did not exist in the Middle Ages,[28] and that the ' *Polis* ' which formed the centre of Aristotle's thoughts on τὰ πόλιτικα

[28] H. W. C. Davis: *Mediæval Europe* (Home Univ. Lib.), p. 93.

could more appropriately be described as ' the city-community ' than as ' the State.' Without inquiry, it is assumed that the State as distinct from what Hooker called the ' ecclesiastical polity,' or from any other organization for the control of men, is an organisation *sui generis*, deserving a science to itself, apart from the study of Society or of the Community.

This assumption is one great *petitio principii*, inherited from an age which wished, for polemical reasons, to regard the State and not the Church as the paramount organization, and as synonymous with the community and with organized society. The assumption is unwarranted, unscientific, and obstructive. It leaves Politics in the difficult position of being the study of a few, very hetero-geneous specimens, incapable of being studied in isolation from each other.[29] It tends to such mis-conceptions as that of a science of civilization,

[29] F. W. Maitland : *Collected Papers* (1911), III, pp. 295 ff. : " If the Creator of the universe had chosen to make a world full of compartments divided by walls touching the heavens, had put into each of these cells a savage race—if at some future time the progress of science had permitted men to scale these walls—I won't say but that this would have been an interesting world . . . but exceedingly unlike the world we live in. In the real world the political organisms have been and are so few and the History of them has been so unique that we have no materials apt for an induction of this sort, we have no means of forming the idea of the *normal* life of the body politic. . . . We do not know, if I may put it so, that Siamese twins are abnormal." This objection must always prove insuperable to a political science so long as we continue to establish comparisons between a few vast states, and not between the countless political actions of our neigh-bours which we see going on under our eyes. Politics, to be a science, must concentrate its attention on the essential political act—the establishment of a relationship between wills.

whereas a science, to acquire body, must be based on the observation of innumerable acts, illustrative of recurrent processes. Such processes are to be discovered in the political field as in the economic field. In the latter case the student is called upon to consider the aspects of that group of processes known as the ' business transaction.' In the former case the suitable subject for study is ready before his eyes in the relations of individuals to each other in society, regarded in respect of the relationship itself. Here the political processes are illustrated, not by a few states in different stages of growth, but by acts repeated innumerable times every day. It is essential for a science that it shall be based on the study of myriads of instances, capable of comparison as like and as different. Politics, therefore, if it is to be a science, must be based on the study of some act which is repeated countless times a day, not on the study of sixty states, or thereabouts, at different and not comparable stages of civilization. As the student of Economics studies the innumerable instances of the business transaction, so the student of Politics must study the innumerable instances of the political act. He must first satisfy himself about what the political act, κατ' ἐξοχήν, is, whether it is the act of control, by domination or collaboration, of one will by another, or some other act equally frequent and fundamental. But it must be some such commonplace act of an individual person or group. By admitting that the subject-matter of Politics is the acts of individuals, not of states, and that the individual will is the political unit,[30] a clear principle is given to the study of the science of the relationship of wills or the science of social action.

Conclusion regarding the Method to be Adopted. There is, then, such a study as Politics ; there is as yet no such thing as a political science in any admissible sense. To construct such a science out of the statesman's or citizen's experience, as Economics has been constructed out of the business man's experience, is a task which it is not *a priori* improbable will succeed. To pretend that this goal is as yet attained is but to obscure the road with a dust of words.[31] Politics must for the present confine itself to the humble task of collecting, where possible measuring, and sorting the historical material, past and contemporary ; and following up probable clues

[30] *Vide* a paper delivered before the American Political Science Association by the present writer, December, 1924, entitled The Doctrine of Power and Party Conflict (*Amer. Pol. Sci. Review*, November, 1925). Herbert Spencer had the merit of emphasizing that the concern of social studies was with the permutations and combinations of individual units, although he tended to forget that the result of these combinations might be a molecule or group acting towards the outside world as an individual unity.

[31] Sir John Seeley wrote, indeed, in 1896, a brilliant book which he chose to call an *Introduction to Political Science*, but this rather contains political wisdom about liberty and such things than a statement of the doctrine of an existent science. At present we have isolated observations and guesses at principle such as, e.g. R. Kjellen's Law of the Bridge-head (*Der Staat als Lebensform*, German trans.), or attempts to educe a science directly out of human history in general, such as those, e.g. of Professor Cheyney (*Amer. Hist. Rev. :* Law in History, Jan., 1924) or Dr. W. Vogel (*Hist. Zeitschrift*, CXXIV, i, 1923 : Uber den Rythmus im geschichtlichen Leben des Abendländischen Europa).

to the discovery of permanent forms and general principles of action.

Did, indeed, the study of Politics merely promise to confute bad politics, it would, as Sir Frederick Pollock has pointed out, be abundantly justified. Hitherto the unguarded field of political theory has been a veritable Valley of Hinnom wherein men have been permitted to cast without challenge the rubbish of uncritical speculation and the burning oil of enthusiasm, to fling the bodies of opponents and to sacrifice to strange idols. Much good critical work can be done by the testing of definitions and old generalizations. As philosophical concepts we cannot expect, as did G. C. Lewis,[32] to get a fixed usage in political terms. But as statements about human method they admit of an objective test, and of refutation by experience or of exposure as inadequate.

It is reasonable, however, to expect that political science will prove to be more than this, that it will give us some insight into the possibility of controlling the social situation, and will show us, if not what it is wise to do, at least what, human nature being what it is, it is unwise to do, because such action will cut across the grain of the social structure and athwart the lines of activity of the deeper forces which have built up this structure.

The difficulty in the way of a science of Politics does not lie in the nature of the case, but in the lack

[32] G. C. Lewis : *Remarks on the Use and Abuse of Some Political Terms* (1832).

hitherto of a suitable method. If the method of
Politics is to be purely empirical and discursive,
then Politics is a mere heaped-up garner of the
harvest of the stateman's experience. And this it
has hitherto been   it has provided not science but
shrewd seemings, not grounded knowledge but well-
argued opinions. We have looked in vain for some
simple indications of why the structure of human
society bears, in its many examples, such marked
similarity, and why there is so pronounced a tendency
of human beings to use certain well-worn methods in
coping with difficulties in their relations with each
other and with other groups. For, as Ratzel well
says, " universal history is monotonous." But
Psychology may supply us with certain clues for
the understanding of the general forms of political
action, as distinct from prediction of the particular
event. Owing, however, to the imperfect condition
of our psychological knowledge, it seems advisable
to take some one tendency and to follow out its
operations in society, and especially in that field of
social action and that succession of similar situations
in which it appears to be particularly dominant.

It is not improbable that Politics, supposing that
it can find some such governing tendency in its
particular field, is capable of becoming a science
or part of a social science, a late-born child of
theoretic principle and of actual practice, of Idea
and Experience. If this be true, it may be possible
to ' think through ' political history, and thought
will be justified in control. But, despite much

brilliant generalization and laying down of isolated principles, this possibility is not yet actual. Modern writers, such as Ratzenhofer, have usually stated the scientific 'if this be, then that is,' as a pseudo-scientific 'must be.' Thomas Hobbes spent his great energies in an attempt, obstinately persevered in, to delineate his private 'ought to be' under the dogmatic form of a 'this is.' Science, as such, is concerned neither with what ought to be nor with what happens to be, but with what must be when the conditions are fulfilled, with '*what must be, if.*' All that it is here proposed to do is to experiment, e.g. with the hypothesis that man in his political actions is moved by the desire for power, or, more precisely, 'to execute his own will'; and to inquire whether the consequences which must tend to flow from this hypothesis are in fact borne out by political experience. By 'political experience' we shall, chiefly, mean that conduct popularly called 'political' and which more peculiarly falls within the range of activities of the politician and active citizen. But, in order to see how much of total experience our hypothesis can account for, we shall not exclude all those ranges of conduct which seem likely to illustrate the operation of the same motive force. 'Situation' and 'hypothesis' will be used as mutually corrective concepts, the test being that of convincing explanation of observed conduct and established social structure. Sufficient, if it has been shown above that this method is neither inherently unsound, nor predestined to be sterile.

L

CHAPTER II

The Present Plight of the Study of Political Science.
The endeavour of various kinds of scientists, anthropologists, psychologists, economists, jurisprudents, to annex to their own realm a middle province, the difficulties into which the attempt has led them, and the unsatisfactory nature of the provisional frontiers drawn, force upon the student the conviction that this middle province, of Politics, is a realm in its own right, at least as susceptible of scientific ordering as any of its neighbours, and one more likely to prosper if treated independently.

No small portion of the problems—problems, on the one hand, of the imperative nature of an absolute ethic and, on the other, of the necessities of national security ; problems, on the one hand, of public morality, and, on the other, of private liberty; problems of the many poor and the few rich ; problems of Church and State—which the Nineteenth Century, with its philanthropy and imperialism, its conventionality and individualism, its democracy and its secularism, has bequeathed to the Twentieth Century for solution, is insoluble so long as our political knowledge remains rhetorical and vague, while our administrative methods remain amateur. These difficulties remain so grave a concern not only of our intellectual but also of our social life, owing to the singular absence in this field of all accepted and objective standards whereby to estimate the strength of the passing winds of party doctrine.

The great objection to a political science in the mind of the ordinary man is that the subject pompously so named has hitherto conspicuously failed to ' make good ' ; it has made a great display of packing for the journey, but has never as yet been known to arrive at a destination beyond the everyday knowledge of any layman. The failure, it may be suggested, is due to the discursive fashion in which the subject has been treated, and to the omission to consider its proper limitations and frontiers. As has been pointed out, the concept of a Science of History (though doubtless containing some germ of truth as does that of a general Natural Science) has stood in the way of fruitful development. The field, moreover, of social phenomena which Aristotle referred to as ' political ' has been treated by philosophers, not only in conjunction with Ethics, but as the theatre of the realization of ethical principles. It has had its superstructure, the details of legislation and administration, appropriated by lawyers and the historians of government, who proclaim themselves free from all obligation to ground themselves on social theory ; it has had its foundations, the fundamental forms of social organization and human motive, annexed by economists and social psychologists, who disclaim any responsibility for acquainting themselves intimately with the upper stories.

Just, however, as Economics has worked outwards in its studies from the nucleus of financial and business experience, so Politics must work outwards from the nucleus of governmental experience. But it must not permit itself to be limited by any traditional and arbitrary notion of the field of government or of politics, or be satisfied with the examination of superficial phenomena and mere machinery. In order to satisfy ourselves that we are not going to start off on a false path, treating this experience too narrowly or too superficially, we must ask ourselves, What is Politics? What is the kind of social situation most appropriately treated by the politicist? What situation is it which evokes action of the nature especially termed political? This inquiry will probably lead us far beyond civil service offices and parliamentary chambers. Without such an inquiry into the correct method, no investigation is likely to be otherwise than sterile. But, before we can discover what facts the politicist is called upon to interpret and how, it may be well to discuss briefly how and with what success the field of human social activities has hitherto been interpreted.

The Interpretation of History by the Decrees of Princes and Legislatures. When thinkers turned from the exposition of what ought to be to the reflective consideration of what was, one of the earliest keys to the interpretation of History was found, appropriately enough, in the study of law. Laws, the expression of the free wills of legislators, it was naïvely believed, determined the social structure. Although Machiavelli might endorse the dictum of Tacitus that "the worse the state, the more the laws," Machiavelli himself, Vico, and Rousseau all considered right legislation and political institutions so decisive of the weal and woe of a community, that they write lamenting that men can no longer aspire to have demigods as their legislators, in order to correct from their secure seat the depraved customs of men and set the social machine again running smoothly. It is Rousseau, who protests against the complacency of the author of the *Esprit des Lois* for whom men are the creatures of their customs, who himself says that, in the last resort, everything depends upon politics ; and that, whatever men may do, "no nation will ever be anything but what the nature of its government may make it."[1] Even for Rousseau, the government stands over against the people and can influence them as a *deus ex machina*.

But the Legislative or Juristic interpretation of History was too obviously an argument in a circle to remain for long satisfactory. Already in the writings of Hume we are left uncertain whether to interpret the history of peoples by the bias of their governments or, as would a modern anthropologist, by manners corrupted by the evil communications and

[1] J. J. Rousseau : *Œuvres* (ed. Hachette), VII, *Confessions*, p. 288.

dominating traditions of their ancestors.[2] Wicked governments and institutions may account for bad customs, but it has yet to be explained what accounts for wicked institutions. Human nature may be naturally good but, if so, it is futile to thrust the responsibility for evil, as does Condorcet, upon the shoulders of the privileged classes. The old explanation of the social structure as built up by the statecraft and priestcraft of an interested few is too simple to explain the acquiescence of the many. Some of the most fruitful suggestions and data for the science of Politics may be derived from the study of law, but it must be studied, as Savigny and Palgrave studied it, as custom underlying the changing policies of governments, rather than as emanating from the creative will of legislative bodies who seek to make human nature ' better by Act of Parliament.' The social structure is less subject than Bentham and his predecessors imagined to conscious manipulation, whether malicious or benevolent ; it is rather the result of the interaction of non-human factors and of deep-seated human impulses. We must look elsewhere than to the edicts of Benevolent Despots for an explanation of the conventions of civilization. We must look away from the lawyers, who trace, as did the theologians, explanations from above. We find a sounder theory with the early economists, who sought their explanation in the earth beneath. No men were, in their

[2] D. Hume : *Essays, Moral, Political and Literary*, ed. Green and Grose, 1882, I, pp. 85, 249.

day, more trustful believers in the power of government to reform the hearts of men than were the French Physiocrats, but it was to be from these economists that the germ of a new and more satisfactory system of historical hermeneutics was to be forthcoming.

The Interpretation of History by the Influence of Material Things. The Economic Interpretation of History is, nevertheless, strictly neither economic nor an interpretation. Its exponents often so use the phrase that it might with equal propriety be called the meteorological or the geographical interpretation. As thus used, it is to be carefully distinguished from the interpretation of history in the light of the ' psychology of acquisitiveness.' And, as an exclusive interpretation, it fails to interpret. The latter charge may indeed be urged against any naïvely materialistic explanation of social phenomena. Crude matter (of which the soil of the Physiocrat school is but one example, the manure to which Maitland ironically referred another) may in every case be a *causa remota*, but, so long as we do not confound the two phenomenal aspects of Stuff, namely matter and consciousness, it cannot justly be called sole efficient cause.[3]   Memory also is a determinant.

[3] Such recent writers as Herr Kautsky (*Ethics and the Materialistic Conception of History*, Amer. trans. 1907, p. 118) admit that the phrase ' materialistic interpretation ' of Marx and Engels is merely retained for polemical purposes, and that some more philosophical but less startling term such as ' monistic ' (in the sense of Haeckel and Ostwald) or ' realistic ' might with academic advantage be substituted.

A. *Climate*. Much harm has been done to the deterministic treatment of human events, adopted as a scientific hypothesis with a view to results, by a too exclusive attention to external determination. But we have no wish to deny that this theory of determination, which receives its classic expression in the writings of Marx, is *pro tanto* valid. Climatic conditions may lead to vast emigrations ; climate may convert a nomadic into an agricultural folk. That climate had some influence on human destinies, even a profound influence, was pointed out, long before Marx and Montesquieu, by Hippocrates and Aristotle, Dubois and Bodin. It may remove all incentive to industry, or it may compel a people by hard toil to extract its food from a niggard earth. It may produce a desert to which only a peculiar type of social structure is adapted, a society of which the members must travel light and for whom manufactured articles are redundant.[4] Its effects may be more subtle. It may ripen men like fruits early or late ;[5] it may alter their morality as it varies the form of their sensuality, and change their cast of thought with the type of their mentality ; it may stimulate the imagination or chill to a cool reserve their passions, lead to long dreamy fasts and *tædium vitæ* or to exercise and the practical life. It may tend to leisure and meditation, on the one hand, or, upon the other, to industriousness and

[4] J. L. Myers : *The Dawn of History*, 1911, p. 18.

[5] *Vide* A. M. Carr Saunders : *The Population Problem* (1922), p. 91. Cf. also Professor J. A. Thompson (*New Statesman*, Nov., 1924) on the spawning of Suez Sea-urchins.

business. It will, nevertheless, be observed, in limitation of these remarks, that southern Phœnician and northern Viking were alike traders, and that the damp moors of Scotland and the broiling plains of India alike produce men reputed metaphysical.

B. *The Earth.* It is not difficult to see the intimate connection between climatic and geographic influences, that of the skies and that of the ground. The sands of the desert are a fact of geography and a consequence of climate ; afforestation alters alike the face of a land and the humours of its skies. The fertility of a country and the affluence of an agricultural people are the product of both climate and soil. But this predetermining influence of the lie of the land is even more irresistible than that of climate. The climate changes with the seasons, and, if occasionally it determines that this or that territory is not a ' white man's land,' its influence, though suspected, is often elusive. It is perhaps clearest when climate, determining the flora and lower fauna, renders certain countries only habitable for races which possess immunity from the diseases which blot out immigrant civilizations.[6] But the rivers which form a highway and fertilizing flood and the mountains which form a barrier of desolation do not change. Geography determines the trade routes and thus the wealth of nations ; geography determines also the strategy and thus the policy of peoples.[7]

[6] Cf. N. Leys : *Kenya*, 1924, p. 31.

[7] F. Ratzel : *Politische Geographie* (Munich, 1897) : " Wenn wir von einem Staate reden, meinen wir, gerade wie bei einer Stadt oder

C. *Race.* There may, however, be a more intimate determinant than either climate or land. The men, it may be said, who go to make up a state are all of a piece with the soil of the land which goes to form that country. But although, like the flowers of the field, a man may be indigenous in one country, he may become naturalized in another. The immigrant will, nevertheless, carry his social characteristics with him. A superficial change of culture may be easy, but far slower will be the change in the physiognomy which betrays the more deeply-seated characteristics of race. Change of country may lead to modification of the more mixed or unstable breeds. Slow selection may have altered the pigmentation perhaps given to the skin of primitive man by the tropical sun. The diet of the Chinaman may have affected his stature. Language may be changed markedly in a century, or a mother-tongue forgotten by a wandering or a subject people. But ' skulls are harder than consonants,' and with the form of the skull and of the brain a limit may perhaps be placed upon the aptitudes of a race. The phrenology of Gall is dead but, from our present knowledge, it would be rash to assert that a new localization of the

einem Weg, immer ein Stück Menscheit und ein menschliches Werk und zugleich ein Stück Erdboden " (p. 4). " Die Entwickelung (des Staates) liegt vielmehr darin, dass im Lauf der Geschichte Eigenschaften des Bodens entdeckt werden, die man vorher nicht gekannt hatte " (p. 25). *Vide* L. Metchnikoff : *La Civilisation et les Grands Fleuves Historiques* (1889), and also e.g. H. B. George's *Relations of Geography and History* (1907), and more detailed research such as E. Curtius' *Peloponnesus* (1851) and *Boden und Klima von Athen* (*Alterthum u. Gegenwart,* II Band, 1886, pp. 22 ff.).

functions of the brain which correspond to the faculties of the mind may not take place. The uniform education of the mind may assimilate the operations of the brain in the most diverse of people, but the most perfect education cannot produce the same subtle instrument in some primitive peoples as in the normal civilized man with a greater brain weight. To assert that this physiological difference can have no psychological counterpart would appear rash. Similarly, it may prove to be true that emotional differences between races are no acquisitions, derived from social circumstances and tradition, but the result of deep-seated and inherited organic differences. Ethnology may well, then, be a study of social determinants.[8]

D. *Population.* The influence of the climate which ripens and of the earth which gives the fruits may, with a certain verbal latitude, be called, by those

[8] Dr. Rhys Davis' remark about the greater variability of language to bodily structure must be held to be qualified by Professor Boas' researches into the modifications undergone by the skulls of descendants of immigrants in America.

But these modifications have as yet shown no indication of bridging the difference between pure-bred negro and white. Cf. also Sir F. W. Mott's article on The Biological Foundations of Human Character (*Edinburgh Review*, July, 1923) for further suggestions as to biological determinants. It seems probable that races are kept apart more by the unlikeness of their emotional life than by the inequality of their intellectual capacity. That the laudation of the superiority of certain racial strains, where isolable, e.g. by Gobineau (*Essai sur l'Inégalité des Races Humaines*), Houston Chamberlain, Lothrop Stoddart, etc., has small scientific foundation, is, at the least, probable. When Mycenæ was in its glory and the Pharaohs ruled in Africa, the chief monuments of the Nordic race were fish-middens. If the ' Nordic Race ' is indeed superior inherently, its eulogists have yet to prove their case.

who are attached to the term, economic. The effects of the fertility of men may be called biological or, again, economic. The millions which seethe in the cauldron of southern China cannot be the human basis for a civilization of the same type as the stationary numbers of France or the growing but sparse population of Canada. When comparing the social conditions of the United States with those of England, it is essential to remember that we are comparing two lands, the first of which has sixty times the size but only three times the population of the other. The reactions of supply and demand in the labour market, the struggle for subsistence and the fear of penury determine men's actions throughout adult life under the heaviest penalties against those of an independent mind—and not merely the action of individuals but of peoples. The adjective by which we choose to denominate these determinants of climate, soil, race and fertility, is perhaps indifferent. That we should recognize that the nature of the particular civilization or social structure is determined by them, is important.

E. *Technical Inventions.* Likewise, and perhaps most important of all, must be emphasized the dependence of civilization in its progress upon the discovery, at a previous stage of development, of the required instruments ; the dependence of all civilization upon fire, of the Roman Empire upon roads, of the British Empire upon steam and electricity, of Western culture upon printing, of Natural Science on the microscope. All this may be treated in one aspect as the result of the genius of the human mind, in another as the limitation of human culture by its material tools. This limitation may extend yet further ; it may not only set a bound to human accomplishment in any given age, but the accomplishments effected in any age by any particular instrumental paraphernalia may bias the type of thinking of that age. This century or craft will tend to think in terms of machinery, that in terms of electricity.[9]

To explain these influences here in detail would be irrelevant. It is sufficient to concede the general validity, for scientific purposes, of the doctrine of ' economic determination ' of the social structure and of human activities, to those who are desirous of including under so accommodating a term meteorological, geographical, ethnological, and biological factors, and factors economic in the stricter sense.

The Interpretation of History by the Psychology of Acquisitiveness. A more precise meaning, however, may be attached to the phrase ' economic interpretation of History,' if we mean, not that so-called ' economic ' or natural factors, such as land, have determined the course of History, but that the desire to possess the produce of the land has determined it. A mountain barrier is a determinant, whatever a people desire to do, and in a very different sense from that in which mineral wealth is a determinant for a people avaricious of wealth. In the former case one's

[9] T. Veblen : *Instinct of Workmanship*, 1914, p. 303.

attention is called to an external or material determinant, in the latter to a psychological and possibly
modifiable one, perhaps stronger in its motive power
in one civilization than in another.[10] The former
meaning gives all its impressive appearance of
ineluctable fate to the doctrine of the economic
determination of History. The latter meaning
much more precisely warrants the use of the term
' economic,' but has no such cogency. In certain
civilizations, and in certain situations of every
civilization, men will be dominantly influenced by
the ' economic motive ' to possess wealth, even in
excess of their need to consume it. But there is no
necessity that they should be so influenced.

The ' economic situation,' therefore, of action
conducive to production or acquisition, and the
economic desire to have and hold, are no more to
be treated as the sole suitable bases for a theory
of human conduct in History than any different
situation or relationship, or a different species of
desire which might prove itself serviceable as a clue
in scientific inquiry into human behaviour. This is
a simple question of actual success in coherent
historical interpretation. A more elaborate distinction between Economics and Politics will be
attempted later.[11] It will be enough to suggest

[10] R. H. Tawney : *The Acquisitive Society*, 1921, chap. iii.
[11] *Infra*, pp. 207 ff. The distinction here drawn may be usefully
compared with that made by Professor J. R. Commons : *Legal
Foundations of Capitalism*, 1924, p. 3 : " These many sciences of
human nature furnish increasingly a foundation for economic theory,
which is concerned with both physical nature and human nature,

here that the economic interpretation of History (in this more compassable and exact use of the term) will tend to describe human conduct as dominated by the will to relate itself to *things*, to consumable goods. The problem of human life appears as one of how to produce, exchange and secure the consumption of what is valuable, because we want to *have* it. Hence the economic attitude in interpretation can be distinguished from that of Politics, which will tend to describe human conduct as dominated by the will to stand in a relation to other *willing beings*, which shall be a controlling or, at least, not a subject relation.[12] The problem of

In one direction economy is a relation of man to nature, in another it is a relation of man to man. The first is Engineering Economy ; the second is Business Economy and Political Economy. The first has given us theories of Production, Exchange, and Consumption of Wealth, while Business Economy and Political Economy give us a variety of theories specialized in different branches of learning. . . . And finally, Politics deals with the mass movements and mass psychologies which define, exact, and enforce private rights and official responsibilities according to notions pertaining to ethics, politics and economics." With the first sentence we can only agree if the ambiguous word ' concern ' be interpreted in the light of a subsequent limiting passage :   " Thus economic theory runs into other theories of man and nature, or else *assumes* certain common-sense notions regarding them " (italics mine). The last sentence, however, seems to condemn Politics to become a species of crowd-psychology, indeed likely to be productive of a ' variety of theories.'

[12] J. A. Hobson : *Free Thought in the Social Sciences*, 1926, p. 181 : " I have named ' power ' as the most prevalent among the interfering interests. Self-assertion, the craving for power, to be a cause, to see things and men more in the fulfilment of our will, is everywhere an operative, often the dominant, motive in Politics. . . . But the sense of power which enters Politics is primarily power over persons, not things. The main defect of the economic interpretation of history lies here. . . . When, as we shall see, the economic motive enters, and often governs, Politics, it is, as a rule, none the less the

human life here appears as one of how to gain, by assertion or co-operation, freedom for the play of our own wills, for doing what we want to *do*.

The economic interpretation of History, in whatever sense, tends to magnify the importance of the part played in human conduct by material things, whether directly or indirectly in the desire to have possession—a possession which, because they are material things, tends to be ' adverse possession.' There has been a certain amount of very justifiable prejudice against the opponents of this theory, on the supposition that they desired to minimize the great part played by the external world, not changeable by individual wishes or ideals, in determining conduct. But it is forgotten that there are many determinants besides the tangible, which are nevertheless emphatically objective, and unmodifiable by individual thought or whim. We must protest that, great though the significance of the economic determinants, physical and psychological, may be,[13] this is not to concede any justification for the attempt to treat the study of natural phenomena or business experience as the only significant angles from which to study the determinant factors in social life.

servant of this instinct of self-assertion.'' Although ' interests ' may bias the scientific interpretations of political data, perhaps the desire for power is not so much an interfering factor in the political conduct which it is the scientists' business to study as, in its results and method, the very theme of that study itself, the woof of political action crossing the warp of events.

[13] The remark of Marx in *Zur Kritik der politischen Oekonomie* is worth recalling : '' The anatomy of civil society must be sought in

Non-Economic Determinants. The past experience of man and his habits cannot with propriety be put among the ' external,' still less among the ' economic,' factors. This past experience abides on in memory, and memory along with present awareness constitutes the very content of the so-called ' self.' Physical conditions, it may be, are the perpetual matrix of psychological facts. Certainly, the whole of reality cannot be dirempted into two independent and self-sufficient portions, mind and matter ; the regularity which obtains in either sphere must leave an ordering impress on the other. But it is most important to remember that the present external determining factors may prove powerless to deflect the course of human events when the past determination, enshrined in tradition and memory, the *inner determination* of the individual or nation, declares itself strongly. The perseverence of Cato, the stand of Leonidas, the resurgence of the Poles, the persistence to this day as a people of the children of Abraham, are instances in point of this traditional determination. The history of religion will furnish no few cases of churches declining to turn aside from the determination to realize their own ' world-

economics " ; and in the light of this Signor Labriola endeavours to explain the period of the Reformation (*Essays on the Materialistic Conception of History,* 1904, p. 108), and Professor Achille Loria to point out that professors who are salaried by capitalism must necessarily expend their energies in bolstering up that system. These doctrines are not so much false as in need of qualification as half-truths. This economic doctrine ignores all human psychological motive which is not economic, such as the lust for self-indulgence, the lust for power, and the lust for gratification in the infinite.

M

scheme,' however seemingly hopeless the enterprise. Ideals are the tutelary deities which wisdom, selecting from the more heroic experiences of the past, has set up as stars in the heavens of the future. They are not to be supposed to direct human life in disregard of all the other factors which determine our experience ; but they are themselves determinants of conduct, too important to be neglected.

It is as question-begging and slovenly in thought as it may be convenient in popular speech, to refer to whatever is external as ' material.' To allude to ' public opinion,' an undoubted external determinant, as ' material,' darkens counsel. To do so is merely to burden ourselves with a moribund metaphysic of materialism, and to stifle ourselves with dust from the embers of last night's intellectual fires. The conflict of materialist and idealist appears to be obsolescent, and it is becoming possible to perceive that a denial of dualism neither involves identifying consciousness with the red glow of the furnaces of matter-in-action, nor involves an assertion that the furnace does not go on burning apart from being cognized as appearance and glow. Men use the term ' material ' and its gloss ' economic,' because they are attached to them as seeming to emphasize the hard, unpleasant, non-ideal side of a social system which those who benefit by it seek to describe as rational, preordained and divine. But, scientifically, this use is not helpful.

The study of human relations, with the emphasis

on the volitional element (the relationship of wills in society), as distinct from the emphasis on work upon material in order to produce a thing (relationships of men and things and, secondarily, of men and men in order to produce, or exchange when produced, consumable articles), is best not undertaken for the moment by Economics, with its question-begging implications. This study is more profitably treated as the province of a separate science, standing on as good, though no better basis ; to wit, Politics.

The treatment, from the angle of economic experience and with the prepossessions of economic theory, of social phenomena, such as those of trade unionism, of the standard of living of the worker, of contract, which are indeed essentially political in nature and involve problems of citizenship, has had a most baneful effect in its influence on the thought of a century. The confusion of ideas, by which citizens are treated as first and foremost employees, is indicated by the phrase ' political economy,' which has come to mean the study of men's actions from the angle of business, and not merely the study of ' city house-keeping ' or of national trade policy.

To pass from political to economic theory is like passing from sea-fogs to mountain air. But the economists owe their superior system to the fact that they had the courage to divorce the study of Economics from those of Politics and Ethics, as the Aristotelian tradition had not done. Naturally, in the economically minded Nineteenth Century, they appropriated to themselves all border areas as well.

It is because the students of Politics have been short-sightedly groping in unscientific investigations of the activities of the State or even of Government, that the economist continues to concern himself with the old vague field of 'Political Economy,' and to include within his sphere even the study of judicial decisions or of Labour Party programmes when they bear upon business transactions.[14] As a result many questions, which are peculiarly social problems of the relation of man and man, have been approached from the angle, not of citizenship, but of a business transaction about commodities, and in the atmosphere of profit and loss values, and of demand and supply standards of efficiency.

If the so-called 'economic interpretation of history,' when exaggerated, may prove seriously misleading and practically dangerous, it remains to be seen whether Politics can offer a helpful 'political interpretation of history.' We may find ourselves led to the conclusion that the field which, on any thought-out definition, might be treated as the subject-matter of Economics, could be, with

[14] " In fact, these transactions have become the meeting-place of economics, physics, psychology, ethics, jurisprudence and politics. . . . Thus economic theory began with a Commodity as its ultimate scientific unit, then shifted to a feeling in order to explain a Transaction which is its practical problem " (J. R. Commons : *op. oit.*, p. 5). Thus the student of Politics is warned off the ground. No wonder that, his matter being so impoverished, his theory has been so anæmic.

advantage, much more limited than is usually the case.

Social Facts. It must immediately be pointed out that such a political interpretation need be no more ' subjective ' than that of Economics. There are such things as ' social facts,' folk-ways, almost as persistent as those of Economics. Coal-fields may become exhausted, the technology of coal-mining changes, and the organization of the mining industry may be altered by legislative action over-night, but to alter the parliamentary system, or those conventions about religion, patriotism and class sentiment which form the background of the thought of a people, is not so simple. We have here traditions which are ingrained in a people, are determinant of the form which their social structure shall take as it is slowly modified with the passage of time, and are as much beyond the power of any one individual to change, whether they remain mere ' atmosphere ' or express themselves in institutional form, as are the dominant facts of the economic situation. These ' social facts ' not only must be accepted and are beyond the power of a few persons to ignore at will, but they make and mould the individual, externally by deciding by convention how he may be permitted to act, and also more subtly by providing the matter of his thoughts and the verbal forms into which he casts them. The man bears the impress of the ' social mind,' the currently accepted opinion, of his day ; he cannot greatly outstrip the knowledge of his times, and even in the fashion of revolt from them he shows himself, in his very negations, the child of his age.[15]

Not only are there social facts as much as there are geological facts, and as much beyond the power of the individual by an exercise of free will to alter in his lifetime—the British House of Lords seems as hard to abolish as the Simplon Tunnel to bore—but these social facts and values, conventions and institutions, are ' given,' i.e. data, so far as the statesman, and in his smaller sphere the citizen, are concerned. Only with time and in part can the statesman alter these facts, since he cannot be an institutional nihilist. But he can so make his plans as not to come into collision with the deeper prejudices.

There is a certain elasticity in the social situation, and it is the statesman's business, by intuition or

[15] E. Durkheim : *Les Règles de la Méthode Sociologique*, ed. 1904, p. 19 : " A social fact is distinguished by the power of external coercion which it exercises or is able to exercise over individuals ; and the presence of this power is in its turn marked by some determinate sanction or it may be only by the resistance which the fact opposes to every individual enterprise which tends to run counter to it." The ' fait social ' is more precisely defined on p. 19, but in a fashion more suspect of the heresy of positing a ' social mind ' independent of the individual minds in group form. Sociology M. Durkheim defines as " the science of institutions, of their genesis and of their functioning." He includes under the term ' institutions ' modes of collective conduct in the text referred to as ' conventions,' while the term ' institutions ' is reserved in the text for the determinate body or organ in which the convention is incarnate or through which it functions. On the inability of the individual to invent an ' original attitude of mind,' of which the thought-content is detached from and uncontrolled (positively or negatively) by the thought of his age and place, cf. Balfour : *Foundations of Belief*, 1897, p. 236.

experiment, to discover what opinion is patient of in the way of more desirable adjustment. There is, however, certainly a limit beyond which the situation is not to be treated as viable with any hope of affecting one's ends. Given a certain 'state of affairs,' many results may follow or, negatively, certain results cannot follow. There is implicit in every situation a necessity about which we can frequently make at least negative statements; there is a logic of the social situation.[16] Although men may entertain the belief, probably psychologically false, that they can change their convictions at any time in the twinkling of an eye, it is clear that public opinion, rooted in history, cannot be so changed, but requires the use of appropriate means. It is the fallacy of all utopianism to ignore this. The use of the appropriate means of contro of these 'hard' facts is statesmanship; and the discovery of these means depends on judgment in appreciating the specific situation, coupled with a 'common-sense' knowledge of the general form of the social structure. But this 'common-sense' knowledge is something more rare than the opinion of any chance twelve good men and true, and is susceptible of more scientific statement than it has yet received in the political testaments of kings and the *obiter dicta* of statesmen. A far more scientific knowledge is possible than we have had hitherto of the political data. And this knowledge can be fully as objective in treatment as that of the

[16] G. Tarde : *La Logique sociale*, ed. 1895, p. 135.

economist is accustomed to be, since the data here is at least as objective as any modern economist can claim to be the data of Economics.

The Suitable Field for the Methods of Political Interpretation : The Relation of Politics and other Social Sciences. An attempt has been made to show that there are non-material objective determinants of human conduct, such as conventions and social habits, which any social science must take into account at least as much as the material determinants of climate, geography, and physiology. If they are less primary than warmth and food, they are even more deserving of attention, as being more intimate to the problems of Politics and perhaps more susceptible of control, when patiently studied, by manipulation, neutralization, or even such modification as might be hoped for through scientific legislation. But, so soon as we turn our attention to the field of social determinants and of the resultant social behaviour, we find not one social science but many jostling each other in the endeavour to interpret these phenomena in the light each of its own particular discipline. Any attempt precisely to define frontiers must be futile. But as a matter of method, it is likely to save energy and to promote the advancement of knowledge if we consider whether it be desirable to treat this field of human conduct, and of the objective determinants of human conduct (not proper to the physical sciences), as one science or as several. If we are to treat it as several, it will be desirable further to consider whether the field will admit of some rational division, or will provide material for as many sciences as there may happen to be departments of human history demanding reflective consideration. Is there no choice between one all-inclusive social science and a rabbit-warren of little sciences ?

I. *Politics and Sociology.* Economists have not been the sole professional body to aspire to appropriate, under the guise of the ' economic interpretation,'[17] the field of Politics for themselves. The sociologists of the older school also have usually had pretensions to the formal interpretation of the whole field of social activity, but their conclusions have been too often at once so grandiose and so uncertain that despite (or perhaps because of) the almost religious enthusiasm of its exponents, Sociology was probably less in favour at the beginning of this century than in the time of its pristine popularity as the protégée of Herbert Spencer. A more novel claimant is Psychology, for which

[17] This is not, of course, to ignore the fact that many who have not merely emphasized the importance of the economic factors but have used economic theory as an organon whereby to interpret History, instead of leaving it a ' disordered and imperfect dictionary,' have yet been very far from the attempt of the early Whig economists and of the Marxists to treat all political and ethical considerations as epi-phenomenal to ' economic ' factors and economic motives. Cf. Thorold Rogers : *Economic Interpretation of History*, p. 2 ; E. R. A. Seligman : *Economic Interpretation of History*, ed. 1902, p. 141. The writings of Professor Charles Beard are instances of the measured interpretation of political events by examining the importance of the economic factor (in the strict sense) as one determinant of the historical process.

popular enthusiasm has grown in proportion as belief has waned in the ability of Political Economy to propound a solution for all social difficulties, and to provide a key to the motives of the human breast. Certainly sociologists, anthropologists, and psychologists have been no less generous than the economists in appropriating for themselves the Naboth's vineyard of human interrelations. In this they have been aided by the customary meaning attached to the term Politics, which, narrowing it to a field proper for the attention of jurists and students of the art and machinery of government, obviously leaves outside its purview a field of social activity of the highest human interest which is not patently within the province of any other discipline. Before, therefore, proceeding to discuss the problems of Politics in the Aristotelian sense, it is necessary to pursue further our discussion of the legitimacy of the claims of these other sciences to the province.

Sociology as a General Science of Conduct. Sociology and Anthropology may be held to stand to Politics in an ancillary and propædeutic relation. This must be the more emphatically insisted upon, since the danger of merging Politics, as a subdivision, in Sociology, interpreted as 'a general science of human conduct,' is even more serious than that of merging it in a Philosophy of History. The objection to Sociology, as it has in the past often been understood, as a science inclusive of Politics, is threefold: that its method is sterile, its conception of science faulty, and its aims chimerical.

Any scientific research which starts from the central study of the actual conduct of administrators and administered in matters of administration, or from the experience of agriculturist, industrialist, trader, and buyer in the world of business, starts from a rich nuclear experience of wide ramifications, in which abundance of record confirms and checks direct observation. On the contrary, those students of politics who have been guided by the traditional Sociology have been drawn away into the forests of the history of civilization and of things in general. Buckle speaks of our acquaintance with History being so imperfect, while our materials are so numerous, that " it seems desirable that something should be done on a scale far larger than has hitherto been attempted," but, while he discourses largely on ' laws,' we only come to science in the popular meaning when he turns aside to devote a note to the influence on social history of the functioning of the liver and lungs.[18] Had Buckle been less anxious to enlarge the scale, the treatment might have been more systematic, and the ' laws' less vasty and vague.

The historians of civilization, since Hellwald's General History of Culture, have done most valuable work by indexing History under subjects, such as Slavery, Marriage, Law, Democracy, and by elucidating how certain social forms have recurred in history. But when they have aspired, like the philosophers of History, to higher things,

[18] H. T. Buckle : *History of Civilisation in England*, ed. 1903, I, p. III n.

all but a few have tended to produce a farrago of private theory and historical facts more exquisite than select. What has resulted has too often been a disquisition about ' God, the world, man, and things in general.'[19] It may very seriously be questioned whether the stunted condition of Political Theory is not due to this connection with the vague philosophizings of early Sociology, with its love for the accumulative, and discouragement of the abstract and analytical methods, and its damning inheritance of Positivism and of the Spencerian ' Synthetic Philosophy.' Economics, on the other hand, separating from moral and political theory, struck out, before the days of Comte,[20] on a line of its own as a departmental study based on one field of experience. If human affairs are to be treated scientifically in a fruitful fashion, it is

[19] C. Wolff : ' *Vernünftige Gedanken von Gott, der Welt und der Seele des Menschen, auch allen Dingen überhaupt* ' (1719).

[20] To Auguste Comte belongs the honour of being the first to endeavour to convince the world of " the practicability of conceiving of and cultivating the moral sciences after the fashion of the entirely positive sciences." But his earlier sterile preoccupation with the problem of the hierarchy or procession of the sciences, and his later too fertile obsession with the religious aspects of his system, and his adoption, in the tradition of Voltaire and Condorcet, of the grand-scale historical method, contributed to give Sociology a bad name and a faulty method at the start, and to render men suspicious of this " science d'où prévoyance, prévoyance, d'où action " (*Cours de Phil. pos.*, 1830, I, p. 63). It was, moreover, unfortunate that, on the occasions when M. Comte did commit himself to a ' scientific conclusion,' as e.g. in the matter of the status of women, his own followers, such as Lester Ward, have had to state their emphatic disbelief in the soundness of the firstfruits of this *physique sociale* (A. Comte, *ibid.*, IV, p. 569; L. F. Ward : *Dynamic Sociology*, 1883, I, p. 130). Herbert Spencer also, the grandfather of Sociology, is not guiltless of being frequently rather the theorist anxious to expound

necessary that certain human tendencies and activities should be isolated and studied first, before the whole of human life is studied in its infinitely complex interrelations. But such an objection is of a purely practical nature.

To argue, however, that the treatment of the whole field is at present beyond our powers, is not to show that the field is not in theory essentially that of one social science. Here it may be asked whether the belief in the unity of the field is not due to the traditional antithesis between human affairs and the natural world, and to the illusive unity (by contrast) of human history. But, as has been shown, History is not qualitatively to be divided as 'human' and 'natural.' And, in any case, there can be no science of history—human or otherwise. The growth of civilization admits of no comparisons, not even of phylogenetic with ontogenetic development (since civilization cannot be regarded as constituting a genus), and such recurrence as there may be is in form and not in detail.

a synthetic philosophy than the scientist coolly examining. Too often he is rather the protagonist of Individualism, denouncing militarism and Toryism and reproaching even Mr. Gladstone for his backslidings into the dark and slimy waters of ecclesiasticism (illustrated by a close analogy drawn from the life of amphibians) than the dispassionate judge of data. It would be ungracious either to underrate the work of these pioneers or to underestimate the advance made by their successors, but it is important to maintain that science must be distinguished from propaganda, that grandiose treatment lends itself to the mere ventilation of opinion, and that we must return for the present, without *parti pris*, to the controlled examination of phenomena, to the examination of phenomena in a limited field and to the systematic examination of it in that field.

Sciences of civilization, historically considered, it must be repeated are illusory, although the field has an interest which encourages sanguine hopes and popular expectations. But this sense of the unity of the field by virtue of its mere content, of its being human experience, has led the historical school of sociologists to dissipate their efforts, instead of concentrating upon a thorough exploration of some few clues. In part the trouble has arisen from the hypnotic influence of the word ' genetic.' ' A genetic account of an unfolding process ' remains an account ; it cannot give us even formal prediction. Even ' scientific history ' is not a new necromancy. An account of the origin and development of institutions may give to the student possessed of insight a clue to some underlying and persistent characteristic of human nature and, assuming this characteristic, may make possible a comparative study with other institutions superficially dissimilar. Even the original institution itself, instead of appearing as one plant-like growth, takes shape as a series of ' incidents,' of comparable attempts of some human ' instinct ' to find expression or circumvent obstacles. A science becomes possible. But no science is possible from the mere historical and contentual study of *one* institution, from the study of the genesis and growth of *one* plant, be that plant civilization itself. A new presentation of Ethics from a social standpoint may be possible—but that is another matter. No science can come out of the History of Civilization or of Progress,[21] however eruditely written. *Or as a 'Fundamental' Science of the Social Instincts.* Provided, however, that the confusion between History and Science be avoided here as elsewhere, a single science of society, it may yet be urged, is theoretically possible. A *formal* treatment is feasible of the fundamental principles which underlie all social life. This is the position (better grounded for scientific purposes than that of the students of History and of the evolution of civilization or of the 'growth of the social organism') of Simmel and of many modern sociologists. The only difficulty here seems to be that such a study cannot remain ' in general.' There can be no ' fundamental sciences ' in the sense that they do not take into account particular manifestations, but only in the sense that they do not limit themselves to departmental treatments of data. The study must either become a study of the interrelations of wills, such as is indistinguishable from the study of Politics,[22]

[21] F. J. Teggart : *Theory of History*, p. 198.

[22] Simmel : *Soziologie*, 1908, p. 7 : " Dass dieses beides, in der Wirklichkeit untrennbar Vereinte, in der wissenschaftlichen Abstraktion getrennt werde, dass die Formen der Wechselwirkung oder Vergesellschaftung, in gedanklicher Ablösung von den Inhalten, die durch sie erst zu gesellschaftlichen Gesichtspunkt methodisch unterstellt werden,—dies scheint mir die einzige. und die ganze Möglichkeit einer speziellen Wissenschaft von der Gesellschaft als solcher zu begründen. Mit ihr erst wären die Tatsachen, die wir als die gesellschaftlich-historische Realität bezeichnen, wirklich auf die Ebene des bloss Gesellschaftlichen projiziert." Simmel, while admirable in his distinction between form and content, falls into the too customary error of treating Politics and Economics on a par

or it becomes a psychological study of all those manifestations of human association which can be set down to some fundamental social instinct. And, if this, then it is best denominated Psychology.

A study is certainly possible, in all its manifestations, human and animal, of ' consciousness of kind ' or of the alleged gregarious instinct. But the evidences of this instinct, in e.g. political life, need be no more fundamental than the evidences of any other as well ascertained instinct ; perhaps less so than of those biologically more significant, such as the sexual, or that especially studied by Ratzenhofer, Gumplowicz and their school—the self-preservative. And, although the ' social instinct ' may undeniably be held to be *par excellence* the ' instinct ' which maintains ' social life,' nevertheless those who are engaged in the intensive study of some field of social phenomena must be held entitled to examine, without prejudice, and as proper to their province, the fundamental human tendencies which may account for these phenomena. And, as Simmel points out, the ' gregarious instinct ' can account perhaps for herding, but cannot account alone for an articulate society. Society, as we know it, can never be adequately explained by adducing

as special and contentual ' human ' sciences, whereas their nature is fundamentally different. Economics is as susceptible of formal treatment as Sociology, but becomes void of meaning unless the relationship of man with the physical world is considered, whereas Politics is a social science of the pure blood, concerned only with the various possible relations of human wills (Simmel, *ibid.*, pp. 9–13, and N. Spykman : *Social Theory of Georg Simmel*, 1925).

an ' instinct for society,' nor can a science be founded upon, or limited to, the study of such an instinct.

Formal Science of Human Relationships Synonymous with Politics. If, however, by Sociology we mean, not a general study of social activities, but a special study of the *forms* of social relationship, and of this relationship when it is *primary* and not considered as subordinated to a relationship *not* social (as, e.g. the ' engineering ' relationship of men with things, involved in the work of production, or the specific relationship, with its consequences biological rather than political, of men and women to satisfy the demands of the race), then Sociology and Politics are indistinguishable sciences. And no precise definition of the political relationship appears practicable which is any narrower than the relationship here studied by Sociology. In this sense, Politics is Sociology and Sociology is Politics. And Politics is the older term and the one less encumbered with bad philosophy.

The study of Politics, it has been asserted, is something very much more than the study of Government. To treat the two fields as coterminous is a fatal error of method. The study of Government (in the narrower sense of constitutional enactment and administration) is but a study of one function of the State, and the Study of the State is but the study of one form of organization of political life ; Government, in this sense, is but a part of a part of Politics.

Even in the broader sense of government, as rule or control, the field of Politics is broader than the

N

survey of the relationship of dominance or authority or sovereignty, since equal *co-operation*, under the control of a mutually accepted rule of conduct, must be insisted to be just as much a political relationship. That Politics only considers the society organized under sovereign authority or under dominance is a dangerous *petitio principii*. Such dominance may be only one manifestation of the political relationship, and the common principle of this relationship may be more fundamental. It must not be merely assumed that human beings must, in a political society, be under dominance.

Again, to make Politics the study of organized society is misleading. It may be wise to follow the Aristotelian maxim and study the perfect growth—or it may not be. But an organized society is only a superlative form of society. What is fundamental is the study of the form of human mutual relations. The organization is a stage of sophistication and secondary, and is arbitrarily introduced into the definition. A political society might not be organized but be merely, like Dante's chorus of angels, or as in anarchist theory,[23] moved by some common impulse and unregulated by administrative officials. A family may be regarded as not a political society. But it is to be so regarded only because it is often more profitably treated as a biological unit (not a political dyad or triad), and not because it lacks organization in any further sense than that implied in stating that it is a society.

[23] B. Russell : *Roads to Freedom*, 1918, p. 51.

It is the lax use of terminology which has permitted the impression to arise that the study of community life falls well beyond the field of the politicist ; as a consequence the State, instead of being linked with the family (as in de Coulange's work), has been left, at least in its modern manifestations, as a juristic sovereign and a moral absolute, suspended in mid-air for the study of political theorists, while the sociologists have taken to themselves the more ' fundamental ' studies of the family and of the amorphous community.[24] The Greek

[24] Giddings : *Principles of Sociology*, p. 35 : " Political science studies the state within the constitution and shows how it expresses its will in acts of government." With this dissevering of political science from the study of the foundations of political life, I am unable to find myself in any agreement. It leads to the suicidal conclusion, so far as Politics as a serious study is concerned, that " it simply assumes for each nation a national character. . . . It takes the fact of sovereignty and builds upon it, and does not speculate how sovereignty came to be, as did Hobbes and Locke and Rousseau. It starts exactly where Aristotle started, with the dictum that man is a political animal." While agreeing with the Aristotelian, in contrast to the semi-juristic, treatment of Politics, I cannot understand this treatment as Professor Giddings does : " Here, as elsewhere, the best system of examination will be to begin at the beginning and observe things in their growth " (ἐξ ἀρχῆς τα πράγματα φυόμενα βλέψειεν . . . . πόλιν ἐξ ὧν σύγκειται σκοποῦντες ὀψόμεθα. Arist : *Politics*, I, i–ii). That, as Lester Ward contended, Aristotle made a mistake of fact about the political animal has nothing to do with his intentions. Professor Small, on the other hand, insists that Sociology has as its task to co-ordinate the conclusions of the special social sciences. This seems to me to be the work either of philosophy (political or social philosophy), or to be the work of some future science when a few departmental conclusions have been reached, and at present it only provokes premature generalization. But my agreement is so far substantial that further discussion of terms here might degenerate from a discussion of method into a discussion of words. For a critique of the notion of sciences of evolution, *vide* H. W. B. Joseph : *Concept of Evolution* (Herbert Spencer Lecture, 1924). Professors

word *Polis* has a far broader significance than its modern mis-translation ' State,' and Politics cannot be limited to the study of the State either with convenience of scientific principle or with respect for etymology. By Politics must be meant the study of τὰ πόλιτικα, and nothing less.

It is not, indeed, to be denied that these social studies have had their influence in modifying the modern theory of the State, although probably less profoundly so than have the theories of jurists and philosophers confronting practical problems—for example, of federalism and of the new trade union and ecclesiastical movements. But it is for the economist or politicist himself to work back from the superficial phenomena to the underlying structure, to be his

Small (*General Sociology*, ed. 1905, p. 117) and Ross (*Foundations of Sociology*, ed. 1905, p. 79) themselves accuse the earlier sociologists of working "instinctively, accidentally and without system," and of "recognizing only a few large causes." Professor Gumplowicz is particularly gloomy about the value of the work of his predecessors (*Grundriss der Soziologie*, 1885, pp. 72–3). But it may properly be argued that the remark of Leslie Stephen that " there is no science of sociology properly scientific—merely a heap of empirical observations, too flimsy to be useful in strict logical inference " (*Presidential Address*, 1892, Soc. and Pol. Educ. League) is no longer applicable, and that the attitude of historians such as, e.g. M. Seignobos (*La Méthode Historique*, ed. 1901, p. 7) is not helpful : "The word sociology was invented by philosophers, it fitted an attempt to group under one philosophic concept the branches of science which were left over in isolation. It bids fair to have the same lot befall it which has befallen this philosophic concept : that of dropping out of the language, after a brief vogue." But cf. D. G. Ritchie : *Studies in Social and Political Ethics*, 1902, p. 3 : "The sociologist is apt to regard the historian as merely occupied with the higher gossip ; on the other hand . . . ' Evolution ' and ' development ' seem only grand names for History treated inaccurately"; and B. Croce : *Historical Materialism*, p. 40, *et passim*.

own physiologist, morphologist and pathologist, and to do his own ' fundamental studies.'

Sociology as a ' Concrete' Science of the Social Organism. It may, then, be shrewdly doubted whether Sociology in the limited sense of a formal science of all human relations, family and industrial as well as political, is—or is likely for long to be—a science at all. As a science of association only, where the investigation is into the inherent conditions and consequences of the very fact of association, there is hope of a useful treatment which would not belie the word ' scientific.' But the study seems indistinguishable from a political science in any thorough conception of this latter. A science, however, of the *content* of human conduct, or any ' science ' which plumes itself upon being based on a study of the concrete alone, is doomed from the start. It is but the mythical ' science of history ' under another name. It may lead to most useful preliminary investigations, and empirical similarities, revealed by comparisons, may provide most useful hints for scientific hypotheses ; but any such historical study has not the germ of a science in itself. At the most we have the mere matrix of a science, such as was ' Natural Philosophy ' and as still is ' Political Philosophy.'

Or as a Social Biology. Nevertheless, it may be asked, may not the biologists, psychologists and anthropologists be permitted to make their contributions to the study of social life ? Assuredly ; nor are they likely to be deterred from applying their conclusions in these fields. But it may be questioned whether any useful purpose is served by intoxicating and confusing them in their path by giving them the title of sociologists whenever they venture cautiously across to conclusions of social significance. They do not thereby become scientists of a new kind ; by their own confrères they must be judged.

We may perhaps appropriately speak of a ' Social Biology,' and it must be judged by the canons of Biology. The organic theory, for example, of society is still alive and may chance to be not misleading metaphor but plain truth. It is not irrelevant, but it is certainly not final, to take exception to the extravagances of a theory which enabled Bluntschli to ascribe to the Church feminine sex, and according to which the nerves were for Cusanus laws and for Herbert Spencer telegraph wires. Are we, with Leslie Stephen, to see in artillery the teeth ? And what are the chemical formulæ of the tissues of this organism, of its albumina and phosphates ? But a new attitude in Physiology may conceivably render it possible to revivify, as more than metaphor, the theory of Lilienfeld, Worms and Schäffle, to which Gierke gave a purely juristic interpretation, and to which Professor McDougall and others have given a psychological one.[25] The theory is difficult to disprove—theories of social life taken *in toto* must necessarily be so general as to be difficult to disprove. But theories which do not admit of proof or disproof are of small value.

[25] Schäffle : *Bau und Leben des sozialen Körpers* (1875), especially I, pp. 53 ff. ; W. S. McDougall : *The Group Mind* (1920). Cf. the recent work of A. Dendy : *Biological Foundations of Society* (1924), especially p. 60.

Explaining all things, they explain nothing. The decisive answer in this matter can probably only be given when Biology has developed further. At least it may be affirmed that this and like questions can only be profitably discussed from an intimate knowledge of Biology.

Or as Social Psychology. Similarly, in the opinion of some, we may have a Social Psychology, as distinct from the study of the mental acts and behaviour of individuals who may happen to live and conduct themselves in society. Hence studies are made of the psychology of crowds and of groups and of the herd instinct.[26] Such studies must *ex hypothesi* be ' concrete,' in that it is their supposition that the individual acts in a qualitatively distinct way when acting as a member of a group. No study of individual psychology, it is alleged, will lead us to anticipate the nature of this group conduct (although whether this assertion be true of the form, as of the content, of action, frequently remains unspecified). Certainly, the individual isolated from all society is a pure logical abstraction. Hence the objection to an ' abstract ' and preference for a ' concrete ' treatment, which too often tends to become an objection to a formal treatment (though it be the form of society itself), and preference for a contentual treatment, which is open to the customary objection to all institutional and historical treatments that it can

[26] G. Lebon : *The Crowd and Psychology of Revolution;* W. Trotter : *Instincts of the Herd in Peace and War,* 1920 ; W. M. Conway : *The Crowd in Peace and War,* 1915; E. D. Martin : *Behaviour of Crowds.* Also W. H. R. Rivers : *Politics and Psychology,* 1923 ; and cf. M. Ginsberg : *Psychology of Society,* 1921, chap. iv.

merely provide us with a narration (no doubt interesting enough) of what has been. To a practical age, tired of the logic of leisured philosophy and of the *a-priorism* of moralists, this limitation is not always sufficiently apparent.

The distinction between Politics and Psychology is discussed below. Social Psychology is not Politics —not even when called Sociology. The questions which it raises, beyond such methodological doubts as that of whether a Social Psychology be any more than a study of socially minded or socially active individuals, are such as only psychologists are competent to discuss. The existence of a ' group mind ' is a psychological conclusion or hypothesis too controversial to be used at present with any confidence by laymen. The social datum, however, of a civilisation of which the constituent individuals are mentally interdependent is one of which the student of Politics can with safety make for himself an untechnical use. Politics certainly cannot afford to be independent of Psychology, but it will not be wisely advised to make use dogmatically of psychological concepts of which psychologists of authority dispute the validity. Its use of these concepts should be hypothetical, selective and derivative, not primary and dogmatic.

Sociology as Social Psychology has one danger in store for the study of Politics. The psychologist of groups tends, for his own purposes, to treat the group as a unit and the individual as member of a group. Although there may be comparisons between societies, societies tend to be treated only as wholes. Hence the study of Society becomes the unanalytical, non-atomic study of a whole. Thus we drop back upon the study of a single growth—upon social studies, historical or philosophical—which may reveal most fruitful data for a science or for reflections on the practical conduct of life, but which does not of itself provide those myriads of comparative instances (such as chemical combinations, biological sequences such as the Mendelian, business transactions, acts of control and rule) out of the observation of which alone can grow a science. These remarks are obviously not to be taken in disparagement of the comparative study of groups. But they are intended to deprecate the obliteration of the very notion of relationship, i.e. of distinct units related, in the name of the study of a common sentiment or instinct moving the whole mass or masses together. This may be the correct method for trained psychologists to study the manifestations of an instinct. It may be very proper for treating a so-called 'natural' group, founded, as is the family, on an affection which negates individuality. But it is far remote from the formal study of the relationships of willing beings.

Or as Social Anthropology or the History of Man's Social Life. Social Anthropology and Social History are both obviously legitimate expressions, if we distinguish the former from an ontogenetical and physiological treatment of the history of man, and the latter from Biography, the History of Law, and similar topics. If Sociology be thus understood, then its task will be that of the purposive selection of historical data,[27] both ' orthodox ' and recondite, both of civilised and of barbarous society, both ancient and contemporary. The Social Historian will not even neglect the History of other parts of Nature than man. As much as the History of the Tasmanian, he will study the History of animal societies, records of this or that ant-heap or hive, its rise, decline, and fall.[28] He will find the paricular record as profitable as that of the life of many a Welsh chieftain. For his task is to study the data of the process of association.

Every historian, in this sense, tends to be an amateur sociologist, even those who, like the genial Father of History, are chiefly concerned to present an attractive narrative, and those who busy themselves with the etiquette of courts or the machinery of parliaments. For not good intentions but circumstantial detail of procedure, the size of the assembly hall or the lateness of the sitting, will determine whether society will be well or ill governed, while

----

[27] Professor Tout takes very reasonable exception to the notion that the social scientist alone is capable of the work of selection while the historian is a mere builder's labourer. But no man, however much he may desire to be his own dry-as-dust, can himself test, at first hand, all the data which may be of comparative value for the building up of a social theory. No one has done more than the members of the Manchester school to moderate the ambitions of research students, and to limit their studies to less grandiose but more compassable fields than used to be selected for investigation (T. F. Tout: *The Place of the Reign of Edward II in English History*, 1914, p. 241).

[28] *Vide* the work of A. Espinas; A. Espinas: *Des Sociétés Animales*, 1924, and W. M. Wheeler: *Social Life Among Insects*.

the etiquette of courts shows all the manner of thought of a society and age. And likewise, every sociologist is an historian, although his task may be more specifically that of selection than of verification, and his attitude may be more that of the publicist than of the recorder. He neglects what is irrelevant to his purpose, however important, as a chemist may neglect the influence of the stars, or Laplace the existence of the Deity. Hence the term ' sociologist' may be reserved for the reflective historian of the type of Montesquieu and Buckle, Lecky and Lea, Westermark and Frazer. Or it may be dropped altogether in favour of that of ' anthropologist.'

Or Sociology as a Portmanteau Science: a general term for all Sciences which bear on the Fact of Association. Lastly, it may be suggested that Sociology is a collective name for all sciences that bear upon the actual relations of human beings, but is not itself a science. The chief use of the term would be adjectival, and would avoid an ambiguity in the use of the word ' social.' A sociological approach would be ' an approach from the side of the study of the social relationship.' It is a pretty conjecture that Economics arises where the realm of Psychology impinges on that of Physics, where mind is conditioned in its endeavours by its material means ; that Genetics[29] arises where Psychology and Biology

---

[29] By Genetics is here meant not only eugenics and the practical study of how to improve human stocks, but the scientific study of the whole field of the phenomena of the growth and movements of population, and the differentiation or cross-breeding of racial stocks ; in brief, the entire field of data which would yield an interpretation

touch, where mind asks something of its body and recognises that happiness is dependent on the *corpus sanum* and this again upon the racial stock ; and that Politics arises where individual mind by its activity conditions individual mind, and individual will conditions individual will. Lovers of rounded systems might argue in favour of three primary sciences of Physics, Biology, and Psychology, and of three secondary ones of Economics, Genetics, and Politics, and for Sociology as the sum of these latter three.

It may, however, be alleged with more assurance that Economics is concerned with the study of the actual relationships of human beings only as secondary to their relationship to the productive sources of wealth, to land, to mines, to men as marketable, to hands, to ' social plant.' Genetics or Eugenics is concerned with men, not as willing individuals, but as members of the human race, impelled by the necessity of their natures to pro-create the next generation and by affection to rear it, whatever controls intelligence may introduce as an afterthought. Precision is gained by distinguishing from these a study of the relationships, as such, of individuals with each other, the sexual relation and relation of the generations apart. Such a study may be called, as by Simmel, Sociology. It is probably better to do so than to call by that name

of history with the Family, a so-called ' Natural Society,' as the fundamental social unit and in the light of the instinct of racial preservation.

treatises, of a social emphasis, appertaining to other sciences. This leads to confusion of method, and a correct method is the first condition of successful scientific discovery. It is, however, proposed here to call this study by the traditional, precise, and more suggestive name of Politics.

II. *The Scope and Contributions of Anthropology.* Anthropology, along with its kindred science of Ethnology, although, unlike Sociology, a subject capable of independent study, is sometimes considered as a ' fundamental ' subject to which Politics should stand in a subsidiary relation.[30] This attitude is not without justification if it is meant to correct a grandiose and ' pseudo-spiritual ' treatment of human history. Anthropology more especially directs attention to man as a fact of natural history, as an animal genus with a certain bodily structure and consequent habits and geographical distribution, points out in its study of human origins what man has in common with the non-human, and serves to link up Physiology and Zoology with Politics.

This collecting science is invaluable for the study

[30] R. R. Marett : *Anthropology*, p. 7 : " Anthropology is the whole history of man as fired and pervaded by the idea of evolution. Man in evolution—that is the subject in its full reach." How far Sociology (as hitherto defined) and Anthropology overlap is shown by the following quotation from Gumplowicz (*op. cit.*, p. 72) : " Since the human race is what lies at the back of all social phenomena, one can indicate this, that is humanity, as the peculiar field and the scientific subject of sociological study." The endeavour of Spencer (*Social Studies*, p. 58) to distinguish Sociology and Anthropology by relegating the latter to ontogenetical studies has not proved generally acceptable.

of Politics, since it expresses the more primitive sides of human conduct, and enables us to correct in the study of society (as psychological experiments may perhaps do in the study of the individual) the sophisticated and conventionalized presentation of orthodox History. It is thus fundamental to Politics in the sense that it collects the data, so far as the human genus is concerned. And it is only by studying the whole field of the development and social organization of living creatures that one may hope to come to a balanced theory of human Politics. But Anthropology is not fundamental in that it aims to provide us with a systematic science of society, apart from which Politics would be as impossible as is the second floor of a building without a ground floor. The true position is quite other. Anthropology, or the natural study of the data of human behaviour, is itself but contributory to general Social Biology (which includes the conduct of animals in society), or to Social Psychology on the historical side,[31] and is misleading if the field of research into human *vestigia* is studied in isolation, except for convenience. Light will probably best be thrown on Anthropology, in part by the general conclusions of Biology, and in part by the application of the scheme of motives and the psychological hypotheses used with success in Economics and Politics, as a clue to the solution of the riddle of the behaviour of animal forms of life with which we

---

[31] Cf. the position maintained by Professor C. E. Ellwood (*Psychology of Human Society*, 1925, p. 9), "The social process is a psychological phenomenon, consequently a psychological explanation is necessary to understand social processes or group behaviour."

cannot yet communicate, and of which the conduct is therefore conveniently called ' instinctive,'[32] and of primitive forms of human life which are no longer extant to be cross-questioned. Anthropology contributes much valuable ' proto-history ' and information about the conduct of barbarous peoples without native chroniclers ; but, when it is a matter of the formulation of principles, the anthropologist, as social historian and collector of data, has to confess that this lies outside his province. Primitive anthropology is therefore an indispensable historical auxiliary ; it is not, as are Biology or Psychology, fundamental to Politics as an abstract science.

III. *The Scope and Contributions of Psychology.* It is probable that Psychology, the formal study of mental action and passion so far as they can be inferred from behaviour or introspection, will be found to contribute more to Politics than does Anthropology, but it is certainly a more dangerous contributor. Many of the hypotheses which the economist can contribute to the study of society are in the last analysis undoubtedly psychological hypotheses, elaborated and corroborated by observation in a particular field of experience and in a particular class of situation. When, however, Psychology claims for its study the entire province of human conduct,[33] it reduces Economics, Ethics, and the

---

[32] J. B. S. Haldane : *Biology Moulding the Future (Forum,* March, 1925).

[33] W. McDougall : *Physiological Psychology,* 1908, p. 1 : " Psychology may be best and most comprehensively defined as the positive science of the conduct of human creatures." Professor McDougall in a more recent work (*Outline of Psychology,* 1923, p. 37) has

science of men's actual relation with their fellows to the rank not only of subordinate subjects, but of subjects vassal exclusively to itself. This claim, were it seriously put forward, while being as bold as that of the Marxian economists, would also be as extravagant. The logical dependence of the material world on mental experience is undeniable, but the actual dependence of the direct mental experience of the individual upon the universe with which he is inferentially acquainted is as well established. What Economics has sometimes claimed in the interests of the material factors, Psychology often, though it be but by implication, tends to claim in the interests of the mental factors, ' instincts ' and the like, as the ultimate term of reference and architectonic energy. It must be admitted as a merit of the Behaviorist school that it has protested against this too facile satisfaction with disconnected mental entities. The psyche cannot be separated, as pure agent, from its environment, but is impregnated with it. On the other hand, it is difficult to concede that the study of human conduct, psychological but with the psyche left out, entitles the newer psychologists to call their own the formal field of the relationship of active beings.

Politics is the science of the conscious relations in society of animate bodies, ruled as much by the laws of the belly as by those of the finite mind,[34] and is

substituted a new definition of Psychology for his earlier one : " The science of the human mind ; we may make the definition more exact by adding the words ' positive ' and ' empirical.' "

[34] I insert as a precaution the qualifying adjective ' finite.' With

concerned with the nature and changes of these relations, whereas Psychology is concerned, not with the social effects of actual conduct and the ensuing system of interrelations thereby built up, but with the forms of conduct which manifest individual ' mental ' performance, as a species of activity susceptible of scientific investigation. It has been rightly felt that Psychology has much to contribute to the understanding of social relations. But this contribution it is perhaps sufficient to ascribe to the fact that the real elements of any society are individuals. These individuals may, indeed, be abnormally stimulated by unusual social intercourse, and may be changed in nervous structure over biological periods by the normalizing of some new grade of social intercourse. There is certainly then, in this limited sense, what may be called ' Social Psychology,' because individuals are unavoidably in social relationship and are modified thereby. But it is unnecessary and even misleading to suppose that social relationships are peculiarly a study for the psychologist. It has been, however, rather owing to the apparent desirability of appropriating an unappropriated and interesting field than from any addiction to a crude belief, alien to

whether the ultimate nature of Stuff is best apprehended as mind, and with the connection between what I have ventured to call ' social logic ' and the Hegelian philosophy, I am not here concerned. I have earlier stated my inclination to regard the conflict between idealist and materialist as ' *vieux jeu*,' and my belief that the important distinction is not between ' matter ' and ' mind,' but between the scientific and the æsthetic attitudes.

o

their training, in the dependence of all things on
'mind,' that the psychologists, like the economists,
have sometimes ventured to put a broad hand over
the whole field of social relations.

The danger arising from the psychological appro-
priation of the field, and from the rash adoption of
psychological contributions, is due to the present
immature state of Psychology itself; by building our
political theory upon psychological premises which
may in a few years become out of date, our labour
may be not merely vain but harmful. That, for the
purposes of interpretating the historical data, we must
borrow much from Psychology is becoming increasingly clear, but it is also prudent to borrow, not
dogmas, but experimental hypotheses, and to borrow
those hypotheses which the history of political
theory indicates that men of genius have used,
with no small success but perhaps not with sufficient
prudence, to explain History in the past.[35]   In so

[35] Bryce : *Modern Democracies*, I, p. 15 : " Politics . . . has
its roots in psychology, the study (in their actuality) of the mental
habits and volitional proclivities of mankind." But cf. J. B. S.
Haldane : *op. cit.*, p. 337 : " Until we have got a sounder neurology,
however, scientific psychology, except of a fragmentary character,
is no more possible than was physiology until chemistry and physics
had reached a certain point. And until psychology is a science,
scientific method cannot be applied to politics." The difficulty,
however, is not unavoidable. Shrewd psychological observations
may be used, as they have been used with distinction by Professor
Graham Wallas, to humanize the study of Politics (which is certainly
much more than Logic applied to the problem of Government) while
repudiating all pretence of constructing an abstract science (*Human
Nature in Politics*, 1909, p. 15). But tentative psychological hypotheses may also be used by students, whether Psychology as a whole
is a science yet or not, for the task of securing the simplicity requisite
for a science of Politics, although the results most emphatically must

far as Politics has to do with the relations of sentient beings in the intellectual and cultural medium of civilization, it has much to learn from Psychology which, in the interpretation of these complexities, it cannot learn from common sense. But, although the principles of Psychology may prove a guide to the form of human conduct, nevertheless the social expression and organized shape taken by that conduct, the expression which, for example, the tendency to pugnacity may take, will be dictated by the conventions and institutions, the civilization of the time, against which background this conduct takes shape. In this connection men are, as it were, things walking ; their passions are not their own in intensity or fashion of expression, but those natural to their time and place. The studies of the form of social relationship and of the form of human conduct are not co-extensive in field. Although these institutions of civilization may be called 'psychological'— are created, that is, by human desires and wishes,

not be " founded on assumptions of which they are unaware and which they have never tested either by experience or study." Professor Graham Wallas would illuminate the study of government by general human experience carefully examined and applied. I submit that this protest against the ossification of political study is recurrently required, but that, if by Psychology be meant a shrewd knowledge of human nature, it will carry us constructively no further than did Machiavelli and less far than did Hobbes. If, however, by Psychology be meant (at least in ideal) a science possessing general concepts and methodical conclusions, i.e. a science abstract as all ' natural sciences ' are abstract, then the hypothetical method of applying psychological suppositions as axioms in Politics is submitted to be one at least as likely as any other to lead to conclusions which, duly allowing for counterbalancing considerations, are likely to prove of practical utility in the management of the actual human society of our street.

seeking a channel—as well as being material, dictated by what is possible under the physical circumstances, no amount of study of Psychology exempts Politics from the obligation to study the social logic of these institutions in the light of their traditional, their economic, their biological, and their geological determinants.

IV. *The Scope and Contribution of Other Social Studies.* A custom exists of distinguishing a ' fundamental Science of Society ' or Sociology (which one sometimes discovers to be an interpretation of the social system in the light of the ' sympathetic ' or of the ' gregarious instinct ') from a rather perfunctory and arbitrary list of ' social sciences,' which includes Criminology and Jurisprudence, as well as History, Statistics, Ethics, and a lesser breed of studies.

As to the impropriety of speaking of History as a science, and as to the obfuscation caused by this use, enough has been said. Why Ethics is misunderstood if treated as a science is a problem to which we propose to return, although there can, of course, be a science of moral ways and means as well as a history of the genesis of ethics, a medical art of mental and spiritual health, and a technique of moral jurisprudence, some of which admit of a scientific and ' naturalistic ' treatment. Such particular studies as Genetics and Eugenics or, again, Criminology, upon which Pearson and the Galton Eugenics Laboratory and the Italian School of criminologists and such British alienists as Sullivan, have contributed much that is of the first interest to political science, are nevertheless for the present[36] contributors to, rather than receivers from or participators in, the social sciences. Workers in these fields are more properly considered as biologists, or medical or social experts, working on clinical experience reinforced by knowledge of the crude historical data or prepared statistics, than as social scientists. Statistics, it is clear, is not a social science, but auxiliary, as a symbolic record or history, to that science for which it supplies the statistics ; it is, unlike Mathematics, not a knowledge for its own sake.[37]

Especially Jurisprudence. A great movement of thought in our time has been away from the juristic or superstructural to the psychological or structural examination of society (although, as has been said, the structure of the social system is by no means solely psychological). But this does not mean that the study of law may be neglected by the social sciences. Whether Jurisprudence is any more a science than heraldry, or is rather to be considered as the general principles of a technique, meaningless (except as conducive to accurate drafting) unless it

[36] Such studies as those of American conditions, e.g. *Criminal Justice in Cleveland*, by R. Moley, F. Frankfurter, R. Pound and others (1922), indicate that social studies, although scarcely yet social theory, are already making positive contributions in the field of crime, as they have done for long in that of pauperism. The ' *Survey of Crime in Missouri* ' (Missouri Association for Criminal Justice) recently made is a most interesting case of the application of the quantitative social study method to the problems of government (*vide* Professor R. Moley's article in the *New York Times*, 4th March, 1926).

[37] A. L. Bowley : *The Nature and Purpose of the Measurement of Social Phenomena* (1915), p. 4.

has some proximate end in view, it is not proposed here to discuss. At least its study (as also that of governmental mechanism, civil, ecclesiastical, and industrial, and of the actual results and efficiency of various governmental expedients) is one of the most important for the politicist. But, whereas the study of the technique of government is of particular value in connection with the knowledge of the structure of institutions, the study of law, it may be suspected, is chiefly to be sought for the insight which it gives into the nature of conventions. The institutional side of law, its courts and executive officials, are rather proper to the sphere of the student of government. But the study of the aims of laws and of the historical theories of law reveals both the crystallization of conventional opinion into the determinate shape of law, and the influence of law in stabilizing opinion. It is probable that law would gain in elasticity and in adaptation to the needs of the times if lawyers were better acquainted with the social sciences, with the conclusions of criminologists and alienists, and with the significance of social statistics.[38] It is certain that social scientists, both economists and politicists, will find in legislation and in judicial decisions some of their most valuable data for the understanding of the growth and stabilization of conventions.

The fields of Jurisprudence and of Politics are,

[38] I hope, in a second volume, to examine this problem of methods of legislation and administration in view of a scientific knowledge of the social situation, and the problem of the ' Expert ' or ' Instrumental ' State.

however, distinct. Nothing can be more harmful than the mistake of treating domestic and international organization as merely a matter of law ' and the rest.'[39] ' The rest ' is determinant of the law, and not conversely. This mistake results in part from the fallacy of identifying Politics with government, and being content when we have pointed out that governmental machinery is established by law. Even were this assumption historically accurate, both the law and the executive agencies are products, and only in a limited measure causes, of the social situation. Law is not something absolute, which it is the business of the State to find and administer ;[40] but law is something ' found ' in the sense that the social situation only admits of certain appropriate measures, and it is the business of the statesman, like a diagnosing physician,[41] to discover and, through the State, to apply the fit remedy. Moreover, a remedy distasteful to the patient will, for psychological reasons, have little or no efficacy. Not only the disease but the remedy is something to be discovered from examination of the particular situation, since society is not only a ' mass ' of people but a public ' opinion,' and by an appropriate measure is meant a measure appropriate to the whole situation, psychological as well as

[39] H. Grotius : *De Jure Belli et Pacis*, proleg. 57 : " Quia ista suam habent artem specialem politicam, quam recte ita solam tractat Aristoteles ut alieni nihil admisceat, contra quam fecit Bodinus, apud quem haec ars cum juris nostri arte confunditur."
[40] R. Pound : *Spirit of the Common Law*, 1921, p. 150.
[41] Plato : *Politicus*, § 297 (ed. Jowett, IV, p. 501).

material. The lawyer will, then, be deeply interested in carrying his researches back to a consideration of the social structure which underlies (although indeed influenced by) law and government alike. But it is no more fitting or conducive to the advancement of learning that Politics should be treated as an afterthought in the study of law, than that Mechanics should, although the younger study, be treated as an afterthought in the study of Engineering. Politics is an independent discipline in relation alike to the ancient studies (such as Jurisprudence) of the various fields of political activities, to co-equal sciences of human conduct, such as Economics, and to fundamental sciences, such as Physics and Psychology, or fundamental investigations, such as Metaphysics and Ethics.

The Field and Method of the Science of Politics. Politics is, then, one of the social sciences. The concept of a social science is a valid one unless we are to adopt so rigid a definition that it becomes disputable whether Physics is a science, in which case the argument tends to degenerate into empty verbalism. There is no inherent reason why the study of political data should not reveal natural regularities of process ; the field admits of treatment by scientific hypothesis, with the causal connection of ' if . . . then ' ; and its conclusions are not incapable of being tested by controlled experiment. Much ink had been wasted over this subject owing to the failure to distinguish between the formal and scientific, and the historical and æsthetic,

treatments of experience. There is, moreover, no inherent reason why the systematisation, in accord
with certain fundamental premises of the science,
possible (and in the last generation carried even too
far) in the case of Economics, should not be possible
and, if prudently undertaken, profitable, in the case
of Politics, the sister study born in the Lyceum.

Politics, with its field properly defined and not
left vague or misdefined, is susceptible of scientific
treatment in the same way as, although no more
than, Economics is susceptible of such treatment.
An increased social control has resulted from the
scientific treatment of a field of social phenomena
of which the nucleus is business experience ; so too
increased control may be expected to result from the
scientific treatment of politics. Politics must be a
positive study of the social facts and, from its own
angle, of actual situations. It must be objective,
approaching its subject-matter where possible without emotion or predilection as to values, and with
a view to applying standards of comparison and
measurement.

Politics is more than the study of the State or of
government, since it is impossible to study either,
thoroughly and intelligently—viewed from the standpoint of the scientist who inquires into the nature
of the structure and of the processes of change, as
distinct from the standpoint of the descriptive
historian or of the technical lawyer—without studying more than either ; i.e. without studying the
system of human interrelationships called society.

But Politics is not Sociology, in the older and more common acceptance of that term, since it does not pretend to be a science underlying and fundamental to Economics and all other possible social sciences. Doubtless, the work of such students as Max Weber in Germany, Fouillée and Lebon in France, Cooley, Giddings, Small and others in America, leaves its mark on all social studies, not to speak of earlier writers such as Spencer, Ratzenhofer, Simmel, Durkheim or Lester Ward (to whom we have elsewhere made specific acknowledgments). Equally without doubt new conceptions of the nature of the State and of social structure owe much to the philosophers, from Hegel to Bosanquet, working against the background of nationalism. They owe much to lawyers, such as Jhering, Gierke, Maitland, and Pound, working in the midst of a conflict between the unitary civilian and the federal Teutonic traditions of law in the German Empire, or of a conflict between eighteenth-century legal individualism with modern social conditions in the United States. They are indebted to students of psychology such as Graham Wallas; to statisticians such as Bowley and Pearson; and to political theorists such as Figgis, Cole, and Laski, developing ideas held to be implicit in new social movements, ecclesiastical, industrial, and civil.

Whether political thought owes more to these departmental workers than to those who adopt the customary sociological methods is a matter of opinion. That Sociology should discard mere political propaganda, or philanthropic and 'good citizen' or 'rotarian' sentiment dressed out in philosophic verbiage, the sociologists would be the first to affirm. As to whether, in these recent years of revision of political theory, the departmentalist owes more to the sociologist than the sociologist to the departmentalist must, in a period of reciprocal influences, be an idle dispute. We learn from high authority of the necessity for a 'sociological legal history.' The living question is not, however, one of names, or of the reputations of scholars, but of the method of study. It must be admitted that historical details, that the machinery of government, that the organization of community life called the State, cannot be studied, save superficially, apart from a study of human methods of organization and of the common forms of such methods. And it is here contended that the investigation of a certain kind of historical data, of which our knowledge is ample but hitherto unsystematized,—the data of and germane to, the political situation,—is to be preferred to an uncentred or multi-centred investigation of all social experience, even in the formal and scientific, as distinct from the philosophic or poetic, sense. Discursive surveys or sporadic investigations furnish a less useful method of throwing light upon social problems than an exhaustive analysis of a limited but entire field, in order to lay bare the form therein of the social mechanism, or (to use a happier phrase) to study social physiology and to discover and trace through their manifestations certain fundamental impulses operative in social conduct. Here, then, the study with which we are concerned is that, not of Sociology in the broad and philosophic sense, but of Politics in the sense above defined.

Admitting a social situation determined, among others, by factors meteorological, geological, biological, by factors of natural wealth and of technical discovery, by factors of conservative tradition and established civilization, and admitting a human nature (i.e. common characteristics in human beings) of a certain, if imperfectly known, constancy, as distinct from inexplicable caprice, our problem is to examine how men have discovered and elaborated a *modus vivendi* in relation to each other without making life worthless for themselves, through restrictions and repressions, or worthless, through oppression, for others. This is a problem not chimerical, as is that of the ' science of History ' ; it is less ambitious than that of the sociologist as usually propounded ; it is less technological than the study of law or of government. From History in the broadest sense, ancient and modern, primæval and contemporary, narrative and symbolical, and from occasional social experimentation, Politics will gather its data, and from Psychology it will derive guiding suggestions. If not all (for the population problem and relationship between the generations does not seem to be proper to either), at least most social phenomena may be mapped out between itself and Economics, from which more mature science it may take much of its method.

This division is to be made, not by the drawing of boundaries necessarily artificial and unserviceable, but by distinguishing between the two nuclear experiences or ' situations '—that of man in his relation to ' things ' in their production and negotiation, and that of man in his relation to the wills of his fellows in control, submission and accommodation. This last relation is the characteristic of the ' political situation,' and the man whose experience is dominated by it and who thinks and acts especially in terms of it, is the ' political man.'

CHAPTER III

THE PROCESS OF POLITICS

Economic Method and Political Theorizing. The objection of the plain man to political science so-called is that after making the bravest of promises, it has hitherto consistently failed to fulfil them ; in the colloquial phrase, ' it has not delivered the goods.'[1] But the endeavour to put Politics as a theoretical study upon a sounder basis may not be desperate. In this attempt to reduce Politics to the compass and system of that science which it has long pretended to be, no subject is likely to prove more instructive for comparative study than that of Economics. By following the methods by which Economics has been built up by Adam Smith and his successors in this last century out of common-sense business experience into a body of knowledge vindicating for itself the title of a science, a clue may be furnished for the reduction of Politics to a similar regularity. The decrying of Adam Smith and of the classical economists, now in vogue, may be a healthy symptom in the history

[1] E. Barker : *Political Thought from Spencer to To-day,* 1915, p. 157. The criticism here made of Professor McDougall, that " he seems to do a great deal of packing in preparation for a journey in which he never starts," could be applied with even greater force to the political scientists of all schools.

of economic thought. It may, however, prove misleading in the development of political science. Just, indeed, as the business man prefers common sense to economic science, finding it easier to arrive at a decision as it were by a trained ' sense of smell ' than by applying theory, so this regularity of political method is likely to appeal rather to the student who desires to see some plan in the social hurly-burly, than to the practical politician who reflects how many of his successes have been due to no assignable reason. We are, however, here concerned, not with a political technology, but with the study of those permanent political forms which limit and shape the policies of the hour.

The subject-matter of Politics is sufficiently similar to that of Economics to encourage the hope that the brilliant and sudden development of the one out of the ground of business experience may, in the course of this century, not be unparalleled by the development of the other out ·of all the wealth of experience of statecraft. Economics and Politics are alike concerned with the conduct of human beings in a certain type of relationship or situation, and the methods of overcoming the difficulties of the one study are likely to be indicated by the methods of the other.

Economics, observing certain factors to be operative and making hypothetically certain assumptions about human nature, is able to predict—i.e. to state a uniform rule holding for past and future—so long as these factors are uncomplicated. And complications, although never absent, are frequently negligible. Economics is thus able to satisfy the chief requirement by which a science is tested, to wit, that it is able to make deductive statements which subsequent experience will in fact corroborate.

Nor must the distinction between Economics and the ' physical sciences ' be unduly emphasized. Chemistry is a science of prediction, not merely a classificatory historical science, but its assertions only hold when the chemical materials are pure and laboratory conditions are preserved ; its predictions are ' *true, if* . . .' The conclusions of Astronomy are implications of, and (so far as their practical significance is concerned) are conditional upon, the general continuance of the general body of observed facts of the solar and stellar systems. Their apparent accuracy is due to their approximation to the formal purity of Mathematics ; the individual characteristics of these celestial bodies are largely irrelevant to the astronomer's purpose.

Economics in the same way is not incapable of conditional prediction ; it is thus a science and not a mere collection of observations. But it is less so capable than Chemistry, because its materials are less pure and with difficulty admit isolation from complicating circumstances, its phenomena are more complex and adventitious and further removed from mathematical simplicity, and hence its theoretical forecasts are possessed of less practical validity. Economics is less able to satisfy the ' if ' of its own conditions, and is less capable of actualizing its own hypotheses. Too often it finds itself, in Francis Bacon's phrase, *subtilitate rerum humanarum longe impar*.

The laws of Economics, true as a logical gymnastic, only hold in part true in practice, since the premises of the particular forecast are inadequately descriptive of the situation. Especially the endeavour to enunciate economic laws depends for its success upon the degree to which hypotheses about constants in human conduct are adequately descriptive of that conduct for experimental use. But, if it is justifiable to postulate any such constants in human conduct as orthodox Economics has assumed, there seems to be no reason why the study of mutual human relations, that is, of Politics, should not prove as susceptible of systematization as are the economic relations set up in the negotiation of things. In both cases we are studying the relations of assumed constants. Did Economics not assume human nature to be, for its purposes, a constant or constant variable, as (in the alternative) the relations of a known and an unknown —matter and man—it would be fruitless. Economics does not assume human nature to be for its purpose an unknown, and there is no inherent reason why Politics should be stultified by being treated as the study of the interrelation of two unknowns, i.e. two wills.

The Field of Economics further discussed. The field of Economics is that of the relation of men with things, and with each other in the negotiation of

P

things.[2] Economics is a social science because men co-operate for the purposes of this negotiation, both as touching production and exchange, and society takes on certain structural forms adapted for these purposes. In the broad Crocean sense of the word 'economic,' it may be distinguished from Ethics, as having to do with means and not with ends—with the *modus vivendi* and not with the *causas vivendi*. But here Economics is understood in the narrower sense, whereby it is distinguishable from Politics as being concerned with things, with the association of men for the negotiation of things, and with trafficking with men as 'animate tools'[3] who turn themselves into things by renouncing their wills in return for food.

The Field of Politics Compared. Politics, as a theoretical study, is concerned with the relations of men, in association and competition, submission and

[2] *Trend of Economics*, ed. by R. G. Tugwell, 1924, p. 261 : " Thus economic theory has in practice come to be restricted to the analysis of social inter-action and co-ordination through the price mechanism, that is, of organization through the competitive sale for money by individuals (really families) of productive services (of person and ' property ') to business enterprises, and the competitive purchase from business enterprises with the money obtained of goods for consumption."

[3] Aristotle : *Politics*, I, iv. Professor Veblen, in his brilliant satire *The Theory of a Leisure Class* (1889, p. 80), distinguishes between industry and exploitation in a fashion roughly corresponding to my distinction between the economic and the political : " any effort is accounted industrial only so far as its ultimate purpose is the utilization of non-human things." But much immediate utilization of human ' hands ' is involved in genuinely economic operations. And political control has an ethical neutrality lacking in the phrase ' exploitation,' adopted by Professor Veblen, when used popularly as a term of appraisal.

control, in so far as they seek, not the production and consumption of some article, but to have their way with their fellows. The conflict is not with a reluctant Nature and, indirectly, with those induced to submit to organized toil for its mastery, but directly with the obduracy of man and in order to secure co-operators or servants, even although for no tangible end.

The extreme instance of simple economic relationship is that of Robinson Crusoe sitting in the midst of his desert island, stitching skins for clothes. There is here no social relation ; there is only the relation of a willing being with inanimate things, entered into as work, with a view to consumption. The equally extreme instance of a simple political relationship is that of the angels in Heaven rising in rebellion against the Almighty. Here there are no material needs, or ' production,' or ' exchange of articles ' ; there is only the relationship of wills striving to avoid or assert control.

In the economic sphere the end is to secure material wealth in order (save with perverted misers) to convert it to minister to such satisfactions as one may think fit.[4] In the political sphere the end is to secure good will or good service, in order that one may turn this control to such purposes as, again, one may think fit. In its first and crudest form, economic

[4] J. N. Keynes : *Scope and Method of Political Economics*, 1891, p. 118 : " This abstraction . . . the desire for wealth, is in its immediate economic effects the same, whatever its ulterior object may be." In the same way, in Politics, we shall be concerned with the consequences of the desire for power without feeling ourselves called upon to answer the question ' powers for what ? '

endeavour arises in the effort to ward off penury and starvation. Similarly political organization extends beyond the circle of the blood-kin in order to assure preservation, τοῦ ζῆν ἑνεκέν—' for the sake of life.' It hereby distinguishes itself from the natural family built on the sexual and maternal instincts and the sense of affection, without antagonistic assertion of will. Even to-day the private person is probably more interested in this organization as a means of protecting him from the interference of others, than as providing facilities for expressing himself and for ministering to his own ' good life ' as he sees it.

Not all control of men need be treated as political. The overseer and foreman are indeed put in control over men, but they receive pay as conducing by their organizing and supervising abilities to increase the output of the undertaking, and not, as a provincial governor, specifically by reason of their ability and tact in producing order and contentment among those under them. The relationship of control, however important, is secondary, although, taken in itself, Politics may treat of this industrial mastery and control with entire appropriateness. On the other hand, captains of industry, commercial princes and merchant venturers, competing for the control of the trade of an area, even where accommodation is possible, stand to each other in an essentially political relationship ; they are primarily interested in the control and respect of men, not in the mere acquisition of shares in a concern. Still more obviously political are the alliances and rivalry of trade unions, and the candidatures and administrative work of their officials. All these relationships are the fit concern of the student of Politics.

The Economic Man, with the Desire for Acquisition. If Economics has reared its head into the air of logic, Antæus-like its feet have been grounded on the observed fact of human acquisitiveness. The axioms on which its laws, however abstract, were based, have had a real counterpart in a natural impulse, the ' will to possess.'[5] It is indubitable that men, even in the economic situation, are influenced by other impulses ; and not by any means all who have the will to possess have the intelligence to acquire. But it is also indubitable that our present economic structure is built up chiefly on the desire for acquisition, even if not unlimited,—upon the principle of not buying in the dearest market—and upon the fact that the maximum of production does not result from the minimum of work.

Economics has met the difficulty of the inconstancy of human nature by constructing the ' economic man,' an ideal being whose reactions to given circumstances are known. Whether the economic man exists or ever has existed is immaterial. It is

[5] I abstain from speaking of an instinct (but hereon *vide* L. L. Bernard : *Instinct,* 1924, *passim*) in order to avoid the implication that these impulses are susceptible of actual isolation from each other and even act as uncaused causes, detached from the context of their environment. The primary factors in Economics are scarcity and wants, and wants are themselves grounded on the involuntary need for things to be procured from nature or man.

sufficient that, in the study of our social organization, we observe that, in the economic relationship,
the will to possess with a minimum of labour is a
dominant psychological factor ; that men should act
as if they were economic men is a condition fulfilled
in the business world of our day with remarkable
frequency. Nor is the desire for the maximum of
pay, the minimum of compulsory work, and tolerable
conditions, entirely one produced by ' capitalist
psychology.' It is of general applicability. The
fiction, in short, as a scientific hypothesis, can
' work.' Thus on the psychological side in desire,
as well as on the material side of the economic
relationship in measurable products, it is possible,
for the purposes of science, to point to a constant
(or known variable). The economic man is an
abstraction, constant in his reactions and freed from
the vagaries of human sentiment, as well as from the
distracting influence of all minor motives. But he
is not a mere fiction, since he is constructed in
accord with human nature, although by the isolation
of one tendency in it ; namely, the acquisitive
tendency. The ' economic man ' is indeed so much
more than a caricature that philosophers from
Hobbes to Helvetius have held up, as the type of the
rational man, a being who acted towards all life in
every respect as the economic man acts in economic
affairs. Even in Condorcet there is the same notion
that the world would be well if men intelligently
followed their natural desires. And although men
are far too little intelligent and too little moved by a

few simple, unsophisticated instincts to do anything of the kind, generally and consistently the structure of our society is shaped by the slow pressure of these and other dominant tendencies.

The Political Man with the Desire for Power. There is nothing inherently impossible in the attempt to construct in the same manner a ' political man,' who seeks so far as possible to direct the wills of others in accordance with his will and as little as possible to be thwarted or controlled by their wills. It must not be expected that the ' political man ' will bear any closer relation to that more commonplace abstraction, ' the average citizen,' than does the ' economic man.' It is merely requisite, in order that this scientific Frankenstein may be serviceable, that he should be not more remote in likeness from the men of our acquaintance than is his ' economic ' fellow ; that the psychological conditions which are postulated (for lack of a more adequate psychological knowledge) in his construction should not be conspicuously more improbable.

Nor is it relevant to object that the doctrine of the economic man has done much harm. That the fiction has been misinterpreted as fact, does not render the proper and judicious use of the fiction vain. Even if it be true that the economists have, in the past, turned a convenient fiction into a dogma about reality, it does not follow that we, in our turn, need confound a hypothesis made for laboratory convenience with a philosophy of human nature. For we are not concerned with what ' is,' (only the philosopher is so concerned), but, as scientists, with results. It may, however, be well to remember in defence of our use of fiction, were defence needed, that in every field of social research, the method of an Adam Smith must precede the corrective theories of a Ruskin.

The History of Egoistic Philosophy. Implicitly the doctrine of a political man is indeed not new. From the infancy of political theory the assertion that man has built up the social structure for self-preservation has gone along with the thesis that man was not a solitary animal—*solivagum genus*—but 'politically,' or better, 'socially,' inclined by nature. Naturally he associates. But the greatest of political theorists and observers have in succeeding centuries, in their endeavours to secure a clue to the interpretation of history, gone beyond this merely negative theory of passive association, as gratifying in itself and a protection against enemies. In the imperfect social organizations known to history, in order to escape restriction in the impulse to express oneself, it is necessary to do more than lethargically avoid hindrances ; such conduct is ineffective. It is necessary to have active control. The State, all social life which involves a relationship of independent wills—that is, all political life—may be, in the Greek sense, a 'natural' product, but it is not an instinctive and unpremeditated product, such as is the biological family. The political society arises with the consciousness of an independent will. For Machiavelli, for Hobbes, for Spinoza, for Treitschke, for Ratzenhofer, the interpretation of Politics is to be found in the desire to gain or maintain power, whether of individuals or of groups.[6] These writers stated as a dogma, and thus with exaggeration, what is indeed but a generalization upon one aspect of human conduct. They have thus evoked reactions of thought which have stressed, as did the writings of Locke, the merely negative desire of the individual for security, or which have emphasized, as recent writers have emphasized, the gregarious aspect of human society with its organization in families and sentimental units, and have demanded study of the ' concrete group.'

Attacked by the individualism of the eighteenth century, which minimized the inexorable nature of the social and governmental relationship, and, from the opposite side, by the anti-intellectualist doctrines of the twentieth century, the theory has been stated with a certain vacillation. Hobbes endeavoured to reconcile the self-will with an obligation, almost final, to preserve one's political allegiance to the sovereign. Treitschke has attempted to moralise it

[6] Machiavelli : *Opere*, 1820, III, p. 247, *Discorsi*, I, v : " for it never seems to men that a man possesses securely what he has unless he acquires something further from another." Hobbes : *Leviathan*, I, xi : " So that in the first place I put for a general inclination of all mankind a perpetual and restless desire of power after power, that ceaseth only in death." Spinoza : *Tract. Pol.*, § v : " All are equally eager to be first." " Furthermore it is certain that everyone would rather rule than be ruled. . . . For by ambition all of us are chiefly led." Treitschke ; *Politics*, Eng. trans., ed. 1916, I, p. 65 : " Wars will endure to the end of history, as long as there is multiplicity of States. The laws of human thought and of human nature forbid any alternative." Ratzenhofer : *Wesen und Zweck der Politik*, 1893, I, p. 47 : " Political conflicts are thus a particular manifestation of the general struggle for existence in nature."

by an Hegelian baptism, Nietzsche to paganize it in his new gospel of inverted ethics, and Ratzenhofer to bind it up with organic theories of society. Although, then, the doctrine has been exaggerated as a statement of fact, its awkward consciousness of this has made it timid as a statement of hypothetical theory. Whether because of the political exigencies of the age of the Stuarts or because of the ethical prepossessions of the epoch influenced by Hegel, the endeavour to explain the political structure as the product of the quest for power has never been carried through as thoroughly as could have been wished. The exponents of the theory have always been concerned to defend the product. They have not been guided—not even Machiavelli—by a purely scientific interest. But that, implicitly if not explicitly, the assertive tendency in human nature has been seized upon by the most fruitful thinkers in Politics, as was the acquisitive tendency by the classical economists, seems beyond reasonable doubt. The only novelty which it is proposed to introduce into the present study is that an explicit hypothesis will be substituted for an implicit assumption of fact.

The difference, however, is of the first importance. In the eleventh chapter of the *Leviathan* Hobbes outlined the features of the ' political man,' which are *mutatis mutandis* those of the ' economic man.' But Hobbes asserts these features to be detectable in ' all mankind,' that is, he considers his description to be an adequate one of human nature as a whole. The purely political nature of the political man

(Hobbes' quite proper concern in a treatise on the
" Matter, Form, and Power of a Commonwealth,
Ecclesiastical and Civil ") is lost sight of, and the
political man is identified with the actual ' man one
meets in the street,' to the confusion of both. This
error is one which Hobbes' successors only accentu-
ated. It becomes more conspicuous as we proceed
on from Hobbes, with his political background, to
the more universal and metaphysical comments of
Spinoza (" *virtus est ipsa humana potentia* "), and to
the hedonistic philosophy of Holbach (" The good
man is he to whom true ideas have shown his own
interest to lie in such a way of acting that others
are forced to love and approve for their own sakes ")
and of Helvetius : (" If the physical universe is
subject to the laws of motion, the moral universe is
not less subject to the laws of interest "). The same
general principle of intellectually appreciated self-
interest was taken over by the Utilitarians, although
as early as Bentham with noticeable modifications.
Few were prepared flatly to deny the two principles
of the desire for power over means, and of enlightened
self-interest guiding the choice of proximate ends—
not even theologians such as Paley and Whateley.
That it explained all human behaviour, few were
prepared to agree. But so deeply rooted has been
the belief that this doctrine, first systematically
enunciated by Hobbes, " *irritabile Malmesburense
animal*," stood or fell as an explanation of human
nature in its entirety, that not many have stopped
to explain, or indeed to consider, to what sides of

human activity, or to what type of stimulus-providing situation, it is applicable. The notion of the hypothetical treatment of a ' political situation ' has not been developed.

The Hypothesis of Self-assertion. It seemed impossible to disrupt human nature into ' sides ' ; it was not perceived that the concrete complex of motives in the individual was susceptible of analysis and of abstract schematization. Although human nature may have, as philosophers such as Professor Lloyd Morgan think, one fundamental *nisus* or (perhaps purposeless) ' on-drive,' it is not so simple that all its expressions can be brought under one rubric, whether the Hobbesian or that of the psycho-analysts and ' soul-doctors ' of our own age. Even in love there is, as well as *abandon*, the ardent seeking that one's will (even to give) shall prevail. Even in politics there is emotional affection for one's country, the dear love of friends,[7] the enriching sense of community and interdependence, as well as the egoistic demand for justice. All that we can say is that these different tendencies dominate in different situations and, by slow pressure on conventions, build up different institutions in the social structure. Although we cannot tear up the man into tendencies and leave him human, or (without caricature) see only one tendency in him, we can profitably distinguish between situations, and speak

[7] Miss M. P. Follett prefers to express this by the phrase ' sympathetic interpenetration of personalities.' For a presentation of this point of view *vide* her book ' *The New State* ' (1918). Cf. also Cooley : *Human Nature and the Social Order*, 1902.

of the conduct especially manifested in a particular type of situation.

To do that which I will to do is positive freedom and power ; not to do that which others will me to do because they will it, is negative freedom and liberty.[8] As often as this doctrine has been put forward with the emphasis of an egoistic philosophy, so often it has been rejected with contumely by moralists who thought better of human nature or, thinking no better, yet believed in the possibility of universal and instantaneous conversion from original sin. It appeared intolerable that a bloodless political science should represent men, as a matter of nature and not of perversion, as seeking after power to carry out not what was right, but whatsoever they might in fact happen to will, whether this were good or bad (and the fundamental question was not put whether they could indeed pursue after evident bad). It was insufferable that countenance should be given to them in this vicious pursuit by seeming, even in theory, to recognize it as a permanent principle of social life. The exponents of the doctrine, relying rather on the base motive of fear than on the subtler influence of tradition to secure the harmony of social justice, were too little optimistic about human nature to show the force of their own case by demonstrating how genuinely men might come to will the will of others, and make conformity to an intelligent social authority their own interested choice. The opponents

---

[8] Lord Hugh Cecil : *Liberty and Authority*, 1910, p. 25 : " Liberty consists in the power of doing what others disapprove of."

of the doctrine, on the other hand, forgot that moral perfection is but the consummate development of a nature in its origins brutal, formed from the dust, even if in its progress inspired, and is not a final repression and quenching of that human nature. The Puritan had no relish for a pragmatic treatment of Politics, and preferred an exposition of ' godly discipline.'

It is not by refusing to admit the force of the desires which actually exist that we advance to a more perfect condition, but by understanding those desires in order to defecate and purge them. The principle of acquisitiveness is not abrogated because we seek to acquire for the sake of our fellows ; probably the family has been responsible for more acquisitive conduct in the world than the selfishness of individuals. Nor are the laws of power a study useless to him who would seek to allay mundane strife in the interests even of religious harmony. The prophet looks to make that will of which he is the instrument prevail, and believes that the truth of which he bears witness is not only mighty but the mightiest power of all. The influence of the religious leader or moral reformer is a form of power, and illustrates the laws of power.[9]

Concerning Eminent and Conspicuous Power. It is not to be supposed that the desire for power is satisfied by what is required to effect our immediate needs, or even, with many, by what is required under a sober calculation of their future individual needs.

[9] W. B. Munro : *Personality in Politics*, § i.

As there is a happiness of the millionaire as such, although his possessions exceed his needs, so there is of the successful tyrant or party manipulator, although his autocratic power is in excess of what is needed to remove social obstacles from his way as a plain citizen. It is the happiness of 'having more' (πλεονεξία). So, too, as there is a happiness, and this more generous, of the philanthropic and paternal capitalist, who feels an untroubled satisfaction in riches well-administered by himself, as trustee for his fellows' good, so there is a happiness of the statesman who bears down the opposition of his antagonists in the interests of the public welfare, of which he feels himself the elect exponent. As the economic man is moved to do the best for himself (and thus, perhaps, instrumentally for others) by securing possession of things, so the political man is moved to do the best for himself (and thus, perhaps, for others) by gaining a hold over men, in either case to avoid a possible frustration of will, whether by things or by other wills.

The question before the political man is ever : How can I carry out my will so that it will be forwarded and not frustrated by my fellows ? Out of such questionings, and their related experience, arises the intelligent socially-trained citizen, and the tradition of good citizenship. For it is not to be supposed that every man's interest upon sufficient reflection will be seen to be opposed to his neighbour's. To decide whether the primitive promptings are moral, or to assess the respective values of the different contents of what is actually willed, we are not now concerned. Our business is with the *form* of political willing, to which all kinds of individual wills in their relation to other wills conform, and thus our business is with all the actual willing of men so far as it is political, and not only with their ideal willing. Just as the tendency to acquisition, assumed in some form to be general and made the ground of a logical hypothesis, is the basis of a scientific Economics, so the desire (however incapable of real isolation) to attain one's ends among one's fellows—to ' execute one's will '—is the basis of a scientific Politics.

The love of possessions may be satisfied either by the secret hoarding of wealth, or by its extravagant display and by its garnering, by daring means, with great risks and great gains. Similarly, self-assertion and the display of power is considered good, not only as in fact clearing obstacles from our road and, if prudently used, as laying up a capital by the *éclat* of its success whereby to cope with future difficulties, but also as being a good in itself. In order to have his way a man is impelled and compelled to dominate his neighbours by oratorical appeal, by more cogent reasoning, by physical might or by other superior power whether of craft or of character, or (if he lack the necessary forcefulness) to see that, instead of being domineered over, he is at least on the side of those who dominate. It follows, by power of association, that, in time, not only the end but the means—nay, as with the plutocrat's money, the very insignia of power, the crown, the senator's chair, the laticlave or the ribbon,—come to be valued for themselves ; or, on the other hand, that to feel one's fingers on the controls of power, though one's hand be hidden, one's intentions disinterested, has fascination.

As there is a temptation to go from wealth to wealth, beyond our immediate or probable personal needs, in order to satisfy the secondary and ' sophisticated ' desire to live impressively in our social station or to outshine our fellows (a desire for ' conspicuous consumption ' which can, on analysis, be detected to be political in nature), so there is a desire for power for its own sake, whether, like the spendthrift's wealth, as commanding admiration from others or, like the miser's wealth, as secretly flattering to our vanity, beyond any present need for it in order to surmount obstacles to our will.

It may, however, be noted that ostentation, like the following of the latest and extreme vogue of fashion, is a sign of weakness, of being petitioners rather than assured possessors. Ostentation, in wealth or in power, arises because men are most proud of that which they desire most to have, not of that which they have most.

The Psychology of Self-assertion. The theory that the first principle of human nature is self-conservation and (one with it ; for with life there is movement, and that more truly in men than in most animals) self-expression ;[10] that when men fear

[10] H. Spencer, in a significant passage, remarks: " This rivalry which man maintains with his fellows has become the leading

Q

constraint from material want, they seek to possess themselves of property ample for their needs ; that, when they fear the more subtle, if sometimes less harsh, constraint of their neighbours, they become moved by a desire to control the wills of others, has received recent corroboration from the observations of psychologists. Even when this desire to escape limitations—which in the infant arouses rage[11] and in the philosopher leads to the contemplation of the Absolute—appears to be absent, the appearance, it may be hazarded, is deceptive. The devoted follower in the train of his leader, the affectionate friend, the weaker brethren, the submissive subjects, attain their purposes and are satisfied in the success of their hero ; his glory is theirs, and through his will they prevail and become more fully persons.

and dominant feature of our civilisation. . . . We shall have to recognise that the first and principal thought in the minds of the vast majority of us is how to hold our own therein." Cf. Spinoza : *Ethics*, pars. IV, prop. xx, and note, and xxi ; also Ward : *Realm of Ends*, pp. 288–9. Professor J. Dewey strenuously combats (*Human Nature and Conduct*, 1922, p. 220) all attempts to assimilate other human activities to the economic (defined, abstractly, as calculated pursuit of gain), or attempts to erect a system of Politics on the basis of fear or of any such gross force or entity. But Politics has no need of a tough, particular ' political or self-assertive instinct,' nor does it deny that men merely react generally in a self-preservative manner and in various ways, such as are appropriate to the whole circumstances ; it merely supposes that these circumstances are sufficiently often the same for all practical purposes for the reaction, or evoked or released impulse, to be susceptible of formal treatment. There is nothing here comparable with the assumption of a ' pugnacious ' or ' political ' instinct, inherent, like some ' dormative virtue ' and capable of itself of explaining all conduct, such as Professor Dewey censures (p. 132).

[11] J. B. Watson : *Psychology from the Standpoint of a Behaviorist* (1919), p. 200.

That they act without any conscious reflection that they are compassing self-regarding ends, does but prove the merging of the one personality into that of the other to be complete. Such, too, is the *amor Dei*, in which men merge themselves in a personality constructed according to the ideal of their own personality.

Where there is none of this reverential ardour, where, moreover, no cool calculation reassures the weak that the strength of the strong serves his purpose, and where yet there is submission in action to the will of another, it must not be supposed that the will to do one's own will, by mastering the master-will, is absent. Rather, irritated, our will like a fettered devil becomes vividly present, causing the mind to turn in upon itself and to make its grievance a subject for morbid meditation.[12] The father, the husband, the king ' father of his people,' the aristocrat born and bred as a leader of men, the master-craftsmen of the guild-fraternity, once

[12] A. Adler : *Neurotic Constitution* (Eng. trans. 1917), p. 35. If I owe much of the theory set forth in the text to the pressure of the problems of the war and the peace influencing my thinking, I also owe much to the fact that I happened to come across Dr. Adler's suggestive, if controvertible, book soon after completing a brief sketch of the philosophy of Hobbes. I am, however, unwilling to salute Accident as the presiding goddess of this theory. There are the debts which I have acknowledged in the preface. *Et in memoriam veterum bib imus.* Had it not been for an early and immature, but for me profoundly impressive, reading of Spinoza and Hegel, I am conscious that I should not have had that to express which, however meanly and inadequately, I have endeavoured in the text to express. To those who may, not unreasonably, distrust psycho-analytical sources, the bearings of the Platonic θύμος may be a more profitable subject for consideration.

followed and revered, become hated, even though the hatred do but smoulder in impotent indignation or in venomous resentment against conditions of inferiority. An irrational attachment and loyalty is replaced by a semi-rational, logic-lacking suspicion of the idol ; the nemesis that we have seen in Russia of a merely instinctive affection for the Czar as ' little White Father ' is a blind and ignorant distrust of the Czar as Autocrat of all the Russias. In unstable characters the continued frustration of the assertive self may result in mental perturbation and disease, just as ill-adjusted social conditions may be symptomized by the neurotic restlessness of an age.

The Will-to-execute-my-Will Operates both through Domination and Submission. As a man may prosper not as an owner, but as employee in a flourishing concern, so too the love of advantages, of social advancement, of political vantage ground, may be satisfied either by the successful use of self-assertion or, no less, by the astute use of submissiveness in conduct. Uriah Heep is always with us. Moreover, to know when to rule, when to obey for the common and the individual interest, has been the characteristic of peoples untainted by obsequiousness. The fulfilment, then, of the will of the individual (or individual group) by the bending of the wills of his fellows to further that will, is attained on the self-assertive side when the small subserves the will of the great ; it is attained on the submissive side when the great man agrees to lead and to protect the small. In either case there is not only the rational satisfaction of procuring the means to some ulterior end, but also the instinctive satisfaction arising from the primitive wish to assert oneself or to find oneself by being the centre of care and attention from others. That these psychological tendencies, both the more superficial one of acquisitiveness, and the political ones of assertion and submission, have been evolved for the sake of race preservation, is indeed probable ; but to suppose that they (especially the last) owe their immediate satisfaction to the consciousness that the race, or even the individual, is thereby removed a step further from physical destruction, would be mistaken. The satisfaction is, by sophistication, dissociable from its biological complement. That, however, action, apparently passive and submissive, is in reality a ' having one's own way,' will be clear to anyone who will ask himself how the weak man is to execute his will otherwise than by bringing one stronger into alliance. So wilful small children seek, by attracting the compassion of their elders, to get their own way. As Hobbes says, ' desire of ease, and sensual delight, disposeth men to obey a common power ' in that their wishes are easily gratified by such a power — from which can be deduced the sedative effects of national sports, and the best political argument for the tavern. History shows that, on occasion, this conservatism is not mere indifference, but a violent, dogged resolve to continue in an old allegiance or custom ; to do neither more nor less than heretofore.

Their will is to go on as their nature is, such as
it is ; each desires *perseverare in esse suo*. Those
are not bond who do not feel their chains, and
it is reform which produces resistance and revolution. To this observation we must later
return.

It should, moreover, be observed that, if it would
be difficult, it is also unnecessary for the politicist to
enter upon the discussion of what precisely the
tendency to follow and to venerate owes, in religion,
patriotism and personal devotion, to the sexual
instinct in its more sublimated manifestations, and
what to the cunning working of the more political
desire to ' make one's way ' (as a means of ' finding
oneself ' or of ' finding one's place ') amongst one's
kind. This boundary drawing, approximate at the
best, between genetic and political science, can be
neglected at this stage. It will be sufficient for
Politics if, ignoring the negative and satellite
varieties, it direct its attention to the more
positively assertive types and consider only those
who lead in the contest. This has been the method
of Economics, of which the orthodox assumptions
come to have more than speculative interest by
reason of the exploits of the man of enterprise, and
not by reason of the employment of the less initiating
sort. Many of this kind might be content to sweat
as their fathers did along with the fellaheen and
coolies, and to find power and delights in heaven
along with the dervish and the fakir, leaving little
impress on the structure of modern society. We

may agree with Professor Dewey[13] that " the most surprising thing about modern industry is the small number of persons who have any effective interests in the acquisition of wealth." But, although the needs excited by his education may be too small to give him any motives for undertaking the arduous labour of becoming a man of wealth, it may be suggested that the man with the pick and can is quite effectively interested in the economics of the avoidance of an empty stomach.

So, too, in Politics, we may object to being threatened by the fist of our drunken neighbour without therefore desiring to become a cabinet minister. Political enterprise and responsibility on the great scale involves as much toil, opposition, and hatreds as great industrial or financial enterprise, and no more people have the desire to embark upon it. But whether it be or be not true that the small man, in his small way, is as effectively motived by the characteristic economic or political motives as those who more significantly contribute to the building and shaping of our social structure, it is convenient and legitimate to treat human nature, for the purpose of scientific study, when it shows itself under its most pronounced and distinguishable forms. While therefore affirming that the submissive type is but the negative variety of the assertive type, and that with both alike the dominant interest is that of control, it is not necessary to make this hypothesis one *standi aut cadendi*. Rather we

[13] J. Dewey : *Human Nature and Conduct*, p. 144.

must concentrate attention, in our study of the social structure, upon the moving spirits. Basing upon these clear instances our hypothesis of the political man, we shall observe how far deductions from this hypothesis serve to explain the rest of political phenomena, and how much is left over as a residue unaccounted for by the theory. Our present hypothesis as to the political man may be by no means the only tenable hypothesis of the rules of conduct of the consumer of social goods.

There can, however, be little doubt that the tendency to bring the wills of others to subserve our ends (righteous ends perchance) by influence, control, and rule or choice of a ruler, is one which it is merely puerile to dismiss as easily eradicable selfishness and sin. It is a tendency perhaps even more profound than the tendency to safeguard ourselves against limitations by Nature by means of the acquisition of personal property. The animal world knows permanent leadership, but it does not know individual private property apart from immediate consumption. If the Roman lawyers, as distinct from the Church Fathers, usually place private property among the institutions of Nature, and rule among the institutions *jure gentium*, it is because they have in mind rather the rule over slaves than political control.[14] In this respect, Politics stands in an advantageous position as

---

[14] *Digest* : xii. 6, 64 : " Liberty appertains to the law of nature and domination has been introduced by the conventional law." Cf. Sommerlad : *Das Wirtschaftsprogramm der Kirche des Mittelalters*, 1903.

compared with Economics in its endeavour to interpret human action, since political activities probably flow from deeper psychological springs than do economic activities.

Even so, political activities must not be expected to be found pure and uncontaminated by considerations of an ethical, economic or other character. The mere reference, made above, to reverence and devotion shows how a quite different set of ' lusts ' from the ' lust for power ' may intrude themselves into the very heart of politics.

Economic and Political Elements Compared : The Demand for Freedom of Action. Politics has as yet no axioms ; that is its scandal. No principles have as yet been detected underlying the confusion of political activities of such a nature as to throw light upon the entire field of political phenomena. In part this has been due to the absence of any delimitation of the field itself which was not of the most patently superficial nature, and in part it has been due to the unwillingness to hazard an hypothesis, which must be less than a ripe conclusion, for fear that it turn into a dogmatism in our hands. The readiness to make a hypothesis from *prima facie* observation or, as the atomic theory, to suit the convenience of experiment, and the willingness to modify it in accord with further observation, which have been so markedly present in the physical sciences, have been too absent from the social sciences so-called.

To the grave detriment of Politics, its subject matter, as we have earlier pointed out, has often appeared so obvious as to stand in no need of definition.[15] For to say that the subject matter of Politics is the ' State ' is as unsatisfactory as it would be to say that the subject matter of Economics is ' the Business Enterprise.' The study of the welfare and wills of the work-people is germane only to Applied Economics, into which political and ethical considerations must also enter, and the study of Public Finance and of Treasury methods is similarly germane only to Applied Politics.

If, however, the subject matter of Politics is often only perfunctorily or erroneously defined, quite undefined are the political analogues of that motive which leads men in the field of Economics to do things with a view to consumption, or of the motive which makes them hold back in these activities of production. And yet it is, on the surface, not improbable that something similar to what influences men's conduct in the economic field will influence them in the political field. At least, the fundamental concepts which have been found of use in building up a theory of Economics, demand the closest attention if we are to see our way to the construction of a science of Politics. For a science of Politics, let us turn back to Adam Smith.

The economist assumes that every man is moved by the physical need of, and psychological desire for, consumption. If a man cannot satisfy these needs

---

[15] W. T. Marvin : *The New Realism* (1912), p. 56 : " To be able to define a science rigorously and correctly is to pass a most important milestone in the course of human history."

for things, he perishes. And, in order that he may be able to consume, he seeks to acquire. In the political relation, which is that of man with man (not things), nothing would appear to be equally fundamental to the demand for things consumable save the demand for a measure of freedom of action ; freedom, that is, to execute my will unfrustrated by others. And, in order that a man may be able to be free, he seeks to gain the assurance of power.

Equally, the economist makes it his assumption that there is limitation of supply, owing to natural scarcity, the time and energy and skill required to produce a useful article, and the irksomeness of obligatory labour. Were there unlimited supply, the economic processes and system of organization to which they give rise would not come into being. In order to acquire, it is necessary to submit to the labour of production, or someone must be induced to undergo it for us. We eat bread at least by the sweat of somebody's brow. And it is from the clash or tension of the two motives of desire to consume and of reluctance to produce, that, in the field of Economics, the organisation of men and materials with a view to production and exchange results.

Similarly, in the political field, freedom of action must be won from other men by a toilsome process. As, indeed, there are goods ready to our hand, useful in their natural condition, so some men by a native gift for popularity acquire power without struggle. But this is the exception. Just as the primitive man,

who knows no system of trade and barter, must yet
usually labour to satisfy his private requirements, so
those who merely desire a limited range of influence
over their immediate neighbours or a barbaric
personal dominance, such as necessitates no very
intricate scheme of personal relationships, must yet
submit themselves to restraint and self-discipline in
order to attain their end. They must go to the
trouble of learning how to manage their neighbours.
But, where the persistent pressure of men's need for
consumable articles or for assurance of freedom has
called into being an elaborate system of interdependent units, men come to lose the old freedom of
when and where to work in return for a greater
certainty of avoiding starvation or beggary, and
they are likewise compelled to substitute for the
erratic cunning and uncertain discipline of the
barbarian, the regular obedience of a man living in
the security given by civil government. A world
comes into being of organized civil, ecclesiastical and
industrial authorities.

There are exceptions. Some men under certain
conditions may labour, as Prince Kropotkin thought
natural to men, from the joy of employment. The
sense of compulsion may be quite absent. Similarly,
some men may repudiate the notion that obedience
is for them anything of a burden ; they may gladly
obey law and custom. But for the mass of men toil
may usually be regarded as irksome, and it must
always be assumed that it may be regarded as such.
And for the mass of men it must not be assumed

that they sacrifice willingly any freedom of action, in a matter on which they happen in fact to wish to act. Obedience is a yoke ; it is the political equivalent of labour. Civil obedience is equivalent to labour under organized industrial conditions.

The Labour of Social Obligation. We have already taken it as our hypothesis, for interpretative purposes, that the fundamental motive in political action is the impulse to make one's will prevail with, over, or against one's fellows. Behind this impulse is the smart of the frustration, or anticipated frustration, of one's desires, because one's will is overruled by the will of others. The power sought, whatever be its specific character, is the guarantee of freedom of action ; and the search for it is distinctive of political action in general. And, as has just been pointed out, over against this impulse to make one's will prevail, which is generalised as a desire for power in order that one may be assured that one's will at any time will prevail, must be set the reluctance of men to submit to irksome restraints in order that they may thereby gain assurance of being able to execute their wills (' having their own way ') in specific directions.

The whole political process arises from the paradox that, in order to gain assurance of freedom in one direction, we must submit to certain restrictions which curtail our sense of general freedom. Not being almighty, if I am to be wealthy and enjoy the fruits of labour, I must give, in return for this desirable good, another less desirable, my leisure, and labour myself, or I must, by an exchange of wealth, induce someone else to labour. Similarly, if I am to be sure of being able to have my will in certain directions, I must give pledge in return that I will not interfere with the plans of other men. And to these obligations, being restrictions of my complete freedom to do what in fact I will to do, it is contrary to the general desire for power that I should submit, as good in themselves, and without expectation of compensation.

In Politics, this sense of being irked by restraint, even though the restraints be means to one's own ends, is often termed the love of liberty, and is not infrequently coupled with a naïve belief, characteristic of Whig England and of pioneer America, in the sufficiency of one's own individual powers to deal with the emergencies of the social situation. One often observes that the lover of liberty declines the end for fear of having his liberty restricted by the means ; he declines the helm for fear that it may gall his hands. That he who wills the end, e.g. of a purity in local politics, must also will the means, by being prepared to undergo the heat and dust of voting and electioneering himself, is one of the most difficult of lessons for free human nature to learn.

It is hence that men are so often unwilling to undergo the discipline or pay the cost of what they quite ingenuously declare to be their ideals, civil or religious. Idealists do not love trudging through the mud of detail, or remember with Napoleon that ' detail is everything.' The believers in liberty do not love to recognize that, when it comes to a fight, discipline must be the means if their cause is to triumph. They prefer " a perilous liberty to a quiet servitude," and, like the Polish aristocrats who uttered the vaunt, end by losing their independence. Talk of ' natural rights,' and of a return to ' the primitive simplicity of a state of Nature,' is not mere spinning of myths ; it is a protest of the fighting savage in every man against the servitude of civilization, and against entering into the yet more exacting social contract which a new stage in its development involves.

The love of liberty is frequently a convenient name given to the sentiment of those who are slow of adaptation, who object to the new restraints required by a more elaborate and easily disarranged social system, and who refuse, while they have the strength, to recognize the necessities of the new organization. Prosperity or other grounds for personal lack of concern may make the determinant social considerations seem to them quite remote, unreal, and speculative. The troubles of the pauper do not agitate the club member. Willingness to undertake the stern labour of elaborating practicable methods, and the discipline involved in joining means to ends, is a necessary preliminary in training in co-operative civilization. But to submit their necks to such a yoke cannot be expected from men not goaded by some stinging need.

An apparent indifference to ' liberty ' may, indeed, be remarked among peoples of a strongly conservative disposition. But this indifference is only to a

liberty of a kind which they do not want. Theirs is
an active unwillingness to change their habitual
wills ; it is reform and the machinery of freedom
which means for them disturbance, discomfort, and
irritation. ' To be compelled to be free ' is none the
less compulsion. What others might name reform
was, for the Lowlanders suffering under Joseph II,
a yoke, an external imposed thing ; the liberty
conferred by the Revolutionary French was " red
ruin and the breaking up of laws," the destruction
of the *mores*, immorality. There is an indolent satisfaction which, seeming passive, may flare up against
oppressive disturbers as an indignant vindication of
the ancient customs and ' liberties.'

Freedom is, amongst other things, freedom from
responsibility. That man is free who submits to no
burden of responsibility ; the question is not of his
good fortune in being free, but of the improbability
of his remaining so. The conservation and attachment to the ancient customs, which appears most
distantly removed from the love of liberty, is often
but a method for shirking the heavy toil and unavoidable unpleasantness of the endeavour, for
good or ill, to restrain and, if need be, to fight others.
Herd action is for the individual a labour-saving
and releasing device. As all responsibility, so the
obligations of political control, are something of
which normally contented men would feel themselves well-rid. Genuine democracy, for example,
is too irksome to be an elementary form of government, or one from which men do not naturally tend

to relapse. The non-voter is in the same position as the medieval boroughs, such as Torrington, which petitioned the King for a charter exempting them from sending representatives to Parliament. Freedom in political responsibility is not a notion which can be embraced until men have learned by bitter experience the vanity of freedom from political responsibility.

Superficially, could consciousness be still preserved, a world would be preferable in which desire was automatically followed without conflict by fulfilment ;[16] where there were required no struggles with nature or adjustments with men ; where the grimmer strife would be in abeyance and the grimmer virtue have lost its meaning. The nearer men come to relapsing into a vegetative sleep, the more there may be of happiness, but the less there is of political activity. The idealist, on the other hand, who exercises the human privilege of being miserable, is one of the most disturbing elements in politics. With prosperity comes conservatism ; with disappointment and obstacles, recognized but not surmounted, comes radicalism. A Paradise of ends without means, the burlesque heaven of the mediocre, is fortunately not the world of our experience ; but it does not follow that struggle and sacrifice are good abstractly and in themselves. The

---

[16] Cf. Semon's doctrine of the dependence of memory upon " irritability " (*Die Mneme*), and the theories which claim that consciousness arises in the course of the striving of organic matter to overcome the obstacles opposed to life ; also E. L. Thorndike : *Elements of Psychology*, 1905, p. 167.

R

history of human 'going forward' (progress), it
may be conjectured, is that of the supersession of
maladjusted and irrational means, and of the
substitution for them of subtler means and of more
exacting demands. It is not a progress in happiness
but in complexity ; but it is happiness and not
complexity which most men continue to desire.
It is, however, out of these conflicts, in which desire
drives men forward, and the irksomeness of work
and authority, the laboriousness of attaining control
over matter or over man, holds them back—it is out
of this real logic of the circumstances that the
economic and political techniques are born, whereby
men find by an intelligent method a way to surmount
their difficulties. And it is a reflection upon the
methods and forms of these techniques which gives
us the economic and political sciences.

There is, then, a *vis inertiæ*, which can be counted
on as a constant factor in political calculations.
There is an economy of an energy physically and
nervously costly, a distrust of a new-fangled and
unwanted restriction which is felt as a burden, and a
restiveness under restraint, even when this is clearly
perceived to be the means to a desired end. Men
enjoy the task of adjusting their wills to those of others
by the disciplined battle for control, or by apprenticeship in the art of mutual accommodation, as little
as they enjoy the manual or mental toil necessary in
order to preserve for themselves a livelihood.

The conative force, then, in Politics, is the impulse
to make one's will prevail with, over, or against

one's fellows ; the proximate compelling force is the smart of the frustration or anticipated frustration of one's desires because one's will is overruled by the will of others. There is, further, a retarding impulse, which, alike in Economics and in Politics, is the irksomeness of undertaking any labour or of undergoing any restraint compulsorily or against our wills.

Conventions as Social Goods. The conative force in Economics is the striving to have, possess, and consume things ; while the compelling force is the physiological and psychological effect upon the individual of the shortage or want of things, and the fear which this invokes. There is the hope, by power over and through material things or ' goods, to compass happiness so far as material things can give it, and there is the dread of limitation by reason of lack of these material goods. But happiness is dependent not only upon food and clothing, upon the certitude of power over such things, and upon the consequent feeling of security given by wealth, but also upon social intercourse, and upon the power of bringing men into some measure of accord with our will. It would indeed be possible (since both seek ' to get their own way ') to subsume the economic man under the profounder psychological concept of the political man, or, conversely, the political man under the economic, since we have at present more precise knowledge of the factors influencing this latter. But an allocation of provinces can usefully be made which limits our consideration of the political man, save indirectly, to the consumption of social goods, as distinct from tangible, and shows him as a creature fleeing from the miserable situation in which the individual will is overruled by the brute force of other men, in order to possess himself of the riches of order and justice.

The concept, of this flight from bondage to the will of another, is not a difficult one. The individual will may be, as is that of the criminal, hostile to and overcome by a social will which represses it, in which case there results frustration of purpose and the misery of the outcast, the 'kinless man,' the man " without brotherhood, without law, without hearth."[17] Or this will may be in harmony with society by a delicate mutual adjustment. Or it may secure the happiness of finding other wills working at one with its will. In this last instance the individual attains his end through willing service or spontaneous affection, or because the wills of others are subservient and his will is dominant.

The concept of Social Goods is not so simple. The subject matter of Economics is goods, things priced ;[18] the subject matter of Politics is power. Power, again, is either the individual control of one man

[17] *Iliad*, ed. Teubner, ix, 63. Cf. also Vinogradoff, *Historical Jurisprudence*, 1920, I, p. 359. The ' Can you kill me or can I kill you ? ' of Carlyle's famous dictum is an illustration of the fundamental criminal attitude.

[18] H. J. Davenport : *Economics of Enterprise*, p. 25 ; and cf. also Marshall : *Principles of Economics*, 1892, *init.*, Ely : *Introduction to Political Economy*, 1889, pp. 13 ff., and *contra* Professor Fetter's very broad definition (*Principles of Economics*, 1904, *init.*). For an argument that scientific economics means the study of the *economic aspect* of life, *vide* G. Cassel: *Theory of Social Economy*, trans. McCabe, 1923, I, p. 7.

over another, a relation as primitive as that of barter, or that social control produced collectively which is called Convention. This includes all the amenities, traditions, institutions, achievements which human beings have themselves built up in order to live tolerably together, while giving to each an outlet in self-expression and even contributing to enhance each man's sense of power (Spinoza's *virtus*) or independence. These conventions have their direct exchange values as means in holding society together upon the principles of mutual obligation and *do ut des*, apart from the direct æsthetic value which the judgment or whim of the individual may be inclined to set upon them.

In order to satisfy my bodily needs I cannot live as a naked savage, but require for consumption articles of food and dress, for which I am willing to pay a price. In order to satisfy the dictates of my will in the world of men I need facilities from these fellow-men and assurances of their conduct, and, in securing this assistance of submission or co-operation, and this assurance, my own right arm will not aid me far. I shall need authoritative customs or laws imposed on individual caprice, not only by me, in my interest and for my convenience, but by others who share these interests. These facilities, guaranteed by my own strength or, as conventions, collectively guaranteed, are the goods which we utilize and require in our political activities. And it is the impossibility of producing these to any high degree, save by social action, which leads to the perfecting of political organization and enterprises.

To the extent to which these conventions, whether ' customs ' or externalized as ' institutions,' give me the means or freedom to go my own way and to execute my own will for my pleasure, they are political goods, and I desire to consume them in the sense that I desire their maintenance and to benefit from them in a fashion which involves a certain expenditure of public energy. In return I must contribute, by my social activities, and by submitting to burdensome restraints on conduct, to produce or maintain other like conventions such as may be of more immediate utility to others. These conventions *may* do more than prove useful to me. They may give me ethical pleasure, as some vase that I have purchased gives pleasure to my eye. They are nevertheless political goods even if they do not do this, but are merely customs which I have to observe if I am to benefit, as a citizen entitled to rights, by like customs in return.

Politics is, then, concerned with civilization, not in so far as it is a material thing of bricks and stones, of steel and gold, but in so far as it is the externalisation of culture in conventions and institutions. It is, in the same way, concerned with that culture, not in so far as it is the ' character ' of the individual to be æsthetically appreciated, but so far as it is the ' impress ' of social convention, and gives itself collective expression in these conventions as a system of habits whereby men are able to live together and enjoy each other's society. Politics is concerned neither with ideals nor with property, neither with goodness nor with goods, but with conventions, and with the institutions in which these conventions give themselves body. Ethics may decide whether the conventions be righteous ; Politics is solely concerned with the strength of opinions behind the conventions and with their efficiency in producing the smooth running of society. Economic progress may have its technique ; the harnessing of fire and of electricity, the contrivance of hieroglyph and of printing press, the discovery of gunpowder and of anæsthetics—inventions which revolutionize civilization. Politics is not concerned with this machinery of civilization as such and on its technical side, but it is concerned with the new social adjustments of man with man which must result, and with the change of the manners and customs which, by sword or cell, censure or frown, societies are prepared under the new conditions to enforce for their own advantage.

By culture, in the political sense, is meant neither the wealth of spiritual adornment told of in the allegory of the Song of Songs, nor the material ornaments of the oriental tale, but those achievements, acquirements, graces, and behaviours[19] of which the terrestrial Solomon, society, chooses to approve. It is something able to be externalized in

---

[19] Lord Chesterfield : *Letters :* " You have nothing now to think of but the ornaments, and as mankind is made, they are striking and consequently not inconsiderable parts of the whole."

conventions and conventional institutions which
'hold,' and, for the time, alter not, whether their
benefit be or be not appropriated and appreciated
by this or that individual. Certain things may be
and are ' done ' ; to do others is to court failure and
to have one's will baulked. The man who conducts
himself with the maximum of friction to his fellows
is not the man who, however aggressive he may be,
will be able to carry out his will to the fullest extent.
Politics ranges freely from considerations on the
arming of nations to reflections on the apparel of
women, on the conventions which decide or deny
that " thou shalt praise Tyrian garments and
consider Coan ones decent," or with Plato to
reflections on the censorship of liars and lutes, just
in so far as these matters are settled and assessable
by the weight of collective opinion. And it does
this rightly in so far as these may be considered
independently alike of the ideal towards which the
soul strives in solitary flight, and of the traffic and
turn-out of tools and possessions. It does this
rightly in so far as these things concern the smooth
running of society and the mutual satisfaction of its
members, who desire to live as they like without too
much unpleasantness, and in such a fashion as to
enjoy the amenities of social life and to have a good
reputation with their fellows. Politics is concerned
with things immaterial but considered as ethically
neutral. It is not concerned with the goodness of
conventions or legislative measures, any more than
is Economics with the ethics of luxury ; it is only

concerned with the problem of the feasibility of the realization of actual individual wills under the given social conditions. The ' direct consumption ' of the political man is the enjoyment of the social facilities and amenities guaranteed by conventions which constitute for the individual a system of rights.

Wages and Rights. The consumption, then, of political goods may be compared to the consumption of economic goods. And to the wages which a man is paid in return for his production of economic goods, may be compared the political rights which a man has to draw for his own benefit on the reservoir of social security in return for the performance of his obligations as a citizen. The simplest case of the economic relation is that of the potter potting pots to exchange them for food. It is not that the potter finds his heaven in potting mean pots all day, rather than one pot that is a masterpiece of beauty, but that he must have food, he must be free from hunger ; in short, he must ' have.' The simplest case of the political relation is that of one man knocking another down because he neither submits to nor avoids but withstands him. It may not be that the heaven of the strong man is knocking others down ; compelled to accept their company he may prefer to join them and act with them ; but, under all circumstances, he must be free to do what he will ; he must be ' free to do.' The economic man may have his freedom to have—on the condition of labour. But he must perform something, he must labour to produce for his own use or to gain wages for exchange before he can have. The political man may have his freedom to do his will—on the like condition of submission to and aid in supporting (' producing ') social convention, ' doing his duty ' and ' making his contribution as a citizen.' In both cases he is forced to submit to conditions by being caught in the logic of the situation.

The particular individual may be quite uninterested in international peace, the domestic ' reign of law,' education, or courtesy, but indirectly, by diminishing violence, ignorant obstinacy, and morose restlessness and quarrels, if not by direct enjoyment, these social goods enlarge the field of his effective action and satisfaction and free him from restriction. He lives in a freer, co-working society, built up out of organized will-power and established in tradition, constructed by the slow labour of his predecessors in civilized ages, which goods of protection, security, assistance, and guaranteed toleration were largely lacking in a barbarous stage of culture. And what he aids in maintaining, by his own co-operation in upholding certain conventions, he derives an exchange benefit from in other rights, which can be, as it were, cashed at need, as valid and enforceable claims, at the bank of social authority. In return for his support, he becomes a member of a co-operative association, in which each will may, in certain cases, rely upon the support of others. The strength of the collective will is the sanction of law, and the content of this will is the law. The individual becomes a member of a

law-regulated society, and in return for performance
of the obligations of membership he receives the
recompense of rights. These rights, however, no
more than wages, are the same for all or awarded
to the individual according to some abstract theory
of his worth. The amount of the rights of a man, as
individual, or as member of a group, depends upon
the power which that individual group has to force
up the standard of its rights, and, as the Roman
plebs by their secessions, to show its indispensability,
or, as in the case of a dictator, his crucial importance
to society. Rights, as wages, are determined by the
fluctuations of the market, and by how many men
will ' back ' them.

Price and Support : Money and Man-power. The
supreme difficulty of a science of Politics lies not so
much in the establishment of a human constant,
such as Economics had in the ' economic man,'
or in establishing analogues to the desire for consumption and the irksomeness of production, but
in the establishment of a standard and unit of
value. Without measurement Physics, without money
Economics, could not have become sciences ; both
required first a numerical unit. So too Biology
and Psychology, although sciences of life and mind,
and perhaps scarcely susceptible of reduction to
terms of quantity to the degree contemplated, e.g.
by Wundt, owe their advance in no small measure
to the discovery of regular proportions and relations,
and to the use of mathematical methods. It is
impossible to say that a man has succeeded in his
economic enterprises unless we agree upon some

common standard whereby to measure this success, such as the financial. Similarly it will be impossible to say that a man has succeeded in his political enterprises—in. his relationship of control over the wills of others—unless we are prepared to measure his success by some agreed standard such as might measure power.[20]

In Economics, money is the standard of price ; price is the objective symbol of value. Now when, in turning from Economics to Politics, one turns from things to human beings, it is still possible to assign valuations, and valuations which shall be proportionate. Men are not for all purposes ' souls ' of incalculable worth ; for many purposes what counts is what a man is ' good for ' ; in brief, his ' merits ' as a political supporter.[21] As a horse has its merits, so has a man. Mobility of determination, the proud grief, all our groupings and aspirations, our cries *de profundis*, these are indeed what gives enrichment to life ; but their value in the intimacy of very intimate friendship and the reserves which they betoken, is something quite other than their value in intercourse with strangers. Far from our sense of justice

[20] S. and B. Webb : *Constitution for the Socialist Commonwealth of Great Britain* (1920), pp. 195–7. The stress which is here laid upon *measurement* in the forming of judgments upon public affairs is most noteworthy, even if the use made of it is of less general scope than that in the text.

[21] Hobbes : *Leviathan*, § x : " The ' value ' or ' worth ' of a man is, as of all other things, his price ; that is to say, so much as would be given for the use of his power ; and therefore it is not absolute, but a thing dependent on the need and judgment of another. . . . And, as in other things, so in men, not the seller but the buyer determines the price. . . ."

impelling us to expect social recognition of these virtues, true delicacy repels the thought of exposing them to the public view. The political values are something different, and more analogous to the economic. Nor is it ill that men should have to submit themselves to this objective valuation, often hasty and harsh ; for it must be confessed that there are many who, protesting that their wish is ' to be ' and not ' to seem,' contrive to call ' morality ' that which justifies them in their own apparent failure, and turn God's creation and the whole generation in which it is their lot to be born into the defendent arraigned before the bar of their private virtues.

The Classification of Effective Power. It is not difficult, in a primitive condition of first-right, to decide who is the victor and who is the vanquished. Again, it is not difficult, in considering states in their natural and extra-legal relationships, to decide which state is suzerain and imperial and which is vassal and subject, or to arrange in approximate order first, second, and third-class Powers. It would not be misleading here to say that the power to effect the political act of control, subject to certain secondary conditions of leadership, discipline, and military equipment, such as distinguishes a nation using, e.g. cavalry, from one without this force, may be measured in terms of units of equally-trained man-power. In civilized life, however, it is not easy to discover the standard of measurement for the civil relations of individuals which will act as the political equivalent of money.

In looking for these standards of political power, guiding indications are furnished by the study of law, in which the primitive decisions of force are at once tempered and established by an enforcible convention. In the more primitive stages of society the simplest form of civil power, status with privilege, was given explicit recognition, and was even so determinately explicit as to be assessable in the tariff of blood-money. And as the wergild varied according to status, so also did the value of a man's oath in a court of law. " It was whilom, in the laws of the English, that people and law went by ranks,"[22] and these castes could indirectly be placed in a gradation, each individual standing to the others in a numerical relationship of value, which determined his ability to secure control over others. In the last resort this status rested upon an estimate of relative strength. To-day similar assessments must be made in a less ingenuous fashion.

Crimes still stand in numerical proportions. For one crime society is of the opinion, as expressed through the customary penalty imposed by the Bench or (as to maximum) determined by statute, that a man should spend so many days in the purgatory of prison ; for another crime so many months, for another so many years. We are thus able to gain, if the facts are used with intelligence, some objective judgment of the relative importance which society attaches to crimes and some judgment of the degree of their disreputability, whether

[22] Stubbs : *Charters*, 1913 edit., p. 88.

to-day or in the days when Tacitus found that the
three capital offences of the Germans were treason,
cowardice, and sexual immorality.[23] Again, degrees
of reputability are capable of, at least indirect,
objective assessment. It is not difficult to compare
in different generations the number of honours
conferred upon bankers and newspaper proprietors
with the number conferred on landowners ; or to
compare the number of squires elected to Parliament
with the number of hand-workers ; or to calculate
the proportion of lawyers to men without university
education sent to Congress.

In contemporary England, the right to vote is an
indication of social value. The criminal classes have
no vote, the ordinary citizen has one, the propertied
and educated classes often have two. These votes
indirectly affect legislation and the fashion in which
men shall be governed and controlled. The vote of
the peer directly affects it, his vote counting one in
the Upper House to about 70,000 counting one in
the Lower Chamber.

Wage is also one (although it is not the only)
indication of relative social value and of power to
effect one's ends in society. In a slave-owning
civilization, it is not difficult to assess the value of
a slave through the common market ; and yet this
valuation, for example, in the case of a Syrian slave-
pedagogue in the Roman market, was by no means

[23] V. Ihering : *Recht als Zweck*, trans. by I. Husik, *Modern
Legal Philosophy Series*, p. 367 : " The list of penalties gives the
standard of values for social goods. What price is for business,
that punishment is for criminal law."

based on mere working capacity and productive efficiency, as of some subtle machine, but on his whole ability and acceptability as a man. Similarly, in the more important positions in the modern world of affairs, a man is not remunerated at a ' just wage ' in proportion to his time-work or even to his piece-work, but in accordance with what he can command against his fellows in a competitive labour market. The estimate made of him is not a truly economic one in terms of productivity, but in terms of his power to control those who need his services. An inanimate article, other than perishables and a few things such as wines, does not, by internal changes, alter its own value. It may be rare, but the fluctuations of its value depend for the individual article upon the market established by sellers and purchasers. So also a ' hand ' in some low-grade manual work is much as any other ' hand,' and, even if he accrete value by experience and lose it by age, his wage is decided apart at least from his individual action. This may be true even of a high-grade workman who has rarity value, in so far as he acts only as a workman and not as a politician. But, in so far as men act (individually or collectively) politically, their remuneration will be a measure of their power, and only in part be measured to them from the market value of their productions ; the producer, not the product, will be the dominant factor in the market. When the reward of ability is considered, economic terms become patently inadequate, because rivals are interested in other than pecuniary compensations. In some cases it may be of actual advantage to be without great pecuniary power.[24] Nevertheless the money-price or money-power of a man is a genuine, if incomplete, indication óf his social power in the estimate of his fellows, and of his potential control as a rival over their fortunes and wills. As such it cannot be neglected in a catalogue of objective means of social assessment.

But wealth and salary and wage as signs of relative social utility, are only indirect indications of probable political strength. They are not intrinsic to the political act of controlling the will of another, and can furnish no measure of the ability to effect it. Grades, again, of status and titles of honour, or degrees of dishonour consequent upon crime, although they may furnish useful hints in the objective measurement of social acceptability, and prove interesting as revealing changes in the customary measures used from age to age, are too artificial and limited to satisfy our demand for a standard whereby to measure quantities of political power.

Once again this standard of measurement, whereby we may estimate the probability of any party to a political relationship being able to secure control, is perhaps to be discovered in man-power, and the sought unit of measurement, comparable to the dollar or pound sterling, may perhaps be found in units of man-power of a given grade of political

---

[24] It is stated to be of advantage to a candidate for the Presidency of the U.S.A. to be the son of parents of no great wealth.

S

competence. In a military age, as in the age of barter, the relationship is chiefly a two-party one only, and the unit of measurement is crude and uncertain ; one chieftain has behind him so many ' blades ' and another has so many. In modern society, however, the relationship of will and will is not customarily a straight relationship of physical force. Law cannot to-day with sobriety be described as made by military conquerors for the advantage and facilities of the victor. Heads are not now customarily cracked but counted. In order to procure a change in law, which change is for me a political good as increasing my social freedom and power, I have to make a calculation of how much support I can count upon. The calculation becomes a calculation of votes, and the unit of measurement in assessing the possibility of effecting the political act of control, and of the adaptation of the conduct of others in accord with my own plan, is the vote.

Where a contest is involved which will show the strength of the two protagonists, the question becomes one of the number of supporters (or, more vaguely, the ' backing ') which each, whether in electorate, legislature, company meeting or family council, can be skilful enough to muster. The majority is no more certain, by mere numbers, to win, than is the lowest tender to receive the contract. As in the latter case, so in the former, a myriad of considerations may enter in to render one man's money less valuable than another's. But the number of votes, in so far as they represent numbers of individuals, indicate the direction in which, *in discrimine*, the decision would go. The matter is, indeed, not so simple as a mere question of counting the heads ; the ' backing ' also depends upon how many further heads each person present at the count may be relied upon to have behind him. It is not merely a question of cash against cash, but also of credit against credit. It is, moreover, the *validor pars*, according to Marsiglio's valuable distinction, which ultimately decides, not the majority ; but at least this ' stronger part,' to be such, must be sure of its control of a large minority or of the acquiescence of the majority. The voting strength is, then, a satisfactory measurement of the power of protagonists in a political relation, provided that the coin is of equal purity, that is, that the electorate is actively interested and of approximately equal intelligence, intensity or persistence of conviction, and military strength.

In ordinary political acts, such as a decision on the rules of a golf-club or balloting on the admission of a member to a West End club under majority-enacted rules deciding the form of election, it is absurd and irrelevant to introduce qualifying clauses about military strength. Whether Mr Jones or even a Latin Dictator shall be admitted to my social circle is not a question to be decided by Mr Jones' or the Dictator's ' military might.' Equally, it is not a question to be decided by Mr Jones' ' voting strength,' whatever that might under the circumstances mean. But here either the relationship is not genuinely political, but one of affection—I do not think of Mr Jones' will as standing over against mine —or else some kind of calculation is probably made of whether Mr Jones is ' popular,' or of how many people Mr Jones' presence will offend, and of whether the few people he will offend stand for many others—which is a rudimentary voting calculation. For it will, again, be observed that all men are not ' equal.' Some men represent groups and count as such.[25]

Voting is not some rare and solemn function, but one taking place every day and every hour. This consideration cannot be over-emphasized. It is a social action to which the student of Politics will give peculiar attention, since the data of voting do not provide merely ordinary information, descriptive of social structure and behaviour, as do most other social data. Support, measurable as votes, is the condition of the performance of the supreme political act (in the most humble as well as the most exalted affairs) of ' getting things done ' by establishing a controlling relationship. We pay for the political goods of having custom and law on our side and meeting our demands, by always having behind us adequate support in voices which will favour our demands and uphold our claims and rights. And this wealth of support we earn by toiling to maintain, and submitting to the restrictions of, those

[25] Cf. the remarks of Professor W. Y. Elliott in the *Round Table* on Politics and Psychology, Third National Conference on the Science of Politics, 1925, reported in the *Amer. Pol. Sci. Review*, ii., 1926, p. 127. Also *vide ibid.*, p. 137.

conventions which are the political goods pleasing to those upon whose support we desire to count.

It would be fantastic to imagine that we could state the voting units of every expression of will—whether social in the shape of convention or an individual act of dominance—as we would state the price of every article in a modern market. We have not yet reached the stage where we are able to state the precise support backing our social regulations or the influence of dominant individuals. And the study of voting is not the method most applicable to primitive relationships of force, which can better be estimated by means of armament statistics and military estimates.

But the study of the vote, where ascertainable, is very near to the heart of the political relationship. It is the study of the fluctuations in the investment of power in the stocks of the political market. Sometimes it may come to be the study of the reluctance of investors to lend support at all, e.g. to party-governmental ventures with their offer of political goods of a party-governmental brand.[26] It may be developed as a study of the relationship in the fluctuations of the investment of power to the periodic and local changes in social and economic background ; or as the study of the amount of support commanded by certain policies, laws, customs, and like goods promising social order ;

[26] C. E. Merriam and H. F. Gosnell : *Non-Voting (University of Chicago Studies in Social Science)*, 1924. *Vide* the recent important pioneer work of Professor F. H. Allport : 'The Measurement and Motivation of Atypical Opinion in a Certain Group,' *Amer. Pol. Sci. Rev.* xi, 1925 ; and of Professor S. H. Rice : 'Some Applications of Statistical Method to Political Research,' *Amer. Pol. Sci. Rev.* v, 1926.

or as the study of the extent of the part in commanding support played by certain methods of organization or by personal factors. It thus might become a valuable study of political power treated quantitatively, and assessed according to the influence upon its distribution of environmental need, purposive interest, and response to leadership. The vote, in whatever field of human activities it may be exercised, is the money of Politics ; it provides the best unit of political calculations of what is and of what is not feasible. The study of its fluctuations, in whatever place or occasion that a vote is taken, is a study of the distribution of power and of the kind of policy to which men are at the moment prepared to submit, and the kind of control which they are willing to support.

Markets of Things, Measures, and Men. What men seek in their political negotiations is power, whether as a ' right,' which is assured by co-operative labour and a general social convention, or as ' control ' by the acquisition of a personal superiority over their neighbours by direct dominance, or as the ' influence ' which comes with great support, or as the ' prestige ' which declares it. Hence the political arena becomes a market for power in which men seek to acquire prestige by social consensus, or to gain to themselves those who have influence and represent others, as well as a theatre for an exhibition of that individual ability by which men are able to dominate over others or to win them over to their will.

In the political market men separate out according to the degree to which they ' stand for ' what is acceptable to, and supported by, their society, or else fail to ' distinguish ' themselves, and are judged, not as individuals, but ' in the lump,' like army units. It is not the case that this deliberate measurement of each against each, according to his power to control others or to accomplish his will, is some strange rarity. Whenever two men meet, in friendly or unfriendly manner, two personalities square up, look each other down, and size each other up. It should, perhaps, be added that it is the falsely, rather than the truly, humble who will shun this ' summing up ' of what a man is good for, and by a gesture of modesty indicate with how large men they might compare themselves, if they would but accept the judgment of the world. Expressed humility is the prerogative of the great and is an impudence in little men. The wise man is he who is prepared to wait until the quotation of his value— that is, of the measure of support which he will receive—is ultimately stabilized in a larger market. Or he may be careless of reputation, and will merely be concerned with the final appraisal which the world puts upon what he has stood for. If so, he will be in no hurry, but reflect that ' *der Weltgeist hat Zeit genug.*'

A cynic might see in this market a pawn-shop of souls, where men redeem their independence of public opinion when they have secured beyond challenge a reputation and support, and thereby power and permission to do as they will. Or he might see an Ibsenesque world where most folk, those of the submissive type, roll through life like a collection of indistinguishable leaden buttons, serving even when in use only to hitch up their neighbours' clothes, until they roll back into the melting-pot of the button-moulder. Both views, as views of life ' steady and whole,' would be inadequate and distorted. But as parables of practical political life and, still more, as parables of the kind of conduct presumed in human inter-relations by certain political theories currently accepted, they merit the most patient consideration.

There are many markets of prestige, that is, of power, great and small. A man who is a ' good fellow ' or a ' man of weight ' in his own tavern or village, his manner oracular, his words law, his following large, may be a mere boor of no account in the great market of metropolitan or international society, where the type of dandy and ' clever fellow ' at whom the ale-house would have jeered is able to find supporters for himself, and to become a sought and valued addition to social groups, just as exotic fruits, which find no favour with rustics, fetch high prices in the city. The man who seeks the loud praise of his provincial circle will, likely enough, find that this praise re-echoes faint and damning in a sale-room where not common service-able china, but novelties, rarities, and things of finest paste or of strange and beautiful design are exposed for inspection, and capture the public taste.

Middling men, again—their work being of such a nature that in all the opportunities which they have to show ' what is in them,' the merits of each is to the casual eye indistinguishable from the merits of the other—are first auctioned in a wider market, as men likely to prove acceptable, carry weight and ' accomplish things,' thanks to the influence of friends who are prepared to stake their credit on some potential talents of leadership or gift of tact which they fancy that they detect. Such auctioneering satisfies the collector's pride in his ability to discern and promote merit, and also raises his own reputation and influence, while he who accepts the recommendation procures something which has in it the genuine qualities which he requires, whether economic and of business ability, or political and social tact. A clever politician can detect, even in the most unlikely quarter, a future Premier or a man of ' Presidential timbre '—a man of such an æsthetic quality—of such an appeal to the popular taste—as is likely to command a high measure of support. Mere sentimental recommendations, being felt as dishonest, destroy the ability of the smaller market to pass on goods to the larger. An even rate of exchange is, however, no more established between all political than between all economic markets.

Although ' good society ' may seek (the valued here being the valuers, as it were the big ewers of precious metal and fine porcelain valuing the commoner water-pots) to give or to refuse its cachet

to those of whom it approves or disapproves,[27] yet
there are diverse kinds of markets, with diverse
kinds of goods, within *le beau monde* itself. Just as
the public will often pay high prices for deleterious
luxuries or meretricious extravagances, so, by a
like aberration or perversion of judgment, the
vicious or vulgar may be remarkably well received
and, having on a gold ring and goodly apparel, be
given for their wealth and gay clothing a front seat
among the mighty. In brief, they will be influential,
whether from birth, wealth, publicity, or other
causes. Or the proper preference for a decent
demeanour may be such that the turn of a man's
nose or the closeness of his eyes, the angle of his
chin or the manner of his gait, may very reasonably
be his ruin. He will lack co-operation in his plans,
because his characteristics are not such as render
him agreeable and winsome to his neighbours.

[27] Beatrice Webb : *My Apprenticeship*, 1926, pp. 51–2 : " There
seemed in fact to be a sort of invisible stock exchange in constant
communication with the leading hostesses in London and in the
country ; the stock being social reputations and the reasons for
appreciation or depreciation being worldly success or failure however obtained. Some stocks were gilt-edged, royal personages or
persons who were at once outstandingly wealthy and genuinely
aristocratic, their value could neither be ' bulled ' nor ' beared ' by
current rumours ; but the social value of the ruck of individuals
who trooped to the political receptions or foregathered in the houses
of the less well-known hostesses, went up and down as rapidly and
unexpectedly as do the shares of the less well-known and more
hazardous ' industrials ' in the money market." Mrs. Webb's remarks are not devoid of truth because their asperity is edged by a
certain animus. Noteworthy also is her remark (p. 49) that the test
of fitness of membership of the governing class was (and is this
merely the phenomenon of an age, from which we may hope soon to
emerge ?) " the possession of some sort of power over other people."

Market Values. If we turn to observe the workings of the market, we shall observe that men are politically esteemed (apart from the æsthetic estimate of'their friends and intimates) according as they are felt, as individuals or a class, to be in fact useful at the moment to the community or to a portion of it ; that is, to the degree to which they are judged to ' have something in them ' for which there is a function or place, in so far as they are felt to ' stand for something ' which renders their aid desirable as facilitating the will of society, or to ' be somebody ' by the accident of position. Men are esteemed in terms of possible co-operation. The esteem for the retired general or for the squire represents the acknowledgment of the reputed past services of the man or of his class to the community ; or of their actual present services of a subtler kind to civilization and good society, in keeping up that exacting standard of taste in the art of life by which man is distinguished from an honest animal ; or of their potential services as men of ability and culture. So, too, much is tolerated from a baron or man of wealth or parish rector in a society which is not in fact prepared entirely to dispense with feudalism or capitalism or ecclesiastical establishment. Thus each age has to rule it the idols of its own making, men who can be sure of commanding its support.

The great tradition-makers are great because, at whatever cost of bloodshed, yet to them—a Henry V or a Napoleon—their countries owe their heightened sense of self-respect. They gave means of expression for the confused and repressed wills of the men of their age ; in a sense they were liberators, power-givers. Even such barbarians as an Attila, or such princely criminals as a Cesare Borgia, awaken our respect because a certain honour is due to any ruler who calls forth a free submission from so many, and is found by them a leader of men, inspiring them with a vigour whereby they, also, become personalities.[28] In each of these cases the hero or leader is actually of value to his society, and the recognition of this value is, necessarily, neither given nor taken away by mere conventional phraseology, but is indicated by the use of influence and power which is in fact permitted to him. He is acceptable to his age and time. His fellows want him. So too within narrow limits and for certain purposes, the elected representative of the people is peculiarly the acceptable man to his electorate. What may cause scandal or amusement to the delicacy of his opponents may be but a sign of bonhomie, and very proof to his adherents that he is no dreamer. The cinematograph-film producer and the journalist wield power in the same manner ; whatever a critical few may think of the more popular kind of these, to the many they are in fact acceptable and, in a democratically-minded community, powerful. Any class, on the other hand, which has the insignia of honour, but has decreasing, not increasing, effective power to sway the actions of men as it would will, may be known to belong to another age, and to be out of place in the social

[28] Cf. Plato : *Hippias Major.*

situation of the present. The streams are silted
up which nourished it from the sources of
power.

Political valuation is not synonymous with, it
is not even always convertible into, a financial
valuation in the same ratio. In many countries
the earl or lord of ancient lineage and broad
tradition but of constricted revenue, has a position
above that of the millionaire, is more acceptable,
and would be admitted into circles of influence
from which the other might be excluded. And what
is true among the few in such exalted ranks is
parallel in the rivalries of baker and candle-stick
maker. It will be observed that this high estimation and consequent influence which the ' great man '
and the ' man of position,' the ' somebody ' are
accorded, and the small man and the wealthy
' nobody ' are refused, bring in their train not only
social amenities but also political power. Money is
often worth while sacrificing in a measure for
prestige, and if the economist object that this
implies that prestige has its money equivalent, the
politicist may retort that money has its prestige
equivalent. If the former is more indispensable,
the latter is more desirable ; if without wealth
power has no durability, without power wealth has
no security. The political valuation, then, announces
an estimate of power (whereby I may carry out
what I happen to want to carry out, from the
promotion of a nephew to the overturning of a
kingdom) and, like any other credit, contributes to

the unembarrassed use of opportunities ; conversely, the possession of power is a sign of political valuation by one's fellows. These holders of power are men in fact influential by reason of a certain merit which is to the taste of their age.

There may be extravagant assessments, but from this market which men (putting up their own auction-hall) have established, wherein to prefer one man to another, there is no escape. Neither is it entirely desirable that there should be, in so far as a man's use to his neighbour, ' what he is good for,' is here assessed. The price of a man is the power which he demands, and which his society is willing to accord him by the quantity of its support. It is irrelevant whether a Coolidge or a Wilson, a Lloyd George or a Cecil of Chelwood, is the ' greater man in himself.' The political market is, indeed, less fluid than is now the economic ; the standard of exchange is less precise ; it is not so easy to assess the power of a man as to decide the trade qualities of a cloth. But in the higgling of the market all that we have to work upon as the political equivalent of Price is Command of Support. The equivalent of barter or money is military strength, conventional status, or the control of votes. Like the subjective term in Economics called ' value,' there is in Politics a subjective ' worth ' which we need to have priced in terms of public support. He who, having many things, desires more, inquires the price ; he who, being in authority over many, desires additional supporters, asks as to the advantages, status, or power, which those who are willing to serve demand. A thing, if it is to fetch more, must be improved in quality or find a better market for the estimation of its value ; a man, would he have promotion in 'esteem and power, must improve in the merits of effective co-operation required by his group, or must adventure elsewhere for support and the appreciation by another group of his alleged desert. The metal money of trade is coin, which seems visibly comparable to him who knows nothing of the differences of currency and the shiftings of valuta ; the political commerce has few stamped and entitled coins, and the study of its money markets requires more imagination.

The Value and Limits of the Economic Analogy. It may be urged that comparison between economic articles and human beings, although an entertaining diversion, can scarcely be suggested as offering a serious basis for a science of Politics ; and anyhow can lead to nothing so precise as to render possible prediction of the course of practical affairs. It is not proposed to deny this. Prediction, as has been said before, must be of form, not of content ; not, for example, of the history of this particular revolution but of how revolutions arise, and that, the political constellations remaining as heretofore, a revolution is due to arrive. This prediction, moreover, is no such wonderful matter as Le Verrier's assertion of the existence of a planet as yet unobserved. The forecasting of wars and risings has been the task of political intelligence officers, of army staffs and of party managers, for long years.

What would be new would be, not the fact of prediction but, by an increased knowledge of the structure and laws of the political firmament, to introduce greater rationality and confidence into these predictions.

As to how far the economic comparison will prove of serious service to us in this task, will depend upon the intelligence with which it is used. It is clear that the problems of Economics and of Politics are not the same, nor is there any reason to suppose, with certain theorists who conceive of no other social relationship than those of baronial domination or of the production for exchange of the inoffensive and industrious craftsman, that political activity is merely a pathological variant of economic activity[29] or a pastime for the moneyed classes. Both kinds of activity are permanent in nature, and both kinds of activity are essentially distinct in characteristics, if never isolable in a pure condition.

It is much, however, to have seen the broad similarity between the problems which faced the early economists and the methods by which they were met by Adam Smith and his successors, and the problems which confront the politicist and the methods which he may adopt. The situation arising out of the relation of supply of labour for production and of demand for consumption, the problems of exchange, of wage, of price, of markets, present political parallels too striking to be ignored.

Again, both of these sciences have been alike

[29] F. Oppenheimer : *The State*, 1908, trans. Gotterman, p. 276.

confronted with the initial problem of how to detach
from a general history of human action, or a general
philosophy of life, certain phases and aspects of
human activity for separate and abstract consideration by hypothetical methods, so as to make a
science of the study.

It may be true that the economists of the last
century carried abstraction too far, and that those of
the immediate future, while the present swing of
the pendulum away from logic to history lasts, will
attend rather to an institutional and genetic treatment. But Politics, if it is to raise itself above the
descriptive level, the level which Biology had
reached before Bichat, can afford a generous measure
of abstraction.

Whenever a science of human action is mentioned,
it is inevitable that well-intentioned persons, biassed
by that dualism which, since the Stoics, has inspired
most of our study of the non-human world, should
remark that human action can never be treated
according to the mechanical methods of the natural
sciences. Even were the dictum justified,—which a
more profound consideration of what we mean by
' nature ' and of how far mechanics is representative
of the scientific treatment of phenomena, might lead
us to doubt,—it is irrelevant. The joys and sorrows
of human life can patently never be measured up
by rule, nor the values and purposes of human
activity regulated by law. Nor is it proposed to
attempt to do so. Both Economics and Politics
defend their position as social sciences in that they

T

only lay down the rules according to which, under certain conditions, this or that framework of social activity must obtain. Within this framework, an incalculable variety and riot of values, paupers happy in their condition, powerful men who prefer willing co-operation to ready submission, will doubtless exist. The mystical philosophy of the social organism may be entirely sound and helpful, but in another place. It is entirely out of place here where Economics and Politics alike are concerned, not with ethics and values, but with methods and necessary processes.

It may well be that the consideration of social purpose, of what ought to be, of political utopias, is a more ennobling task than a groping inquiry, a series of experimental analyses of the way in which men actually conduct themselves. We may have none of Plato's confidence in the close connection between good ideals and true understanding of method, and regard only with contempt his predilection for the expert state and his anti-individualist belief, unflattering to our personal esteem, in the significance of the administrative process. It is no part of our purpose here to judge or to estimate the exaggerated humanism which periodically comes into vogue, and which certain German writers have assigned as an attribute of what they choose to call ' Faustian civilization.' It need only here be remarked that neither economist nor politicist is concerned with selecting ideals of the economic or political condition, in order to exhort others to adopt them. They are not, and must not become, moral philosophers. They are plain observers of facts and students of method.

There are, then, conspicuous resemblances both in their task and approach, and in the broad line of their subject matter, between Economics and Politics. If the clues furnished by the development of economic science are adopted in bringing into being a political science, the immediate result may be anticipated that the treatment of Politics (in an age fonder of anecdotes than of theories untranslatable into a simple literary phraseology) will not only be more abstract than it has hitherto been in the hands of Hegel and Bluntschli, but more abstract than Economics in its present mature and self-reflective condition need be.

If we were to choose to explore how far political phenomena might be interpreted on the hypothesis that every man in a political relationship, whether he be saint or knave, self-seeker or patriot, desires the free execution of his own will (a desire which is more misleadingly than helpfully described as ' the will-to-power '), certain clear advantages to political theory might be expected. Various dogmata about states and sovereignty, which masquerade as self-evident axioms, but which in truth rest upon the assumption that men will not forgo power, would for the first time since Hobbes be submitted to a fundamental investigation. Their logical context would be shown, and the reader would then be in a position to judge whether he could or could not accept these consequences as tolerable, and would be led to inquire whether he did or did not accept these premises and dogmata as sound. Hitherto the good citizen has been expected in some part to base his philosophy of political practice on the assumption that men are to each other gentle as doves, and in some part on the assumption that man is to man naturally and irremediably a wolf. Such consistency would give clarity to our political thinking, even if the consistency took the shape of issuing in a *reductio ad absurdum*. A political hypothesis, moreover, if well chosen, need not be anticipated to end by reducing itself to absurdity. It need not, moreover, issue in consequences of a merely palatable kind. The soundest hypothesis will probably be the most economical in its demands upon human goodness, consistent with the avoidance of deductions which caricature human life. Such a parsimonious assumption, if made the foundation of our political thinking, would probably save much of that obstinate blindness, mutual recrimination, and disillusion which results from the· persistent confusion of private standards of conduct with conclusions from men's observed tendencies in behaviour under given conditions.

The object, then, of a consistent political science should be more than to expose the fragmentary character and uncertain assumptions of much current political theory. Its task is more than critical. It must also be constructive, in the purely scientific sense in which any detection of plan and method in the midst of the formless stuff of detail is constructive. But this construction, to be sound, must be approached from an observation, in their 'natural' and unglossed condition, of the facts with the detachment of a student who examines a process, without any prejudices as to its value, rather than from the subjective point of view of a political philosophy, concerned to show the inferiority in ideals of all theories or policy not in harmony with itself. In the case of an ethical philosophy, it is a weakness if it does not expose the baseness of base conduct, while especially concerning itself with indicating the good. In the case of a political science, it is a weakness if its theories do not serve to explain, with as little embarrassment, not only men's nobler, but also their baser conduct, and if it does not pay attention to the characteristics of men's conduct in proportion to their permanence, and not in proportion to their edifying qualities.

Whatever hypothesis, then, we may choose, we must not choose it in order to thrust the facts into the confines of our system, or follow our choice by a selection, as did Spencer, of appropriate facts. We must not even choose it by reason of our interest in its critical value, as forcing the present facts and traditional theory into sharp contrast by compelling consistency. Much of the theory of absolute national sovereignty results, we may suspect, from ill-digested reflections on the supposed fact of the fundamental self-assertiveness of men. But the selection of this supposed fact of psychology, as a hypothesis, has scientific value to the extent to which an impartial consideration of the historical facts seems to demand the testing out of this hypothesis as a partially adequate explanation of the character of those facts. And the kind of hypothesis which is sound must be discovered by its ability to reduce to a comprehensible order deeds and thoughts, policies, *mores*, and opinions, which facts it is our business to survey, without attempting an ethical valuation, merely as facts and as the phenomena of human behaviour.

" It is utterly impossible," said Lord Macaulay in one of his more pontifical moods, " to deduce the science of government from the principles of human nature." This is undoubtedly true in the sense that no man can reduce human nature to a catalogue of simple principles, any more than to a box of compounded instincts. But a science of Politics, and a more business-like treatment of the art of government, may perhaps be expected from the assumption of principles in explanation of phases of activity, which principles human experience is not in general found to contradict.

The treatment of political phenomena by means of the working hypothesis of the political man may give us a new and deeper insight into the political structure of conventions and institutions than we have yet had. That will be worth while. Such a treatment will achieve this end if it reveal causes and connections bringing hitherto disjointed facts into plan, and exhibit the existence of a process which subsequent observations confirm and which we can therefore tentatively affirm. To do this is the work of science. If it can be done, we have a political science.

It must, however, be added that the work still largely awaits the doing, and is not likely to be done until men appreciate the importance of an examination of social facts, methods, and inherent possibilities[30] as distinct from discussion about the principles, purposes, and ideal situations which might be desirable. It is never, indeed, beneficial or even possible to separate the practical consideration of the social ' how ? ' from the consideration of the social ' why ? ' and ' whither ? ' But to distinguish in theory questions of value and of what is desirable, from questions of method and of what is practicable, is important if the significance of a science of Politics is to be apparent. To this question we turn, in order to make it clear that the science of Politics is, on the one hand, no matter of philosophical opinion or moral conviction, or, on the other hand, an empty social algebra, but is an essential study preliminary to the accomplishment of all feasible social designs because it is a study of fundamental human method in the political field.

[30] H. J. Laski : *Grammar of Politics*, ed. 1925, p. 109 : " The fact surely is that we have so little attempted the conscious control of social organization that we have hardly sought to inquire into the principles it involves. If we start from the assumption that we must either, over a period, satisfy the basic impulses of men, or court disaster, it becomes obvious that we must organize the processes of production with the purpose of satisfying those basic impulses. To that end we must end the anarchy of the modern scheme." To end anarchy, moreover, involves at least as much an intelligent appreciation of the possibility of the material, as it involves the possession of a good will.

PART III

POLITICS AND ETHICS

POLITICS AND ETHICS

Scientific Method and Democratic Theory. " When I applied my mind to Politics," says Spinoza, " so that I might examine what belonged to politics with the same precision that we use in mathematics, I have taken my best pains not to laugh at the actions of mankind, not to groan over them, not to be angry with them, but to understand them."[1]

What matters is to understand. All else, before we have understood, smacks of the cheap and charlatan. Spinoza's hope that Politics and Ethics could be reduced to the irrefutable exactitude of a demonstration, the ambition of Hobbes to prove all with mathematical accuracy, of Hume to draw conclusions of detailed certainty, of Locke to reduce all principles to such concise simplicity as to be compassable within one sheet of paper, all these expectations must be abandoned.[2]

But it is necessary not to fall into the opposite error of mere ' common sense ' empiricism or *a priori* moralizing. Politics is a science *in posse*, and

[1] B. Spinoza : *Tractatus Politicus, Opera (ed.* Vloten et Land), II, p. 4.

[2] T. Hobbes : Eng. Works (*ed.* Molesworth), II, xxii ; D. Hume : *Essays* (1892), I, p. 99 : " So great is the force of laws and of particular forms of government, and so little dependence have they upon the humours and tempers of men, that consequences almost as general and certain may sometimes be deduced from them, as any which the mathematical sciences can afford us."

Spinoza's impatient desire for the impartial and impersonal study of the scientist, in lieu of the fulminations of pulpit orators and the dark commonplaces of market orators, many have shared. To men who seek scientifically to understand, who laboriously accumulate evidence of the facts, who with deliberation point out some cause of disorder or who anxiously wait to observe the reactions to, as it were, some imperfect but hopeful social Wasserman test, nothing is more vexatious than the action of those who, feeling strongly about all things, impertinently rush in to deliver a ready-made judgment, cut to fit all cases. Facts are brushed aside with the witticism that statistics are the superlative degree of lying, with the complacent remark that we cannot change nature, which is ' a holy thing,' or with the shrewder but facile observation, with which Mr H. G. Wells seems to come too near to concurring, that " nature is a rum 'un."[3]

Admitting that human nature contains many primitive forces, of which the precise action is not to be listed for docketing in official pigeon-holes or filing in professorial card-indices, these forces will be controlled, so far as they may be controlled, by cool observation, and not by moral denunciation and panic repression. And social ills will be healed not by sympathy only, but also by knowledge of the appropriate treatment and medicine, administered after deliberate diagnosis.

" The search for truth is intolerable to the many,

[3] H. G. Wells : *New Machiavelli*, 1913, p. 217.

and they turn aside by preference to things near at hand." The hauteur of the aristocratic Thucydides is not entirely justified. The search for truth may be equally intolerable to the educated. As Thomas Hobbes wisely remarked, the very axioms of Euclid would become subjects for dispute, did they but arouse enough men's passions. And the desire to receive and stand by a comprehensible doctrine, as men stood by the medical theories of Galen or the physical theories of Aristotle after they had been shown by the experimental method to be false, is natural to those who have been brought up to appreciate this doctrine and to know its advantages, when the alternative is to embark on a sea of experiment, with the compass of morality thrown overboard.

It is at the moment a fashionable philosophy that ideas themselves are labour-saving devices which give definiteness, even at the cost of truth, to an experience too fluid and inchoate to be of profit as a guide to the practical conduct of men. Certainly the realm of morals is full of such stereotypes of thought, which nothing but the keenest experience is capable of breaking up and is insistent enough to reform. The privilege of inspiration from the infallible Delphi of local convention is too valuable lightly to be foregone. A man knows, it is maintained, beforehand (or good men can know), what *ought* to be done. The plainest man, according to Puritan theory, has a conscience, which will instruct him on what is right in all that matters. The common man of the people, according to democratic theory, in any political problem of general concern, knows what ought to be done in the common interest. The plain citizen can dispense with any expert knowledge of detail. Both he and his representative have a practical judgment, and a moral sense.

Politics, hence, became, until recently, a branch of rhetoric, and social problems too difficult to be reduced to any formula were approached in the fashion of a revivalist meeting. If this has, in part, ceased to be the case, the reaction is due rather to the appreciation of the need for importing into the public business some measure of the efficiency demanded in the administration of private affairs, than to the fact that this efficiency has been attained in effect. At the present stage of civilization and in the present correspondingly complex condition of politics, it is inevitable that the judgment of the plain man should be incompetent in matters well outside the purview of his experience and the compass of his imagination. If the extent of his education has increased tenfold beyond that of his grandfathers, the complexity of his problems has increased a hundredfold.

Questions of foreign policy (of the less sensational kind and with no scapegoat or personality to add interest to the case) are regarded with apathy, and the degree of public attention tends to be in inverse proportion to the scale of the interests at stake, and to the measure in which they transcend the concern of the moment. India may contain a seventh of the human race, but, as a late Secretary of State used to complain, the British public is not interested in India. In similar fashion, votes of public credit will be accorded involving millions of pounds, but there will be demur and agitation over a vote for the more comprehensible figure of a few hundred thousand. The fate of a battleship will arouse public interest, but foreign control of something more intimately but less traditionally connected with public safety, such as a Canadian power station, passes without remark. The newspaper has abolished parochialism in space, but has not given a sense of perspective in time.

Unable to comprehend the complete state of affairs of which the details cannot be stated by the press in a marketable form, or to weigh the conditioning circumstances, not only uneducated folk, but those who plume themselves on their general education, are left to grow warm about vague and large concepts, such as self-government, socialism, and denominationalism, little understood and less well defined. In this atmosphere, reverence towards or fanaticism for an idea or symbol is more natural than the intelligent understanding of a tool. The state becomes ' a mortal God,' not an instrument of human welfare demanding painstaking use. It is easier to discuss what ought to be, than laboriously to inquire what may be.

Faith in the justice of political ' causes ' becomes none the less ardent, because information about the bearings of the ' cause ' is lacking. A moral principle can but too easily be detected to guide action in the uncharted seas where we are ignorant of all detail. To the ignorance of the private individual is added the interested exploitation of prejudice and contagious excitèment by the commercial press. The problem of getting correct and proportioned civil information across to the citizen through the throng of competing items of news, less unattractive to an indolent mind or more intimate for a curious one, is a subject by itself, one of the most critical of our time. Much of this misinformation and misguided enthusiasm or disastrous apathy is inevitable, in the vast populous heterogeneous states of modern times, which have so far departed from the Greek ideal of compactness and homogeneity, expressed in the City-State, where public policy was almost as comprehensible to the citizen as his private affairs. What is desirable is that the consequences of the situation should be recognized.

The most important task of democratic education in politics is to inculcate an invincible scepticism about the possible range of lay political knowledge.[4] When men know their ignorance, they can be on

---

[4] Cf. Blackstone's remarks on amateur politicians : " Indeed it is perfectly amazing that there should be no other state of life, no other occupation, art or science, in which some measure of instruction is not looked upon as a requisite, except only in the science of legislation, the noblest and most difficult of any. Apprenticeships are held necessary to almost every art, commercial or mechanical : a long course of reading and study must form the physician and the practical professor of the laws : but every man of superior fortune thinks himself a born legislator." (*Commentaries*, 1800, I, pp. 8–9.)

their guard against the danger of that ignorance. Those who know themselves to be at the best but amateurs can take measures to safeguard the efficient conduct of their affairs, and to protect themselves against lobbying and the self-interested use of inside information. When the critical judgment has been trained, it will be possible for a democracy, as Aristotle suggests, to be a connoisseur of political confections. A man may judge the satisfactory nature of his own experience ; but it is as impossible for him to judge outright the efficiency of a political method for providing him with that experience, as it is for a rural farmer to judge the methods of a metropolitan business house. And the objection to the belief in the competence of the moral sword to cut the Gordian knots of politics, which belief lies behind much democratic theory, is that it obstructs the growth of this critical diffidence. The possession of a conscience is not enough to give any and every man the right to a voice in what should be done in a political crisis. His duty as a citizen demands, in addition, that he exercise his understanding.

Moral Convictions and Social Therapeutics. Ethical intuitions must not be confused with a competent grasp of political methods. They may be as important, but they are not a substitute. If popular moral judgments on complex political questions are to be excused as inevitably dogmatic owing to human indolence, or to that distraction of interest which leads to economy of energy in mastering

U

detail by calling in a ' principle ', they are nevertheless often to be condemned as quackish and ruinous in a civilization of social adjustments so delicate as to require the most patient study. The adjustments required for efficiency in the pursuits of civilization in the world of the twentieth century, which is bound the globe over by lines of communication, and rendered psychologically subtler by education, are not those of the simpler, parochial world of the fourteenth century. The village, the barony, perhaps even the state, are not efficient units for all the purposes of present civilization.[1] From Syria one learns that the structure of village society has notice- ably changed with the coming of the automobile. But larger units of social organization than the rural village are affected.   Counties, such as those of some American States, which were assigned as admini- strative areas appropriate for administrative pur- poses in the days of horse-back riding, are not obviously suitable for to-day.   Our institutions abound in such vestigial remains as had a function once in meeting old needs which have long since given way to new ones.   State organization may itself conceivably be growing obsolete, along with the systems of civilization which in the fifteenth century saw its rise and to which it is adapted.

Only research into mortality statistics and reports of criminal proceedings, not *a priori* generalization, will show how drunkenness is divisible into types of widely differing social import, the one kind

leading to chronic ill-health, the other to sporadic
violence, and how these types tend to be local and
occupational. Only research will show whether
there is any correlation between the decline of the
number of murders in certain countries and the
increase of the suicide rate.[5] Not conventional
generalizations and the taste of individuals, but
technical inventions which disturb and modify,
often in unexpected fashions, an economic and social
environment not completely under the control of
any one generation, are the determining factors in
deciding the structure of the world of industry and,
hence, the scheme of social relationships.

In a political administration which aspired to
approximate even to the efficiency expected in industrial management, committees would exist, not only
to make recommendations (as is already done in
Wisconsin by the Legislative Reference Bureau) on
the uniform drafting of law, but also to point out
where new law required additional legislation to
make its provisions systematic and of a piece with
the old. Still more important, however, would be
the work of some official expert body to suggest
legislation of a preventive nature, such as new
conditions, social or technical, might require, if

[5] The distinction between ' soaking,' resulting in cirrhosis of the
liver, and ' convivial drinking,' resulting often in arrest for being
' drunk and violent,' came to the notice of the present writer when
he was serving on the staff of the Central Control Board (Liquor
Traffic). The statistical incidence, moreover, of drunkenness differs
both according to locality and according to occupation.

The theory mentioned in the text about the suicide rate has been
propounded by Professor Ferri in a paper read before the International Statistical Congress at Rome in 1925.

misdemeanours were not to occur, uncorrected by the present law, and grave social damage to be done for which this law, remedial in its nature and appropriate to an earlier social situation, had not prohibitive provisions. At present, the anticipation of social damage must be left to the ordinary legislator, i.e. to the busy minister who can only be expected to concern himself with matters so obviously vital (from a military point of view) as the control of naval fuel, or to the amateur private member preoccupied with local needs. The growth of slums has been possible owing to the ineffective crudity of the early Tudor repressive measures, and to the lack of any public and important agency for promoting preventive legislation. It is not, of course, to be expected that men will impose upon themselves legislative restrictions, save under the spur of social discomfort. All that is here suggested is that an *ad hoc* agency could supply the information which would render it vividly apparent that such discomfort was to be anticipated. It is, again, neither scientific and productive of the most helpful results, nor does it promote a rational and smoothly working social system, to appoint commissions for the investigation of social problems which construe it to be their task to make their findings conform to public morality as understood at the moment, and to the beliefs of the uninstructed conscience of the appointing body.[6]

[6] Cf. the Vice Commission of Chicago (quoted by Walter Lippmann : *Preface to Politics*, chap. vi), in the Introduction to the *Report on the Social Evil*, 1911, p. 25 : " The Commission . . . has

It is as intelligible that interested parties desire to dictate the results of investigations, as that moral opinion itself may not be entirely disingenuous, but subconsciously prejudiced in the direction of interest. The appeal to morality can only be treated with deference when we do not detect behind it the justification of a custom built up by self-interest, and is to be criticized, favourably or unfavourably, accordingly. But often this desire to hector arises from no more than inability to find any deeper causes for social problems than human perversity and an inexplicable or base refusal to make a change of will. This moralizing attitude frequently goes along with lack of sympathetic imagination and mere absence of the experience requisite for forming a judgment.

Those who are too full of moral impatience to search for the underlying causes and to study with humility the logic of social conduct, those who ever desire a short-cut, must be content to lament the persistence of the symptomatic manifestations of evil. To be forward with moral blame before we have diagnosed the nature of the evil is as profitless as the exercise of those who, from piety, used to thrash lunatics in order to. drive out the devils of which they were believed to be possessed.

kept constantly in mind that to offer a contribution of any value such an offering must be, first, moral ; second, reasonable and practicable ; third, possible under the Constitutional powers of our Courts ; fourth, that which will square with the public conscience of the American people."

It may, however, be replied that we cannot refrain from returning the blow of the man who strikes us on the cheek, until we have completed an inquiry as to why he strikes us. This argument is unanswerable in practical life, in so far as we are there in no small part interested in giving expression to our natural emotions, and not only in the betterment of society. And it is certainly a necessary concern of the political scientist to study these natural reactions in social conduct which result in lynchings, and in illegal and extra-legal associations for the execution of popular justice. But if we are concerned with right methods in moral sanitation, as distinct from explosions of indignation, the argument is irrelevant. To say that it is ' instinctive ' is not enough to justify a moral judgment : it must also be rational. And what a rational judgment depends upon is an extensive knowledge of shifting conditions and obscure causes. The whole history of Charity Organization illustrates this contention, and points the moral that ' instinctive ' promptings may be ill guides to social conduct. In social questions we have a more difficult task than to award praise and use blame *in terrorem,* so as to influence to virtuous action the conduct of an individual or to persuade him by the argument of general consent. Social evils, such as war and prostitution, are probably not so much due to the sudden and inexplicable wickedness of human nature, as they are the results of its profound wants, which, owing to maladjustment in the social system, find satisfaction in perverted courses.

The political situation must, then, be approached, not with preachings and programmes, but in the attitude of a profession of social medicine. The task of the legislator is not that of the evangelist, but of the physician. The popular representative in Parliament or in Congress may be called upon, as he has been since the days of Edward I or John, to provide a sample of the opinion in fact obtaining in the country—the partially informed but power-controlling opinion with which the legislator has to reckon, and which is the opinion of those whose interests he has intelligently to serve. The representative voices the experience of those for whom the legislation and the State itself exists ; he gives expression to the opinion of those who are, as Aristotle rightly affirmed, the judges of the legislator's finished work.

But, if the patient judges the efficiency of the legislator's remedy, the patient has not the skill, knowledge, or confidence, save for simple ailments, to doctor himself. These qualities the legislator, as physician, must possess and use for the country's service. But, if he is to perform his task professionally, he must possess both a knowledge of the general principles of his art or science, and a sufficient knowledge of the detail of the specific case to form an adequate diagnosis of the disease. For this he requires information, reliable and convenient ; in Lord Bryce's echoing words, we

need Facts, Facts, Facts.[7]   And, if we are to avoid
the evils of superciliousness, harshness, and departmental spirit, to which an unchecked bureaucracy or
dictatorial system of 'business-like good government' tends, we shall need not only firmly established means of securing democratic control (as
distinct from the phantom[8] of democratic direction) ;
we shall also need unofficial as well as governmental
agencies, for finding these facts.   Such agencies are
the *sine qua non* of any sound social therapeutics,
and are the chief hope of health in a society burdened
with the load of civilization as no society has
been burdened hitherto.   The whole issue between
Dictatorship and Democracy, between the Expert
State *du sang pur* and the Instrumental State, turns
upon whether absolute authority is or is not the fee
which must be paid for scientific direction ; whether
management retaining the ultimate right of decision
is or is not required in the political field for the
running of a modern state, equivalent to the rights
of the management hitherto obtaining in the
economic field of men's daily industrial life.

This is not to defend an anæmic and repellent
attitude of expert aloofness and of scientific detachment, once established conclusions have been

[7] H. J. Laski : *A Grammar of Politics*, 1925, p. 372 : " Nothing
can ever compensate for the absence in a state of (a) systematic and
organized research, and (b) the accumulation of material likely to
bear on social processes."

[8] *Vide The Phantom Public*, by Walter Lippmann (1925), and a
review of it, entitled *The Sovereign People's Paper Crown*, by the
present writer in the *Cornell Law Quarterly*, April, 1926.

reached. But intolerance of impartial research and of the suspended judgment encourages that habit of make-believe, whereby men, comforted by indulgent dreams, are able to flee from the pain of contemplating what is unpleasant, and from the mental toil of finding new solutions for the problems presented by a changing world of new inventions, new environment, and new outlook. This make-believe would be a blessed solution of all difficulties, did it not lose touch ever more and more with the world of actual causation and of practical happenings, until, in some crisis, the real world impinging and thrusting itself upon the dream world, this latter is shattered, and men wander disconsolate and sceptical in a society without moral traditions.

Political Science and Ethical Theory. It is necessary, then, not to confound the practical observance of Morals with the scientific study of Politics. But it is no less necessary to note the danger lying in the intrusion of ethical theory into the treatment of political method. The result is an unwillingness to reach a dispassionate judgment on the facts so far as the evidence goes and apart from their bearing on ' human values,' which is a grave hindrance to the development of the social sciences, and is prejudicial to disinterestedness in thought. This is not to deny that the irresponsible criticism of matters in one aspect moral is destructive of the great sentimental allegiances in those whose training does not supply them with the means for a balanced independent judgment. There is natural indignation against those who seem to betray the forces of righteousness by intellectual frivolity in dealing with grave practical issues. But the publicist must insist that Politics is a pure science, of which the abstract arguments take no cognizance, save strictly as hypotheses, of considerations of value ; it is for others to decide whether these arguments are useful or beneficial.

Exhortations apart, speculations as to how men may most nobly lead the communal life, such as have not been lacking in the writings of the English disciples of the great Hegelian school, may properly be held to be irrelevant to Politics. What may be my station in society and what is the nature of its duties, is appropriately to be described as an ethical, not a political, study.[9] If our thesis be correct, it may be doubted whether the Greek thinkers did not give a false bias to Politics by their failure to differentiate its field from that of public morals, and by their ethical inquiries into the nature of the good or the perfect State. Still more might Aristotle be held to be at fault when he raises (*Politics, IV*, 1) the preliminary inquiry as to the nature of the desirable life. The science of Politics may reasonably be expected to make great advance, as a study of political method, before ever there is even approximate agreement on these questions of values. It is no more the task of a political scientist to instruct men about political values, than it is the task of a teacher of sculpture to

[9] E. F. Bradley : *Ethical Studies*, Essay V, *My Station and its Duties.*

instruct his pupils in themes and ideals for artistic expression. His business is to teach well the principles of technique, and to tell them what can and what cannot be done with the material.

A political science is needed which need not be contingent for its acceptance upon the acceptance of a political or ethical philosophy. It is perhaps unnecessary to add that this is not for a moment to admit that men do not require such a philosophy. The aim of pure Politics is not, any more than is that of Ethics, to exhort men to good action. Nor is its aim, as is that of Ethics, to give them the vision of all that good action involves, its principles and system. It is no more concerned with this than to decide whether the results which may be obtained by pursuing a certain course will be, in the last analysis and in the context of circumstances, expedient. These things men must decide for themselves.

For similar reasons a sound theory of Politics must regard with suspicion all theories of political phenomena which concern themselves chiefly with a qualitative selection of the facts, and which by implication place more emphasis upon certain approved motives, as guiding and dominant factors, such as a sense of citizenship, than all the facts would seem to warrant.[10] Such explanations are to

[10] B. Bosanquet : *Philosophical Theory of the State*, ed. 1920, p. 49 : Political philosophy " recognizes a difference of the level of degree in the completeness and reality of life, and endeavours to point out when and how, and how far by social aid, the human soul attains the most and best that it has in it to become."

be rejected, not because they may not be sound so far as they go, but because they are complex, reflective, and secondary, induced from observation of or conjecture about the fine products of a highly developed civilization ; not primary, simple, and offering clues to the understanding of why civilization rots as well as of why it grows, and of the behaviour of primitive men and of men when primitive. The study of Politics by a consideration of its qualitatively most valuable data, e.g. that of highly civilized states, as the consideration of Politics through the exclusive study of Law, resembles the action of one who, setting out to investigate the foundations of a house, declines to examine the basement until he has completed an exhaustive survey of the upper stories.

Politics is merely the science of the interrelations of human beings in society, a science quite impersonal. It is not therefore adverse to Ethics, since, as a science, it is irrelevant to Ethics. It will first, as pure science, discover, and then, as applied science, demonstrate the best means, granted the political situation, for any man or society to attain political ends. It is as much concerned with men's means of attaining the unsubliminated desires which they actually have, as with the subliminated and chastened desires which they may also have. *The Prince* and *The Discourses* are written, if with a crude psychology, yet in a very appropriate fashion for works on Politics. The objective treatment of Politics may be said to begin with

Machiavelli, if the systematic treatment begins with Aristotle.

But' the neutrality of Politics is no more to be considered a malevolent neutrality than is the neutrality of Pharmacology in the study of cures of the human body to be considered malevolent. We must know the character of drugs in order that we may know which to avoid and when. So too the effects of military reprisals are worthy of study, in order that we may decide whether, all things considered, we can accept as beneficial these effects with which we are impartially presented, and are willing to defray the necessary costs. Politics, coupled with a knowledge of finance, will tell us the consequences of the repudiation of an international debt. It is for each people to decide whether it will economize on domestic taxation and face these consequences. But nothing is gained, save a solace to sentiment, by the refusal to face the logic of the political situation. Politics will not tell us that it is necessary to procure this or that effect, but only that, if we desire the effect, this or that cost is necessary. It will not supply us with directive maxims. *Salus populi est suprema lex* is a maxim of Ethics and not of Politics, for it involves a question beyond the power of Politics to adjudicate.

Political Science and Moral Detachment. To the argument that the science of Politics should be treated as a study of method, thus cutting the development of the science loose from the vexed problems of values, the moralist may retort,

paraphrasing the words of the Moslem destroyer of
the Library at Alexandria, that, if Politics is a
science of conduct in accordance with what ought
to be, it is redundant, and that, if it is other
than this, it is pernicious. With a doctrine that
teaches how tyrannies are formed and how prudent
assassinations are carried out after the example of
the method adopted by the Duke Valentino when
murdering Vitilezzo Vitelli, with this dreary science
and nefarious art of the deception of enemies, it is
possible for humanity, without loss, to dispense.
A healthy and creative statesmanship can ignore
it. We know what ought to be (as Plato knew in
his *Republic* and More in his *Utopia*) and we should
direct our energies to making it to be, instead of
considering what ought not even to exist. This is
an attitude common among enthusiastic supporters
of liberal projects, such as the League of Nations,
until, their ideal meeting with a practical reverse
from the action of nations inspired with more
primitive sentiments, they lapse into the belief
that all effort is fruitless unless preceded by a
universal miracle of human moral regeneration.

The argument contains its own refutation.
Humanity has not dispensed with the facts, and to
know the cause whereby such things come to be is
the indispensable preliminary to avoiding such
monstrous happenings in the future. For change
of circumstance is as necessary as change of heart ;
and perhaps change of heart depends upon a better
perspective of circumstance. A better nature is the

consequence of a better understanding. Change of circumstances, so far as it is within our power, is a matter of proved method in dealing with a particular type of situation and of an adequate knowledge of the factors of the specific situation, as well as a knowledge of the general direction which the change should take. Instead of ignoring the unpleasant in Politics for six days, until, unable to be longer repressed, it keeps a devil's Sabbath on the seventh, let us rather repeat the words of the godfather of modern inductive science : " Gratias agamus Macciavello et huius modi scriptoribus, qui aperte et indissimulanter proferunt quid homines facere soleant, non quid debeant."[11] As Machiavelli himself said, we are concerned with ' the effectual truth of the matter,' with what will in fact cause or result from, certain acts.

Just as poisonous drugs have their virtues and healing powers in cases of sickness, so political manners and methods, considered at one epoch vicious, because contrary to the current of the best ethical feeling of the time and hence surely betokening in a contemporary an evilly disposed will, may at other times, and under more primitive or disturbed circumstances, be, as despotism has sometimes been, both beneficial in fact and benevolent in intention. In an early age ' a wrong is still a right.'

Great movements, again, whether due to a true or to

[11] Francis Bacon's *Works*, ed. 1862, Boston, III, p. 31 (*De Augmentis Scientiarum*, chap. vii).

a mistaken idealism, have not only been accompanied by what is relatively evil, but have often owed their success, in making headway against and in disrupting repressive custom, to this enterprising evil, to the less than scrupulously honourable assistance of not disinterested persons, and to non-altruistic motives such as the desire for confiscated ecclesiastical estates or for the profits of speeded-up labour.

Men may and do contribute to carry into effect moral reforms in social organization for motives less ethically lofty than those which inspire the pioneers or leaders. To recognize this is a condition of leadership ; to abuse the knowledge is the first step to forfeiting confidence and control. Thus the delicate humane courtesy of the eighteenth century, with its war against what was *barbare*, is connected by its own writers with its self-indulgence. The victory of religious toleration was less due to a firm grasp on the principle of human liberty in the realm of ideals than to a diversion of interest, to *ennui* resulting from the practical failure to enforce laws of uniformity, and to religious indifferentism. The coming of the Christian dominance was due in part to the civil wars of the astute Constantine and his personal rivals and to the decadence of the conservative aristocracy, not at all to the rule of the great Trajan or to the farmer virtues of old Rome. Natural science owes its birth, in large part, to the immorality ascribed to the Greek gods, which released the intelligent mind from affectionate and dutiful allegiance, and set it free for serious interests other than religious. The modern secular state, again, is under no small debt to the fomentors of the Great Schism and to the Borgias, who shook the Catholic international system to its foundations.

A slave state may be founded on a wrong, but the wrong is founded on the mercy and calculation which spares a captive from the sword of a foeman, and thereby renders possible a new stage in civilization. Nor does it seem possible to maintain that the new stage is reached despite the evil in slavery, in any more helpful sense than that in which it could be maintained that the world progresses despite pain and toil.[12] War will not be abolished thanks chiefly to the more heroic and self-sacrificing qualities in humanity, although the war against it may require heroism, any more than the duel was

[12] Professor L. T. Hobhouse maintains that " it is quite one thing to say that there may be good elements in a slave society, and quite another to find slavery a rational institution. What is good may have survived in spite of slavery, and may even have turned some of the consequences of slavery (e.g. industrial organization) to good use (e.g. useful or artistic works) . . . The bad in society lives on the good " (*The Elements of Social Justice*, 1921, p. 15). Certainly slavery is not rational in the sense that it is suitable for every form of society, or that we should consider it suitable in those more ideal forms of society towards which we hope that we ourselves are progressing, but only in the sense that it has been suitable for certain forms of society. Assuredly ' the bad,' by definition, then ' lived on the good.' But the problem is whether what we now consider the good could have lived then, if what we now consider bad had been surgically cut away from it. Is this ideal division historically valid ? Was it practically feasible to separate the two elements ? And are we justified, despite the weight of Lord Acton's opinion, in confounding our appreciation of the manner in which men in the past confronted the difficulties of their age, with our judgment of what of the past deserves imitation in the present ?

x

suppressed by such qualities. Rather the duel was not suppressed without a grievous affront to those more honourable and mettlesome qualities in men insisted upon by its defenders. And wars will be no more when fear and interest, as well as a growth of humane sentiment, dictate that an end be put to them. Great moral movements, again, succeed not only because they give men something to love and approve of, but also because they give men something to hate and fight, and it is often true that love leads to a happy indolence, but that hate leads to action. Neither hate nor war nor servitude nor acquisitiveness are wrong when the circumstances are appropriate and the social effects beneficial. But as society becomes more intimately co-operative, these methods become more unfitting and uncouth in their crude forms.

It is thus not satisfactory to settle political problems, without further inquiry, by an appeal to our direct moral intuitions, or to our first thoughts about what ought to be. What ought to be is limited by what can be : the impracticable ideal is, as a guide to action, a false ideal. Utopianism is the worst foe of practical idealism, since it diverts energies which need to be directed with concentration and sound judgment if they are to be effective. What constitutes Utopianism is, of course, a matter of opinion and vision, to be settled by each man's wisdom and conscience. What ought to be depends not only upon guiding values, often themselves matter of dispute, but also upon the conditions of the society of the time and place, and requires accurate study of the facts of these conditions. Private vices are never public virtues, but apparent public vices require study in their relation to the vital organs and growth of the community, prior to attempted excision by the knife of the first chance moralist. When it comes to the application of ' principles,' there are no static ideal social constructions ; there is no ' Republic ' or ' Utopia ' which is good unreservedly under any conditions. There are no such things as political principles, in any sense in which they might be held to compel on social grounds adhesion to the content of this or that political programme, ' though the heavens fall.' There are ethical principles ; and there are political methods, whereby we may put into effect these principles or realize these values ; methods shown by human experience to be wise and expedient, and which may perhaps be susceptible of reduction to rule.

In the vast flow, or inter-connection and osmosis of cause and effect,[13] which is displayed in History, it is impossible to isolate in any absolute sense the good from the evil—this decaying good—which ' must needs come.' It is impossible to set up a final scheme of the good society which will supply us with an infallible prescription *a priori* for social ills, and thus save us the trouble of making afresh each time a

---

[13] I do not wish to appear hereby to commit myself to the assertion that the phrase ' cause and effect ' is one philosophically satisfying.

social diagnosis. Politics is the science of methods, in accordance with which may be made perpetual readjustments. Ever History will provide, so long as human nature and the changing world endures, new situations ; provide them faster and faster as human wit modifies in geometrical progression the outer environment, and thereby complicates its own civilization. And these new situations will demand new expedients, compared with which the old will appear obsolete, crude, and wrong. The world is full of this débris of past goods, new wrongs because long since in the wrong place.

It is the grandeur of History that it so austerely abates our local, ephemeral pretensions, and reduces us and our would-be moral requirements to their due and proportionate place. For the true Hegelian this may ring with the authentic sound of a faith. At least it is a caution against rash moralization. It is not a caution against the alleviation of present human suffering—which is indeed often impeded, not by this doctrine, but by an inflexible *a priori* morality. Nor is it to proffer the effeminate excuse that all comes to the same in the end. " Progress is not automatic "[14] from the point of view of humanity, since the automatic and self-sufficient process of the universe, the operation of universal law, might result in the progressive elimination of a human race unadaptable and inactive. It may be that the stars in their courses fight against the Siseras of oppression, that the logic of History is

[14] Lord Balfour : *Decadence*, 1908, p. 58.

against those who do wrong, perhaps because our notions of wrong are moulded by the historical experience. But such reflections will, of course, not therefore excuse us, in reaching a personal decision, from troubling to discover where just men are ranging themselves, even though it be on the side of the temporarily smaller battalions—*sed Cato minora*. It will yet be noted that, however strong our conviction of what is valuable, it will still be incumbent upon us to realize these ideals under certain historical conditions, and subject to the objective logic which governs those conditions. It will, therefore, remain necessary for us dispassionately to study and objectively to test these conditions. There cannot be ultimate difference between the conclusions of Ethics and those of Politics. No ethical or political impossibilism can ultimately be satisfactory. They are to be reconciled in the relationship respectively of content and form, of purpose and method.

Ethical Ends and Political Means. The political man, let us recapitulate, seeks to bring into conformity with his own will the wills of others, so that he may the better attain his own ends. It is here irrelevant that a good critical and sentimental education may have rendered his ends entirely unselfish in the generally accepted sense, or that, again, while being effectively selfish, thanks to a process of rationalization, he may be unaware of their self-regarding nature. The knowledge whereby this harmony or co-ordination may be brought about has recently been indicated as the office of Ethics.[15] This purely instrumental treatment, however, of human conduct, according to which virtue is sunk into *virtù*, and in which no judgment is attempted of the value of the ends pursued, would seem rather to appertain and be proper to Politics than to Ethics.

Politics is concerned with means ; Ethics with ends. Ethics has to itself the field of valuation. The province of Politics is matter of science, a question of social mechanics and social engineering. It may indeed be true that whatever conduces to the most perfect social harmony is the most perfect virtue, but, whereas moral discipline leads to a reformation of the person as a partaker in social life, and ethical philosophy to a recognition of the proper proportion between those things which we should be educated to esteem valuable, Politics is only concerned with the method by which, with the minimum adjustment to which the pressure of the social situation compels us, it is possible to carry out our empirical wills. This point of view has been

---

[15] A. C. Laing : *A Study on Moral Problems* (1922), p. 6 : " Ethics' . . . task, accordingly, does not differ from the task of any positive science." " Morality turns upon the possibility of controlling natural processes " (p. 10). " What is desired is a value ; and values are what is desired " (p. 215). Virtue, in short, is technique. To the presentation of Ethics set forth in this recent book I am in debt, but I cannot help feeling that what Mr Laing calls Ethics very largely covers the same field as that which is here termed Politics. That Morality (as distinct from the æsthetic appreciation of values) ' is relative to conditions,' I agree. I, therefore, include morals (*mores et consuetudines*), as matters of fact and social influence, within the political field, although, by doing so, I may perhaps be doing more violence than Mr Laing to the customary use of the term.

admirably indicated by Kant in various passages
where he is treating of the difference between the
transcendental world of the free will, which has
ethical significance, and the determined phenomenal
world, and especially where he says, speaking of
the insistent pressure of factors making for peace,
that the problem of the formation of a federal state,
hard as it sounds, is not insoluble, " even for a race
of devils, if intelligent."[16]

It is unsatisfactory to establish, as the standard
whereby to judge the value of action, the degree to
which it conduces, in a political fashion, to social
harmony. For this has as its consequence the
Platonic identification of ethical training and
political means. But there are other autonomous
ethical goods, good finally and in themselves, besides
that of social harmony. Rather, it may reasonably
be objected that this harmony is good only *as a
means*, i.e. that it is not a genuine ethical good in
itself, but is only a prerequisite condition of a
society in which ethical goods may be realized.
Actual harmony (as distinct from the *love* of
harmony and fair play, which goes to make the
just character, and from the *ability* to ensue
harmony, which belongs to the wise character) is
devoid of value in itself and save on the condition
that it harmonizes that which is valuable. A society
cannot commend our admiration because, ὡς ἔπος
εἰπεῖν, its members ' take in each other's washing.'

[16] I. Kant : *Perpetual Peace*, trans. Campbell Smith, 1903,
pp. 153-4.

Each member must have a personality capable of possessing individual value. And, although the contribution may be social, and although an individual cannot live to himself alone, it is in the component parts, the living and enjoying individuals, and not in the scheme of relations, that all final values, including ethical values, inhere.

Justice, it may reasonably be argued, is not a virtue in itself, but the quality of actions or of a social scheme, whereby the attainment of virtue is facilitated. Self-control is virtuous since it is a characteristic of an individual ; similarly benevolence is a virtue as being an attitude of mind. But justness, like ' adjustedness,' is a quality of actions which establish or maintain a certain objective relationship between individuals. Only if we believe in the existence of ' parts of the soul ' can we hold that the quality of justice, as distinct from the well-proportioned character, is a personal characteristic. And only if, further, with Plato, we regard or come near to regarding society as a person, can we treat justice as a virtue because it inheres as a final quality, good of and for itself, in the character of society. Virtue cannot be a mere substanceless scheme of relationships, whereas harmony may be a harmony, e.g. of the substantially bad, a multitude of one mind in the pursuit of evil. Justice has no more ethical value than efficiency in machinery, save by reason of the value of those between whom just relationships are maintained. A society which holds to the rule of *caveat emptor* may be a perfectly

just society, but its members have not the virtuous
characteristic of generosity and fraternal confidence ;
rather this society sanctions in its members self-
seeking and suspicion.

Justice is indeed much more than legality ; but,
admitting this point, thinkers who here follow Plato
forget that the accord of perfect justice does not
necessarily carry with it any value, in beauty, intelligence, and strength of character, on the part of those
thus in accord. Virtue, on the other hand, may
well be a quality to be judged by its social effects,
and not a mere gratification of conscience or a
subjective feeling[17] enjoyed by those who are in a
state of grace. But virtue is, for all that, a quality of
which the benefit accrues to individuals directly, and
not a social arabesque which can only possess direct
value as pleasing to the contemplation of the
Absolute. The entire field of political method, its
lesser politics and its instrumental ideal of a perfectly unobstructed and harmonious *modus vivendi*,
is a field of means, and is to be distinguished
from that field of final values, of ends, which alone
is the realm of Ethics. Social justice is, hence, a
' natural ' system arising from the balance of social
factors and is neither ethical nor non-ethical ; it is
the condition of an equilibrium of wills each desiring
to execute its own will, good or bad as the case
may be.[18]

The Nature of Ethical Values. A distinction has

[17] G. E. Moore : *Principia Ethica*, 1903, p. 173.

[18] *Vide* L. T. Hobhouse, *op. cit.*, p. 91, for a parallel statement
about social justice cast in ethical language. The point about justice
made in the text is one long maintained by Quaker writers.

been permitted above to pass without challenge between ethical and other final values, as though ethical values were peculiarly concerned with social relationships, and carried necessarily along with them (although we cannot by definition admit them as means to) social effects. On the other hand, other final values, such as mathematical truth and painlessness, seem to be regarded as of no social significance.

It may be doubted whether this distinction is valid. It may be doubted whether all final values are not in the last analysis ethical values. Or, conversely (and more precisely and satisfactorily), it may be doubted whether ethical judgments are not but one species of the general type of judgments which we make upon final matters. Granted that all final values fall into one group, judged by one form of judgment, it appears more accurate to describe this judgment as æsthetic than as ethical.

Ethics, as the study of the good, is not a simple but a compound subject. " It is plain that goods may be so called in two senses, the one class for their own sake, the other as instrumental."[19] When we speak of a ' good ' sword, or refer to the ' virtues ' of a herb, we are using ambiguous words in the second of these two possible senses, in the sense of the good or virtue to be found in the excellent adaptation of means to ends. We are speaking in what may be termed an economic sense. It is in this Crocean

[19] Aristotle : *Nicomachean Ethics*, ed. Bekker, I, 4.

sense only that Politics may be brought under the more general term ' economic.'

But when we speak of a good character, we do not have in mind any ulterior use to which this character can be put. It may be beneficial to the friends of its possessor, but rather by reason of the joy derived from its existence than for any specific utility it can be relied upon to possess, such as would render its exercise convenient to others. Rather it is like a jewel, requiring indeed to be viewed in order to be appreciated and enjoyed, but like a jewel, nevertheless, even when not exposed to public inspection.

It is noteworthy that, when speaking of these final goods, which are not to be tested by their utility as efficient to produce something beyond themselves, but only as giving pleasure in the direct contemplation, we, like the Greeks, tend to make use of such terms as ' a beautiful character,' ' a graceful act,' ' noble behaviour,' ' sweetness and light,' in brief, emphatically terms implying an æsthetic judgment. The ethical judgment is, then, composite ; sometimes an economic judgment, in terms of efficiency, sometimes an æsthetic judgment on things final[20]— things which may be displeasing, to some minds, if

[20] Lord Shaftesbury : *Characteristics*, ed. 1773, II, *An Inquiry Concerning Virtue*, pp. 43 ff. : " A soul, indeed, may as well be without sense, as without admiration in things of which it has knowledge. Coming therefore to a capacity of feeling and admiring in this new way, it must needs find a beauty and deformity as well in actions, minds, and tempers, as in figures, sounds, or colours." Cf. also pp. 28–30.

irrational or sinister, but not necessarily pleasing just because rational or well-intentioned. *Et de gustibus non est disputandum.*

This æsthetic judgment may admit of psychological explanation of why it has arisen, but it does not admit of logical argument as to why it ought not to arise. We can, indeed, show that certain conduct would produce the disruption of social order if persisted in, but this is not cogent unless we set a value upon social order, or condemnatory beyond the degree to which we set a value upon social order. That suicide is wrong because, if committed universally, it would lead to the extinction of the race, is not an argument which would prove convincing to a Buddhist,[21] who, while disapproving of the means, would commend the end. ' To do unto others as you would be done by ' is a maxim which assumes a large measure of equality in the worth and needs of human beings, and will not commend itself, save in the most abstract and empty sense, to those who believe in the value of conduct based on the conviction that men are unequal, and that there ought to be inequality of opportunity. Thus the Golden Rule itself rests on a supposition, to wit, that men have a right to live, and that, since they live, it is socially expedient that they live well, and hence, upon the value we set on life and upon our repugnance to wars and medical methods of extermination. Again,

---

[21] I. Kant : *Grundlegung zur Metaphysik der Sitten*, ed. Vorländer, p. 45.

there is the fundamental maxim of law that we should not act against a man ' arbitrarily,' that is to say, ' by whim instead of by general principle,' but inveterate racial prejudice may be, for legislative purposes, such a reasonable ground for social action. Each axiom rests upon an intuition of value, which it endeavours reasonably to formulate and expound.

No satisfactory system of conduct can be irrational, because a chaotic method is not an efficient means to ends which, by the very fact that they are ends, are something to be attained. But, if the system is rational and consistent, the value of the ends is not therefore arrived at by reason. Controversy is not productive in the matter of values. All that Ethics can do is to expose the logical consequences of inconsistency in judgments of value, and appeal to the value of consistency. Applied Ethics, in giving system and direction to the habits of popular morality, will probably find more profitable matter for study in Medicine, than in the universal harmonies of questionable axioms to which it is tempted by the methods of Logic.[22] For the rest, we can only hope that those we deem ' invincibly ignorant ' of the true values will come to have ' new souls,' thanks to the impinging of new experience (hence the need for a broad-based and fearless education), or will be met by the stark

[22] I do not for a moment wish to appear to join in the common and probably ill-considered attack on the use of general concepts. This book is, indeed, a plea for the use of logic in the field of Politics, where there has been too little abstraction. But Ethics has suffered from an inadequate study of the phenomena of moral experience.

argument of extinction, which Nature meets out
to those whose minds are scored with the pattern
of a long-obsolete environment.

The ethical or æsthetic judgment on ends is one
neither of the pure nor of the practical reason ; it is
neither intellectual nor utilitarian. It is not, therefore, completely anarchic. There is in fact very
general agreement over broad fields of society as to
what is ugly, what is beautiful, whether in things,
persons, or acts. A practical criterion is perhaps, as
Plato thought, to be found in the response to what
is good and beautiful, and in the judgment, of the
man ' beautiful and good,' whose taste we esteem
more universal and finer than our own. The wise
man goes about through life seeking his superior in
order to correct by this inspiration his own judgment ; the vulgar man goes about through life
seeking his inferiors in order to flatter himself by
comparison and to water his self-esteem. The canon
of the beautiful is the judgment of him whom
the best seek out ; it is based on a qualitative
consensus.

Right in Law and in Ethics. That the doctrine has
not very generally commended itself that our judgment on final ethical goods is essentially æsthetic
and matter of taste (although educable as is all
æsthetic sensibility, and subject to the rule and
value of self-consistency), does not prove that it is
not true. The reason why it does not more generally
commend itself is perhaps not far to seek. The
æsthetic judgment has no fixed criterion and,

although by no means naturally anarchic, cannot be brought to order. But most men have the ' police mind.' And the pragmatic and political necessity of refusing to admit any principles which might, in an imperfect state of civilization, encourage social disorder, it is traditional to regard as pressing. Hence, even if it is uncommon to resolve with Hobbes all morals into positive law, men cling obstinately to some permanent rational system of ethics, which can be proven, as the Cambridge Platonists imagined, like logic—however much it may end in an empty and contentless arabesque— or to a moral sense which can be counted on to deliver itself uniformly in all times and places. It is noteworthy, however, as a caution against the martinet rationalizing tendency, that it was the very philosopher who declared that virtue is knowledge who was compelled, when it came to a discussion of the ultimate good, to identify it with beauty.

The requirements of social order render men prone to believe that morality or good citizenship are straightforward matters, on which there is a general consensus supported by practical reason and common sense. Aristotle's pertinent doubt as to whether the good man is a good citizen in a bad state is too inconvenient to be readily remembered. But that the man of practical intelligence is necessarily the man of practical goodness is a belief which will deceive no one who reflects. In so far as it is believed, it is believed because it is pleasant to both parties to believe it. It is at least equally true that the intelligent man is the perpetual criminal, according to the customary, conventional, and habitual standard of what is good and kindly. If the latter contention is an exaggeration which omits the consideration of moral continuity, the former omits that of social change and departure from the ancient folk-ways. Practically, intelligence only conduces to a conforming morality in a perfect society, where the good of the individual and the will of the society are at one. But if, by a rational morality, we mean, not the basing of morality upon what it is possible to convince a jury is no whim but common sense and ' reasonable,' but an ethical system which acknowledges the rule of eternal reason and universal consistency, then the social advantage of such a philosophic system as opposed to the apparent caprice of a system of good taste no longer exists. This Reason, as with the Stoics and Hegelians, will become identified with the absolute mind of God. In this use of the word reasonable, no man is fully reasonable, although he may be inspired by reason. The lawyers' use for a rational scheme of morality is quite other. Here the desideratum is that, instead of alleging as an excuse for action an irresponsible conscience, or taste, or temperament, men should act in a fashion rationally consistent with certain ethical premises upon which, in a given society, there is presumed to be agreement, whether there be or be not satisfactory philosophical proof.

The lawyer's use for an ethical system is essentially a political use. He demands it as a *means* for preserving a valuable social order. His concern is not really the problem of *final* values or to criticize the value of the local *mores*, unless their inefficiency and maladjustment to new conditions presents him with the problem of disorder. He is concerned only with flagrant contradiction of these conventions, whether enacted in law or unwritten. There may be logical inconsistencies of conduct, but, if so, these must be customary and due to the logical incapacity of the many, not criminal and due to the insolence of the individual. The lawyer is concerned, not with the content of the moral practice, but that there shall *be* a moral practice or ethical system which encourages order and discourages social discord. Order only demands a rational and non-arbitrary system of ethics in that social cosmos cannot be founded on ethical chaos and on individual perversity, however dignified by the name of ' objection for conscience sake.' In a given society there must be a general agreement on fundamentals[23]—*in necessariis unitas*—and in other matters give-and-take—*in dubiis diversitas, in omnibus caritas*. But too exacting a sifting out of ideals, with its attendant controversy, may lead not to unity but to division, not to the tolerance of fellowship but to a bigoted enlargement of things requisite for political salvation and safety.

" Must not the content of just law be derived from

[23] Cf. Bryce : *Modern Democracies*, 1921, II, p. 662.

Y

ethical theory ? We deny this absolutely. . . . We must regard it as an elementary fact, generally recognized, that the aim of ethical theory is perfection of character, while the institution of law has to do with the regulation of conduct." . . . " The meaning of law is exhausted in volition which enjoins other persons ; having, for its purpose, not the goodness of their inner life but the rightness of their outer co-operation."[24] This argument is much reinforced, if it be true that Ethics is, in part, a field of values, assessed by the individual æsthetic judgment, and incapable of formulation, like law, into a single system intolerant of diversity and demanding the acceptance of its formulæ from every rational being. The fundamental principles of legality and of orthodoxy are very different. The realm of ends thus becomes a realm of the independent judgment, and Politics can be expected to advance as a science only if it does not tarry to find rational principles for that which has no rules, or final solutions for that which has no ' few, simple, fundamental problems.'

Even were this philosophy of Ethics not sound, the conclusion for the advancement of the science of Politics would be the same. If there be immutable

[24] R. Stammler : *Theory of Just Law*, trans. Husik, p. 39 (German ed., 1902, p. 51). Also p. 57 (p. 74, German ed.) : " Political questions as such belong to the domain of just law and have no direct relation to ethical doctrine. . . . Ethical teaching is only one part of that just volition which stands opposed to brute force. Just law forms its supplement ; and the political problem belongs to the latter. This holds true not only of internal politics and the organization of rights in one's own sphere, but also of foreign relations as exhibited in the contact and treaties of people and states."

eternal values, we are too ignorant to know them.
And if we might know them, the multitude of men
do not know or cannot agree upon them. And if
there is agreement upon a few general principles
(such as, be it added, may be due to the common
environmental training of the æsthetic judgment),
they are too jejune to supply alone detailed content
for a social ideal. In brief, the politicist is confronted in practice with diversity of social ideals.
And he may entertain the theoretical opinion that
he always will be confronted with this diversity
owing to the fact that the field of values is not in
the last analysis subject to argument. The argument
of social utility is an argument in a circle, since to
argue that an action is good because it is socially
beneficial tells us nothing about final good. It is
socially beneficial because it contributes to the good
of individuals ; and the good of these individuals
must not be something only good because, again,
socially beneficial. But to answer that the final
good is their happiness is to cover with one word
many things. Action is ' economically ' good because
it contributes to final goods or values, and final
values are plural.[25]

If this argument be admitted, interesting conclusions follow. There being no one value or system
of values which alone can be held or known to be
laudable or right, the social system cannot be
maintained to be founded, even in its most perfect
or developed form, upon some one such system. The
social system is a harmony of individuals whose

[25] G. E. Moore : *Ethics*, 1912, p. 248.

judgments of value, even in a highly rational and civilized society, need not agree, although in some specific community, such as a Quaker village or a Benedictine monastery, there may, in fact, be this ideal agreement. The politicist, consequently, is not concerned to appraise the final value of the ideals to which individuals happen to be attached, but to co-ordinate them. His appraisal will be merely a utilitarian valuation, in terms of the ethics of means ; that is to say, in terms of efficiency. This thesis has corollaries no less instructive. For example, we can now set a limit to valid political argument from which scientific conclusions can be expected. When we cease to argue about means and begin to argue about social values, when we cease to discuss the effective remedy for a situation of discord with which we are presented, and begin to discuss whether the situation ought to have arisen or the abstractly desirable situation towards which the social process should tend, and debate whether efficient remedies are contrary to principles, we are no longer discussing Politics but Ethics.

To decide what is the ideal society, or which of two associations is the more valuable (save in terms of their efficiency in facilitating the smooth working of a third), is no matter for the politicist. As has been said, the dictum that ' the safety of the people is the supreme law ' is a maxim not of Politics but of Ethics. The problem of ultimate allegiance in cases of conflict of duties can be solved outright no more by Politics than by Law, but is a matter for conscientious ethical argument and for decision in a fashion consistent with the ethos, moulding our judgment of taste, imprinted upon us by a good education and broad experience.

Political Organization as Permissive of the Realization of Values. Politics, abstractly, is separable, and should be separated from Ethics in the æsthetic sense of that term. It studies what is, not what should be. But is it possible to escape from the notion of final values in political organization ? Are political data comprehensible, save in terms of purposive action towards an ideal ? Is not this organization, this co-ordination itself, something finally valuable ? This question we have already answered with a negative. Political organization as such no more has final value than has economic organization as such. Save in the very limited sense in which efficiency of itself has symmetry, beauty, and value, like a steel structure, organization and co-ordination only have final value by virtue of the final value of what is co-ordinated, and this is true even though, in the ' harmony of the spheres,' it were the whole universe which was co-ordinated. The mere fact that it is a society as large as the State, and not some paltry association which is co-ordinated, does not make co-ordination an end in itself and a valuable end. Order is valuable, and the State as having received the mandate to preserve order undertakes a task which is valuable and deserving of respect, but these values are both of them instrumental values, and conditional upon the excellence of the society which this order will protect and maintain. Perfect order, it is true, would imply

the complete satisfaction of human needs, without
even the least quality of discontent. But perfect
order would here be the symptom and consequence
of a happy and valuable state of society, not the
independent cause of it. Political maladjustment,
as the school of Condorcet and later the anarchists
have seen, can prevent happiness. But a Utopia
of political adjustment cannot produce happiness.

We have yet spoken of the State as having a
task. Does not this imply that it has an aim and
purpose ? Is its task no more ethical than that of
my razor, save that the generality of its uses are
more dignified, and more proximate to final goods
and evils ? Food is good ; the health and pleasant
tastes with which it provides us are final goods.
But we do not call the butcher ethical, because he
furnished us with the means of attaining these goods.
Whether food is good as a means to health is a
matter upon which men have long ago made up their
minds. And, if the statesman does no more than
so direct social organization that it provides what all
men are agreed is a simple necessity of human life,
to wit, order, his office is one which calls not for
ethical judgment but for technical good sense. But
is this an adequate description of the office of the
statesman ? Has he, and the State at large, not a
purpose to fulfil in leading the citizens to a better
kind of life ?

*Political Organization as Directed to the Realization
of Values.* Politics may be asserted to be more than
a system of efficient means. Without returning to

the position that social organization is an end in itself, it may be held that a satisfactory political system must be *means* indeed to the attainment of the more ideal life, but means to that *only*. Political organization is the skeleton or the husk ; but mankind striving after freedom seizes upon these forms and gives them substance and vitality. And thereby, it gives them intrinsic value. They bear the divine spirit as it proceeds on from form to form down the ages. These organizations display the *Gang Gottes in dem Welt.*

It is, however, of little assistance in the formation of a political theory to be told that the State, or any other political organization, embodies the march of God in the world, unless we know whither this march tends, and are left, not with a general notion, but with a specific notion of what constitutes the more ideal life. Yet precisely the chief virtue of Hegelianism has been that it has taught reverence for the actual, for the historical process in contrast to abstract utopianism, and has declined to permit the individual to dictate or specify ends to the process of history. Man must study as an act of intelligence, and, as an act of wisdom, must bring himself into accord with the process of the rational spirit displayed in history.

The Hegelian doctrine of State may give us scientific reverence for a process not to be changed by individual whim or party petulance ; it may teach us that the end of man is only fulfilled in the organized community ; but it will not give us the notion of this or that specific ideal, such as that of Plato's *Republic*, which the State seeks to realize as its final goal.[26] In discussing, therefore, whether political organization has not some ultimate purpose, we are committed to the consideration of two questions ; whether this organization does not embody an unknown Purpose, the expression of a more than private Personality, in harmony and co-operation with which individuals find satisfaction ; and whether the State exists for the fulfilment of a series of specific ideals.

The first question cannot indeed be separated entirely from the second. Presumably there is connection in the series of ideals. The State is not merely the sorry instrument of intermittent purpose. Nevertheless the several ideals in the series may alone be sufficiently limited to be known ; the entire design according to which the State fulfils the ends of civilization may be unknown. Although conscious purpose may be required to bring the specific ideal to fruition, the general design of the ideal may include the unknown product of future circumstances—the future expression in consciousness of the phase of development which Reality has yet to reach. But an unknown Purpose, even though it be so specific as to involve the development of freedom

---

[26] The accusation that Hegel saw in the Prussian State of his day, not the highest embodiment of a reasonable civilization hitherto actual and therefore deserving of high respect, but some final form, scarcely demands discussion. Rather Hegel insists on the importance of that ' sense for the state ' as such, to use the late Professor E. Troeltsch's words (*Die Soziallehren der christlichen Kirchen und Gruppen*), which was so conspicuously lacking in the Middle Ages.

or of self-consciousness, if it demands devotion must do so as a matter of faith and not of understanding. The convictions on which this devotion is based transcend experience, and, although they may be corroborated, cannot be contradicted by experience. A man is not a patriot on utilitarian grounds, but because it brings him happiness and self-respect to be so. Similarly the belief in a divine Purpose ruling the conduct of men is a pure judgment of value. This purpose is itself the valuable thing, and not what it proposes. And the State as the embodiment of this purpose is valuable in itself and respectworthy, apart from all question of specific accomplishment. The answer to this argument, then, is that, as a pure judgment of value, this belief concerning the nature of the State is a matter of individual taste, and cannot be the basis of a scientific doctrine of Politics. The connection between Politics and Ethics cannot be established by the mere affirmation of the ultimate and absolute value of the State. All that we can say is that for many people the State in itself is an ethical object of the highest value.

Similarly, values, not always quite consistent, are attached to the nation, and to groups of like speech or of common traditions united as dwellers in one country-side. But for the politicist Nationality is a fact, of biology or of opinion, to be judged and criticized in the light of its effects and susceptibility to co-ordination with other values, not to be accepted as an *a priori* value.

The second question is a different one. We are not here asked to attach value to the State as something which in our judgment is valuable in itself, as the embodiment of the rational purpose which is believed to exist in the universe. We are asked to admit that there are things valuable, that the specific function of the State is to forward the attainment of things valuable, and these only. It is, hence, impossible, even theoretically, to separate Politics and Ethics, because the chief task of the statesman is to select, and direct the machinery of the State towards, what is, or is believed to be, or is by those in power held to be, the valuable. In short, we are here asked to determine, not on a matter of faith, but upon a question of the specific function of the political organization.

The statesman, it may be said, surely has the task of so directing social organization that it will conduce to the good life of the individuals composing it. ' It pertains to the office of a Prince to care for the good life of his people in such a fashion as conduces to the attainment of eternal bliss.'[27] The statesman must select the goal towards which his policies shall tend. He is the architect of the fortune and happy life of his people. He must have a vision of the ideal state which he would facilitate or construct. The legislator has an obligation in conscience to act in accord with this vision. If the State has come into being for the sake of life, it exists for the sake of the good life.

[27] S. Thomas Aquinas : *Tractatus de Regimine Principum*, Bk. I, chap. 15.

Political Purpose v. Political Method. Whether this teleological treatment of social organization is sound may be doubted. It can be disputed whether, e.g. the State can be described as having an end or series of ends, as apart from the maintenance of the means and facilities of social order—which is not an end. Its organization may be a method and an instrument, not a plan with a purpose. It accepts, it does not dictate, the values which it is its task to bring to realization and co-ordination. It is the instrument of the wills of the particular society of individuals whose State it is. It is true that regulation may, in a highly civilized community, far exceed what is needed for the bare preservation of physical life. In a closely packed and intimately interdependent community, violent friction and dislocation may arise from far smaller causes than a direct threat to life. But it does not follow that the aim of the State must be some definite conception of the good life.

In other forms of organization, ecclesiastical systems and business associations, the problem is slightly different. Here there may be more than a mere living together. The specific purpose may, in this case, be the very cause of association ; whereas, in the case of the State, the pursuit of the good life for its citizens cannot exculpate the State from the specific obligation of preserving life and order, while its provision of the means for the good life as it understands it is imperfect in just this, that these citizens had no individual, free choice of what type of good life the State should pursue. ' The State is not an Academy of Arts,'[28] something which can leave its protection to another, while it concerns itself with furthering cultural ends. The State has indeed the power to enforce, as Germany, Japan, and other states have enforced, its cultural *ethos* on the citizens, although they are not members of a voluntary society associated for that purpose. But, if it does so, either it renders more difficult its primary function, as the pure political association, of maintaining order, or it acts because the government is of the opinion that this cultural training and education is a specific instrument, as Machiavelli treated religion, to the maintenance of order and harmony, and is useful as such apart from intrinsic value. All redundant regulation is an added difficulty in the maintenance of order ; hence it is an impediment, and bad.

The argument that the State is concerned to promote the good life has two stages. The first position is that there are degrees of ideality in social conditions, that social organization is constructed with a view to promoting, or at least to destroying hindrances to, the attainment of the more ideal conditions, and that it is judged by its more or less efficient functioning in promoting or facilitating this better life. The State is not merely an efficient instrument, but is an efficient instrument for a final good. To this position the answer is that when we refer to anything as an economic good as

[28] H. v. Treitschke : *Politics* (Eng. trans.), ed. 1916, I, p. 24.

distinct from a natural fact, we imply that it is efficient for something, and our using this instrument implies that we consider it efficient for something useful. But there may be no agreement as to the precise use to which, for instance, our manufactured product is to be put, or of its final value in that use. Similarly, political engineering may facilitate something generally desirable, without inquiring whether this or that movement is especially and truly desirable, or whether even there is any agreement in detail on the truly desirable social scheme. It facilitates what is desirable *as willed*, and not what is desirable as essentially valuable. The statesman carries out the actual will of the people or of such of the people as are politically significant ; he does not, like a benevolent despot, seek to impose on them his own opinion of what is good. He seeks to do, efficiently, and in a fashion consistent with good order, what would anyhow be done, though clumsily, in the actual distribution of social forces. The State is not a censor of the value of the uses to which people put their political liberties, but an executor of the prevalent public will, whatever this may happen to be.

This or that society may in fact be agreed, or may have a majority which agrees, upon a certain ideal of life. This ideal is in fact its will, and the State is its *âme damnée* in executing it, whatever it may be. But this is to record what may happen to be a fact, not to discover an essential function of the State.

This argument and rebuttal may seem to be unsatisfactory in that it omits to consider the directive office of the government and legislature, and the guiding influence of the tradition of the State on the wills of the citizens in bringing them to unanimity in their conception of a good national life. Hence we pass to the second stage of the argument. The State, it may be said, is not indifferent to what ends its citizens, or the majority of them, pursue under its ægis and thanks to the facilities which it provides. It is not only agent of the ' popular will,'[29] but a judge. And since, clearly, there will be difference of opinion as to which is the more ideal life and which the less or unideal life, the State will find itself compelled in all matters of major importance to select and, through education, to inculcate, its own particular ideal. Hence the State finds itself compelled to bring, at least, moral pressure to bear in favour of this ideal or that. It may not do so on religious issues if it consider that what people profess about their relation to and place in the universe is of too philosophical an interest to be of practical import, or if the animosities aroused by interference in doctrine and ritual is out of proportion to the magnitude of the social advantages to be gained by regulation. But in matters of the veritable ideals of the community, whether or whether not religious in a theistic or confessional sense, whether moral, whether economic, whether

[29] Such uncritical phrases as ' the popular will ' and ' public opinion ' are used, for the moment, to avoid periphrasis.

political, ideals which affect their daily conduct as citizens, the State cannot be *ex animo* tolerant, but merely tolerate (which is a very different thing) certain opinions which it holds harmful, and grant them a limited immunity.

If this position be accepted, it is then clear that political conduct will, at every turn, be influenced by ethical convictions. But certain considerations arise to cause us to hesitate. This position involves us in an attitude the soundness of which may be thought to be confuted by historical experience. For it is, in essence, a going back upon the principle maintained, even if on grounds of political expediency, in the Toleration Acts. This principle seems to be that the State is not concerned with the ideals of its citizens so long as their conduct be not such as to infringe the rights of others. And this single and simpler principle of the co-ordination of rights has alone proved sufficiently fertile to lead to the growth of the vast system of liberating restrictions to be found in a modern, secular State— restrictions which are not more contrary to liberty than railway lines are restraints on the freedom of locomotives to reach their destination. It may be doubted whether to go back upon this principle, which limits the action of the State to what it is able to do efficaciously,[30] is not to turn from the more specialized and perfect example of the State to the less specialized and more primitive form of the panto-pragmatic Polis. Moreover, since some

[30] Spinoza: *Tract. Theologico-Politicus* (trans. Elwes), 1883, I, chap. xx, p. 258.

indisputable States do not adopt this enlarged view
of their functions, a survey of political action does
not necessarily or essentially include this problem,
or undertake to solve ethical problems of a choice
between social ideals. To do this may, in fact, be a
part of the activities of some politicians, but it is no
necessary part of an uncomplicated political science.

This does not, of course, mean that practical
politicians can for a moment ignore ethical considerations, any more than they can for a moment,
without risk of folly, ignore geography. Ethical
considerations enter into experience, and are as
indispensable to rational conduct as are geographic
considerations. The politician—and not only the
politician but the State, i.e. the composite of
citizens—is as much obliged by ethical considerations
as is anybody else.

But the politician will view these considerations
from two angles, according to whether they are his
own estimates of value, or the ethical opinions of
others which, whether they are for him values or
not, are social facts which go to the make up of the
system of morality of that time and place. These
beliefs, right or wrong, which in fact exist as *faits
socials*, and regulate the social behaviour of the
community affected, are among, and are a large part
of, the facts of the political situation which, as brute
factors, it will be the business of the politician to
take into account. But he will also be guided,
when in doubt, by his own private estimates of
value, remembering, in those matters in which he

has received no mandate, that these private estimates, however conscientious, are merely private
estimates. They may, however, well be decisive in
stimulating a political leader or legislator to agitate
for certain reforms.

Reforms, nevertheless, seem rather to come, with
more or less foresight, more or less violence, because
the facts of the situation demand them as a formula
of stabilization, and not owing to any definite concept
of a final end. And if politicians, from among many
ideals of what society ought to be like, choose one
under the guidance of their ethical convictions, they
do it just as medical. men, faced with an actual
situation where the choice has to be made between
the value of this life or of that, may be guided by
ethical considerations. It is not that these considerations enter into the canon of the medical or
of the political arts. A physician who obstinately
placed his own opinion of what ought to be good for
a patient in front of the recognized methods of
medical practice, or insisted on applying a general
remedy without diagnosis, would be guilty of
culpable conduct. Similarly, a politician who suffers
the continuance of disorder because he declines on
principle to apply experimentally a probable remedy,
or who applies a party and doctrinaire remedy without informing himself of the facts of the social
situation, is a bad statesman.

Summary of the Non-Teleological Theory of Politics.
Political science is not necessarily architectonic of
the ' perfect city,' and therefore, *a fortiori*, of this or

z

that kind of a ' good city,' any more than medicine
is the technique of producing a good man, even
although it may facilitate the building up of men
more capable of good than are the debilitated.
Nor are the principles of Ethics, in so far as
they govern the details of the conduct of life,
more intimate in their bearing upon the political
situation than upon the religious, the economic, or
the hygienic situations.   The recognition of this
should make for freedom and disinterestedness of
ethical speculation, as well as for the solid grounding
of political theory on a study of objective possibilities.   Unless all sciences having to do with
human action, and all arts, are ethical, Politics is not
indivisible as a science from Ethics, and all political
action is ethical in precisely the sense that every
other voluntary act in life is subject to the ethical
counsel to promote that which is most valuable.

Politics is the science of the method of social
organization.   The method in itself is neither good
nor bad, save as a condition prerequisite to the
accomplishment of human ends, good or bad.   It
gives by regulation a new liberty which may be used
or abused.   Its practical task is no more ethical than
that of engineering.[31]   The organization is sometimes
put to the promotion of this or that ideal, just as
highways of communication enable men to build up
material prosperity or to promote the spread of
knowledge.   Highways presumably would not exist

[31] I hope to return to this matter in a forthcoming volume on
' The Instrumental State.'

if they served no more useful or valuable purpose
than to facilitate the escape of robbers.   But,
although communications are not merely roads
joining places but roads put there to serve useful
purposes, these purposes are many, and it is their
common factor alone, the need for communications,
which concerns the engineer.

The politicist admits that the method which he
discusses is not mere method, but a method which
serves various purposes, but he is not necessarily
by reason of his science any censor of what these
purposes may be.   Similarly, the practical politician
is not such a censor, by virtue of his office as statesman, but only occasionally, as citizen or as agitator
or as educator.   What the better state may be, which
ought to be aimed at, lies outside the scope of
Politics, although not of education in political
matters.   Politics is not concerned with the specific
purpose and its ostensible goal, but with the wills
willing this end, and with their intensity and
strength.   It looks not to the imagined future
satisfaction, but to the lack which this will signifies,
and to the appropriate social remedy for removing
that sense of lack and of discontent.

The only perfection of which the student of
method knows is that of perfect adjustment or
harmony, for good or for evil, for activity or for
apathy, in accordance with the existent factors of
what men will.   It may well be that man in the last
resort does not desire perfect harmony, which he
may stigmatize as ' stagnation,' that a measure of

difference, hailed as change and ‘ progress,’ is good for its own sake, that the satiety of satisfaction of itself breeds dissatisfaction, or, should it fail to do so and leave a race complacent and unaware of the need of modification and adaptation, contains the threat of social disaster. All this may be true. The conclusion to be drawn is that life cannot be limited to or cabined within any static political system. But it is not the business of the study of the method of the political process to provide sports and exceptions in history, but to consider their accommodation and utilization. Politics certainly has to consider the cases of ‘ beasts ’ and ‘ gods ’; it has to take into account their probable appearance. It may even admit the high efficient value of these revolutionary spirits in breaking up old customary harmonies, and forcing the substitution of agreements, more satisfactory and smoothly running, and adapted to the entire social and material environment. But it is not its duty to produce these men, but only to explain the wisdom of giving them release, when produced, in the harmony of an intelligent and tolerant society. This science has no formulæ for the production of genius, but only for the co-ordination of human ability and wills.

The task of Ethics is to hold up before men for their love the pattern of what the finest spirits consider lovable, and to expose relentlessly those inconsistencies of values and those subterfuges whereby baseness and stupidity compromise with a self-consistent virtue in the pursuit of the beautiful and the good. It is the æsthetic judgment which declares the value of the bright sky and the warm air, music, the noble souls of men, the god-like universe, and all that renders civilization finally worth while and satisfying. The task of Politics is to study the actual situation and to discover by what method wills there in discord may be brought into actual harmony, judged by external tests, with the minimum repression of the wills of each. It assumes, as an axiom, that this enduring social harmony is desirable, or, more precisely, it acts on an hypothesis, as if harmony were desirable. The two tasks, each carried out on a different plane, are mutually consistent. But they are quite dissimilar.

Difficulties of the Traditional Treatment. The customary treatment of Politics has been very different. The classical treatises on the subject have been writings almost as much ethical as political. The alternative title of Plato's ' *Republic* ' is *On Justice.* For Aristotle, despite his natural science approach, Ethics and Politics were two parts of one subject. No clear line could, indeed, be drawn for Greek civilization (in which the Polis held together, under the influence of family institutions and, in embryonic form, civil, ecclesiastical and industrial organizations) between the ' beautiful and good ' conduct of life, and the fundamental principles of the civil relationship. No distinction was drawn between the course which men ought to pursue if the ideal life of the commonwealth is to be realized, and the course which men ought to pursue if an orderly society is to be preserved. The problem of the circumstances under which the good man may be the good citizen is indeed discussed, but the conclusion is that the rightly constituted city ought to satisfy all the needs and ideal demands of the good man. Each community has a specific *ethos* which, by education, it inculcates into the minds of its citizens. It excludes emigrants, enslaves the lower orders, and ostracizes recalcitrant members of the upper orders. Thus a political system is maintained, based on one undefiled scheme of values. But when the philosophers of Greece have worked out this system to its logical conclusions, we have something more comparable to a secular monastery than to a modern State.

In the Middle Ages, although the separation of the organization of the Church from that of the State, and their rival claims, have rid us of the notion of the Temporal Power as justified in imposing its ideals on its subjects as a 'public conscience,' the political thought of these ages is too much infused with religious considerations for it to be possible to consider Politics divorced from Ethics, or to examine the efficiency of civil organization apart from its tendency to forward the Christian kingdom of righteousness.

Since the rise of democracy, those who were brought up from the country, as samples of local opinion and representatives of the interests which it was the business of the just monarch and his ministers to conciliate and bring together, have themselves become the legislators. As a consequence, in the hands of parties, the task of law-making and of government has come to be viewed as one of carrying out in practice the opinions embodied in the programme of the victorious party, instead of a matter of impartial administration and of expert technique, such as it was according to the theory, at least, of benevolent despotism. The political thought which has been the product of this period of party rule has, naturally enough, been of a polemic or apologetic character. The political theory of John Locke is an apology for the fact of the Revolution of 1688. The writings of John Stuart Mill are outstanding instances of the treatment of the problems of Politics by essays on first principles. Even the recent magistral work of Professor H. J. Laski discusses the 'purpose of social organization' from the angle of rights, and of the principles of liberty and equality, more emphatically than it inquires what are the functions of social organization demanded by the necessities of the situation.

It is perhaps to the period after the secular state has become specialized and self-conscious, but before the theory of government as the concern of the plain man has grown up with the demand for responsible government, that we must look for a satisfactory method in political theory. Machiavelli is concerned rather with the art of maintaining power in the hands of individuals than with the fundamental structure of society, and relies rather upon the pretence than upon the practice of an historical method. But Machiavelli has grasped the wisdom of using history as the raw material for a science ; he directs his attention to detecting the recurrent political situation, and he is fully alive to the necessity of distinguishing in Politics *probabilia* from *desiderata*. Thomas Hobbes, again, although he disfigures his exhaustive political works by a caustic and too-clever argument against his *bêtes noirs*, the believers in Independency whether in Church or State, sets out to provide a study of Politics at once systematic and scientific. His production is an *ex parte* treatise on Sovereignty ; his plan, however, is a study of the body politic on the analogy of the body natural, and with the accuracy required in the physical and mathematical sciences. The brief *Tractatus Politicus* of Spinoza, remarkable for the refreshing lucidity of its thought, is also characterized by the detachment with which it considers the problem of Politics. And the writings of the Jesuit theorists, if tendentious in purpose, are often marked by realism of treatment.

The great Hegelian school was and is too much dominated by Greek social thought to be prepared to admit any departmental treatment of Politics apart from Ethics or the theory of Law. Consequently, the master's writings on political philosophy are essentially synthetic works of philosophy giving to our views of Politics a certain perspective, rather than analytical works systematically surveying the field, and advancing theories from observation of how, in fact, men do act.

The Positivist school, which might have been expected to be detached alike from the ethical preoccupations of the philosophers and the traditional themes of the writers of the Tory-Conservative and Whig-Liberal party traditions, proves disappointing in its accomplishments. It was, in part, too much influenced by the neo-theology of Comte and, later, by the religion of Evolution and Progress. In part, too, it was too much allured by the will-o'-the-wisp of a Philosophy or Science of History (a child of the theodicy of Bossuet and of the anthropology of Montesquieu and of the Encyclopædists, to which Voltaire administered secular baptism in the sure hope of Human Progress) to hold fast to the methodological tradition of the Seventeenth Century.

The influence of the sociologists, and the scientific prejudices of a Germany newly bureaucratized by Prussia, conspired to produce such works as the *Statslehre* of Bluntschli and the more biassed treatise of Treitschke. The first work, despite certain fantastic notions of the state-organism type entertained by its author, it is not ridiculous to call the first systematic treatise on Politics since Aristotle. It returns, although uncertainly, to the most satisfactory element in the work of ' the master of them that know,' his naturalistic treatment of politics.[32] Most of the important modern work which pretends to be

[32] Bluntschli : *Allgemeine Statslehre, p.* 7 (Eng. trans.), 1892.

systematic suffers, as does that of Burgess, from being too closely connected with Law, or, as with Sidgwick, from too close a connection with description of the machinery of government, or, as with Woodrow Wilson, from passing too easily to merely descriptive, comparative history. The assumption on the whole has been that any work which was not descriptive, but which inquired into fundamental principles, would, *eo ipso*, concern itself with a discussion of morals.

Ethics and Politics are to be distinguished, not because the study of Ethics is not valuable in order to give sanity and good taste to the ends which men pursue through political means, or because the student of Politics can be exempt from studying the facts of moral conduct, but because the preservation of that close alliance diminishes the value of each discipline by confusing the requirements and conclusions of the two.[33]   Generosity is an excellent virtue, and, by any sound standard of ethics, a rational generosity will be encouraged. Generosity, also, is happily a fact in political conduct, as open-handedness is in economic conduct. But self-sacrificing generosity is no more a clue whereby to detect the underlying motives in most political phenomena than is philanthropic conduct with material goods the key to the understanding of the

[33] J. Dewey : *Experience and Nature*, 1926, p. 131 : "The great historic obstacle to science was unwillingness to make this surrender" (of immediate ends, "reducing them to indicative and implying means "), " but moral, æsthetic and religious objects suffer."

economic situation. Both of these virtues would imply a high degree of perfection, were they general, in the political and economic situations. They belong, as general attitudes of conduct, to a specific stage of the development of social order ; they are not factors of permanent intensity in every political or economic situation. It is necessary not to confuse the study of Politics with what may be an irrelevant consideration of values, but, on the one hand, to simplify the already sufficiently complex problems, with which we are confronted, by abstraction, and, on the other, to verify our hypotheses and deductions by a broad and impartial survey of the facts, arranged in such a fashion as to provide an objective test for these theories.

We are not at the moment concerned with whether the conduct which we postulate or observe is or is not in our opinion valuable and commendable. It is enough that it is recurrent, and manifests (even though in a perhaps undesirable fashion) the principles of political action. Upon the axioms of the political situation, upon the permanent structure of political organization, upon the constant elements in political method, and (until our science is riper) upon these alone, it is our business to concentrate our attention. It is not for the chemist to delay his discoveries by considering whether men will put them to use in the preparation of healing drugs or in the manufacture of destructive bombs. His discoveries at least are a way to better things for those who will so use them. So too here ; a political science is desirable in itself. If there be such a science, it may be expected to show us what will result from what, but it cannot be expected to tell us whether those results will be good. It is for the use of both the wicked and the virtuous, of the just and of the unjust.

Public opinion and the interests of the powerful or of the numerous may decide what shall be done. But only a knowledge of how society is constituted and of how alone it can function without strain, only the science which Plato ascribed to his physician-statesman, can ensure that what is done is inherently capable of conducing to the improvement of social conditions by enabling human activities to be conducted with less friction, and individuals to develop their faculties with less impediment and with more systematic encouragement. Legislation cannot be safely enacted, judicial decisions cannot be beneficially given, in accord with principles of party doctrine or of legal lore divorced from an exact and verified knowledge of the social situation in which the citizen or the litigant lives. And, if it be true that the essence of government is administration,[34] the secret of sound administration is a knowledge of the particular facts and of the general method of human behaviour. As Anatole France says : " Sovereignty resides in science and not in

---

[34] H. J. Laski : ' The Civil Service and Parliament ' in *The Development of the Civil Service* (1922), p. 30 : ' I can only say that much thought about politics has convinced me that the essence of government lies in the executive act.'

the people. Foolishness repeated by thirty-six million mouths is none the less foolishness."

But until we attain this knowledge of the means of social control, our civilization, speeded on by conditions and movements which we have unwittingly provoked and which inevitably bear us along, but which we cannot master, is in danger, like the car of the young Phæthon, of being carried, swinging, on its unintended and uncertain course to the destruction brought upon it by the destiny which wreaks vengeance on those who are contemptuous of facts and of science.

INDEX

A